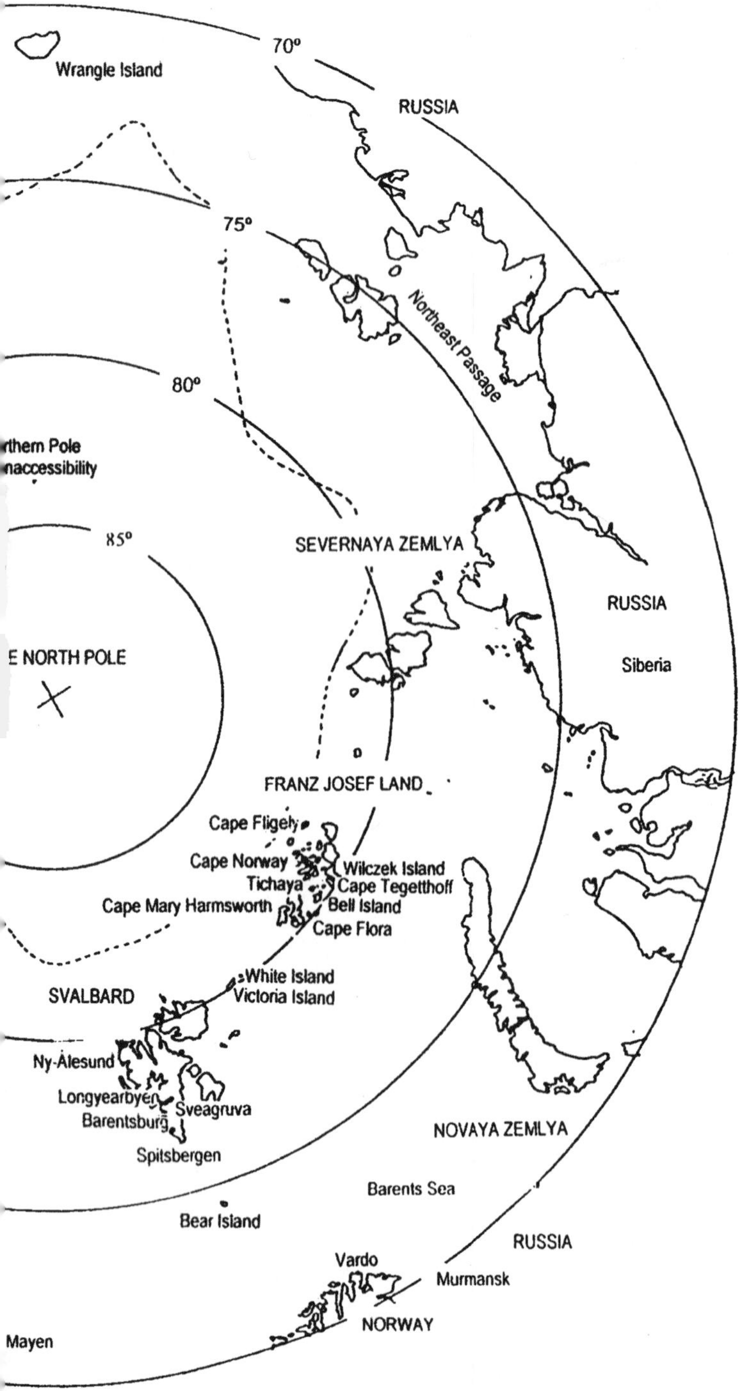

70°
Wrangle Island
RUSSIA
75°
Northeast Passage
80°
rthern Pole
naccessibility
85°
SEVERNAYA ZEMLYA
RUSSIA
Siberia
E NORTH POLE
FRANZ JOSEF LAND
Cape Fligely
Cape Norway
Wilczek Island
Tichaya
Cape Tegetthoff
Cape Mary Harmsworth
Bell Island
Cape Flora
White Island
Victoria Island
SVALBARD
Ny-Ålesund
Longyearbyen
Sveagruva
Barentsburg
Spitsbergen
NOVAYA ZEMLYA
Barents Sea
Bear Island
RUSSIA
Vardo
Murmansk
NORWAY
Mayen

THE NORTH POLE

THE NORTH POLE

Kathan Brown

Crown Point Press
San Francisco

ISBN 1-891300-18-0
Book and cover design: Kathan Brown
Color correction: Rick Levy
Typography: Dave Blake, *turnaround,* Berkeley
Map: Tom Marioni
Production: Sasha Baguskas at Crown Point Press

The photographs are by Kathan Brown with six exceptions:
Photograph of Bob Headland on page 380: Helen Morehouse
Photograph of Gunter Weller on page 124: Randy Brandon
Photographs of Steve Trautman and Sonja Gustafson (page 32),
Fred Sandback (page 188), Jack Brink (page 272),
and Ed Mathez (page 330) were supplied by the subjects.

Printed in China through Colorcraft Ltd. Hong Kong

Crown Point Press
20 Hawthorne Street
San Francisco, CA 94105
415-974-6273
www.crownpoint.com

Acknowledgments

Sasha Baguskas and I built this book. I wrote it and she produced it. We hammered, sawed, and assembled quite a lot of disparate material and eventually managed to give it a shape and a form. My editor, Judith Dunham, helped a great deal, especially in the sawing, and Dave Blake and Rick Levy helped with the finishing. Helen Morehouse provided a needed photograph, and Tom Marioni, Helene Fried, and Richard Tuttle read early drafts and gave useful advice. Bob Headland generously read more than one draft, correcting historical (and other) errors, and Gunter Weller patiently helped me understand the scientific issues and corrected the chapter on weather and climate. Any mistakes that remain are entirely my own responsibility. I am grateful to each of the seventeen people who engaged in the conversations reported here. All of them gave me their time, knowledge, and opinions in ways beyond the obvious. The trip I took to the North Pole on the *Yamal* was sponsored by the American Museum of Natural History and operated by TCS Expeditions, Seattle. Spitsbergen Travel, Svalbard, Norway, organized the trip I took along the coast of the island of Spitsbergen on the *Polar Star*.

—KB

Contents

Introduction

The North Pole is the point at the top of the world on which the axis of the earth turns. A straight line drawn from it into the earth's center, then out again to the equator, forms a right angle, or 90 degrees, so if you stand exactly at the North Pole you are at latitude 90° north. You can bounce a signal from a global positioning device off a network of satellites in outer space to confirm it. But if you check again after remaining in the same spot only a few minutes, you will be at a different latitude. The North Pole has not moved; the ice on which you are standing has drifted. In 1874, the leader of a band of polar explorers discovered that after walking for two months they had traveled only nine miles. They were going south, trying to save themselves, on ice that was drifting north. "I am very much aware that we are probably lost if conditions do not improve," he wrote in his diary. He did, however, succeed in returning home with his entire crew of twenty-two men.

At the North Pole there are no landmarks; there is no land. The North Star is fixed exactly above the pole and has been used for centuries everywhere in the northern hemisphere for navigation, but when you are at the North Pole, you cannot see the star. The sun, which is always out in summer, obscures it. The North Star is visible during the six-month-long winter when the sun never appears, but during that period no warm-blooded creature can survive at the pole. Nevertheless, in order to begin walking when the sun came out, explorers would spend winters a few hundred miles away from the pole in huts on islands or in ships locked in drifting ice floes for four or five months of complete darkness.

In the aftermath of a trip I made to the North Pole, I began to see the condition of polar explorers of a hundred years ago as symbolic, in some ways, of our human condition at present. We drift where we do not wish to go without being aware of it.

We are at the mercy of weather events that become worse and worse. We are in a vast unpredictable space. We have no choice but to move on, yet we suspect that we are lost. I was aware before I set out that the Arctic ice is melting and that the climate of the earth is warming. I had heard many times the cliché that the time occupied by human civilization is that of the blink of an eye in the history of the earth, but I had not grasped its meaning. I knew that a catastrophe of some sort had wiped out the dinosaurs long ago, but not since the 1950s, when we had drills at school in preparation for nuclear war, had I considered the possibility of a sudden disaster that could wipe out civilization as we know it. Until my trip to the North Pole, I had no idea that such a disaster could come from climate change, and that climate change is predictable and probably avoidable in its most immediate and catastrophic form.

Nevertheless, the bulk of this book is not about climate change. Most of its pages are occupied by the stories and reflections of people who went to the North Pole or—in times past—tried to go there. Each chapter begins with a text based on my journey. I traveled to the pole in 2002 on a Russian nuclear-powered icebreaker. Following the text, and illustrating it, is a set of photographs that I took on the journey, and then there is a related excerpt from the diary of Norwegian polar explorer Fridtjof Nansen. Nansen, in 1893, deliberately got his ship locked in the Arctic ice, hoping it would drift to the pole. In 1895, realizing the ship would not drift far enough, he left it in the command of its captain and, with one companion, Hjalmar Johansen, made an attempt to walk to the North Pole over the sea ice. They went farther north than anyone had gone before, and both men survived. In 1897, Nansen published a book called *Farthest North* that contains diary entries and other material. I have drawn from the diary portions, using only words that Nansen wrote while he was on his ship or on the ice.

Along with my narrative and Nansen's, I have included in each chapter a conversation among two or three people who have a connection to the Arctic. My trip to the North Pole changed my attitude toward being in the world, and other passengers I met were also affected. We were able to experience a place that, because of its extreme nature, has been visited by fewer than fourteen thousand people in recorded history. Some of those people speak with one another in conversations in Chapters One, Two, and Four.

Most historians now believe that none of the early explorers reached the pole. However, all but a few of them returned home alive. The most dramatic exception is Sir John Franklin, who led an expedition in 1845 to the Northwest Passage in which he and his entire group of 129 men died. After that, many explorers, at some point in their journeys, shifted their priorities from reaching their goals to retaining their lives. Robert E. Peary, the man commonly listed in history books as having discovered the North Pole in 1909, was probably among those who did this, although he did not admit it. In fact, the North Pole may have been impossible to reach in his time. The first person indisputably to reach it on foot did so in 1969. The first people to see it did so from a dirigible in 1926. The first plane landed there in 1948, bringing twenty-four Russians, who probably were the first people to stand on the spot that explorers had been trying to reach for at least a century.

In Chapter Three, the book shifts briefly to a larger timescale. This chapter is called "The Weather," and in the conversation, two scientists talk about global greenhouse warming and its probable consequences, one of which, paradoxically, might be a new ice age in which human beings would find survival difficult. In Chapter Four, the narrative of my journey resumes as we reach the North Pole. In Chapter Five, on our way back from the pole, we encounter Franz Josef Land, a large group of small islands about six hundred miles from it. These islands belong to Russia. They have been glaciated for at least two million years and have never been inhabited. In this chapter's conversation, a geophysicist and an anthropologist speak about the difficulties faced by human beings who lived in or explored glacier-covered lands.

Chapters Six and Seven focus on stops our ship made at historic spots in Franz Josef Land: Cape Norway, where Nansen and Johansen built a stone hut and stayed over a winter nearly nine months long, and Cape Flora, where another explorer of a different temperament erected an extensive camp of prefabricated wooden buildings. With almost incredible luck, Nansen stumbled on Cape Flora, and he and his companion were saved. In Chapter Six, "Cape Norway," Nansen's narrative speaks of scarce resources frugally used and of the dullness of a mental state close to hibernation that characterized the winter that he and Johansen spent there. The conversation in this chapter, like the conversation on the weather, moves into a larger scale. Near the North Pole, underneath the frozen sea, are smoking volcanoes that provide sustenance for living organisms that have been on the earth for billions of years but were unknown to humans until 1979. A microbiologist and a geologist talk about a new science of extreme environments. Chapter Seven, "Cape Flora," contains the story of Nansen's rescue, and the conversation brings the stories of Arctic explorers into the twentieth century. A polar archivist and an experienced Arctic guide discuss the question of whether Robert E. Peary made it to the pole and talk about trips by hydrogen balloon, dirigible, snowmobile, and—in 1969—the trip (by dogsled) that was the first to be indubitably successful.

My trip to the North Pole began and ended at the island of Spitsbergen, which is part of the Svalbard archipelago of islands. This island group is seven hundred miles from the pole, and is historically a no-man's-land. Since the Spitsbergen Treaty in 1920, it has been an international zone, administered by Norway. After my brief acquaintance with Spitsbergen in 2002, I returned the following year for a weeklong trip along its coast in a small Norwegian icebreaker. That trip is the subject of the last chapter in this book, Chapter Eight. There is no Nansen section in this chapter; Nansen and Johansen never reached Spitsbergen, though they had intended to. People have lived on this island year-round for about three hundred years. In Nansen's day, the population was mainly trappers, but now it is a mix of coal miners, working scientists, and students who attend a small university there. In the conversation, a thirty-three-year old traveler talks with a twenty-five-year old Spitsbergen resident, a student of Arctic technology. The winter night at Spitsbergen is four months long. There are no trees, and few plants or animals, but the presence of polar bears and walruses gives the place a special character. The two young women who converse in this chapter conclude on a note of hope.

"Before every decisive resolution, the dice of death must be thrown," Nansen wrote at the end of the nineteenth century. "Is there too much to venture and too little to gain?" The weather at the North Pole and the consequences of global greenhouse warming there are so important to the rest of the world that at some time in the twenty-first century people in many nations will, of necessity, make decisions concerning this place. As I moderated the conversations in this book, I found that in all of them the subject of climate change appeared; sometimes I had to force a subject change to make room for other topics. I now realize that people who are connected to the Arctic find global warming, as one of them said, "always in the back of our minds." We may already be throwing the dice of death without realizing it.

Scientists are looking for ways to load the dice in our favor, and if our society accepts their recommendations, we may be able to change our priorities, as the Arctic explorers did. They protected their individual lives. For us, changing our priorities may be necessary in order to protect our children's or grandchildren's lives. As time goes on, and more and more extremes of weather and climate occur, we who live outside the Arctic will realize little by little that we must think carefully about what is being ventured there and what it is possible to gain.

CHAPTER ONE
THE POLAR BEAR

Journey: The Polar Bear

The bear's spine unfolded upward from his hind legs like a jointed doll, each vertebrae rising effortlessly above the last. A white unfolding, enormous, ten feet high, and the head only eight or nine feet below me as I leaned over the ship's rail. The steady eyes looked up and caught mine. A little more length below the knee, I thought, and he could be a person, balanced and graceful in a way human beings are in dreams.

Someone asked me later if I could smell him. I don't remember a smell. He was too white, too clean, to have had a smell in the cold air. All the polar bears I have seen in pictures have been yellow, or partly so, but this one was entirely white, except where the black skin showed through on his long nose. If you shaved a polar bear, it would be black. Its hair shafts are hollow and transparent so light can reach the black skin, which is heat absorbing. As the bear ages (especially in less permanently cold places), algae sometimes grows inside the shafts and turns the bear yellow.

We stared at this wild, white animal, and he calmly stared back at us. Although he could not reach the food he smelled, he seemed curious, not desperate. A fellow passenger gave him words: "He's thinking, 'If I could just get this big tin can open—.'"

I smiled, then winced because a picture came into my mind of a sardine can clawed open by a desperate bear. I had seen the can in a close-up photo printed next to a photo of a dead polar bear and two dead cubs, all bleeding from gunshot wounds to the head. They were on the front page of the newspaper at the town of Longyearbyen on the island of Spitsbergen where we had spent a day before boarding our ship.

"They missed the ice," our young guide had said. "The females den here, and when the cubs are born they weigh only one pound and are hairless. They can't travel. If the ice recedes from the island before they are ready, they are trapped and cannot get any seals." A female polar bear needs at least a seal a week to keep herself and a cub alive.

The image of the dead bears stayed only a moment in my mind, supplanted quickly by that of the live one now circling us, pausing to glance up from time to time. Our captain had stopped the ship, and the bear ambled completely around it, a distance of nearly a quarter of a mile.

The ice had locked us in almost as soon as we had stopped, but I wouldn't have guessed that the newly frozen section close to the ship could have supported the bear's weight of something like a thousand pounds. It did, however, and the bear did not seem worried. He stopped to drink at a bright turquoise melt pool, then stepped right through it, confidant that the ice would be solid underneath. It must be fresh water that he is drinking, I thought with surprise. How could it be? For days we had seen nothing but ocean, gradually more crowded with floes of ice.

I found out later that the water in the pool was fresh, or nearly so. When salt water freezes, it discharges some of its salt into the unfrozen water below. Melted pack ice is only about three parts salt per thousand as opposed to seawater with thirty-five parts per thousand. And if any truly fresh water is present, from rain, snow, or melt water from glaciers, it sits on top and melts first. Freshwater pools, pure and transparent, palely expose the color of the sea ice below. The true color of ice is blue —all the other colors are absorbed by it.

Sea ice, either in vast fields or in drifting translucent shards, is pebbly looking, like frosted glass. Frozen seawater is cloudy. Freshwater freezes in relatively transparent layers, but salt water has a different mechanism. At approximately 28.4°F(depending on its saltiness), it reaches its freezing point, and its density increases. Thousands of tiny crystals form, first creating frazil ice in which the crystals are free-floating, then grease ice, which is thick but soft. After that, the ice solidifies quickly, often in just a few minutes. That is how our ship became locked in so rapidly when we stopped to watch the polar bear.

When we began to move again, breaking a path in the ice, our wake solidified behind us, connecting broken ice rubble before our eyes. The freezing was so fast that small ice chunks thrown up by the ship would rain down on already refrozen ice with a tinkling, shattering sound, like glass breaking, and the waves that we pushed over the still-intact ice field could not withdraw.

We were in the summer pack ice when we stopped for the bear. This part of the Arctic Ocean is not permanently frozen. We forced our way through unbroken ice that would frequently vanish. Suddenly, for no reason that we could see, we would be in open water, or what is called a lead. Some leads are very large, and in them ice floes move independently, each with a ledge of startling turquoise just under the water's surface.

Polar bears easily swim through leads where they cannot walk, the males traveling alone, the females usually with cubs. Males and females rarely are together except during the process of mating, which occurs over a week-long period every two and a half years for most females. Cubs stay with their mothers for two or two and a half years, a time of instruction for the young ones, who must be taught to hunt effectively.

The bear we encountered was a young male, and he was in this particular spot because it was a good place to find seals. A polar bear's front legs are thin and flexible, like arms, good for swimming and for wrapping around seals and hauling them up on the ice. The back legs, with their solid haunches, provide an anchor.

Sometimes a bear stalks seals that have come out to sun themselves, but its preferred hunting method is to sit waiting by a breathing hole. It can smell the seal under the ice and prepare itself to pounce as soon as a faint bubble of breath appears. Before we saw an actual bear, there were many tracks, sometimes with staining on the snow that showed the bear's success. On our ten-day trip, we didn't see any seals, though we were sure that they were there. Unlike the bear, they must have been frightened by our noisy approach.

Polar bears and seals are not related, but their heads are so similarly shaped that beginning students of animal anatomy often confuse their skulls. The polar bear's Latin name is *Ursus maritimus*, the "sea bear," but the Inuit natives of northern Canada, who know the animal well, use a name that emphasizes a different quality. They call the polar bear Tornarssuk, the name they also give to the most powerful god in their lexicon of gods.

When I leaned over our ship's rail and held the bear's eyes in mine, I understood that name. If I had not been safely out of reach, things might have been different, but since I had no reason to feel fear, I studied his demeanor: he was confident and unhurried in his investigation. He has enormous size and strength, I thought, but his power comes from his confidence. Then I realized that his confidence was his only vulnerability. If we had become frightened, or if (like the explorers before us) we had wanted to eat this animal, we could have pulled out our guns and the animal would not have had a chance.

The Journal of Fridtjof Nansen
December 12 to December 14, 1893

Tuesday, December 12

Had a long walk southeast this morning. The ice is in much the same condition there as it is to the west, packed or pressed up into mounds, with flat floes between. This evening the dogs suddenly began to make a great commotion on deck. We were all deep in cards, some playing whist, others "marriage." I had no shoes on, so said that someone else must go up and see what was the matter. Mogstad went. The noise grew worse and worse. Presently Mogstad came down and said that all the dogs that could get at the rail were up on it, barking out into the dark towards the north. He was sure there must be an animal of some sort there, but perhaps it was only a fox, for he thought he had heard the bark of a fox far in the north; but he was not sure. Well, it must be a devil of a fox to excite the dogs like that. As the disturbance continued, I at last went up myself, followed by Johansen.

From different positions we looked long and hard into the darkness in the direction in which the dogs were barking, but we could see nothing moving. I struck about with my arms to get a little heat into me, then went below and to bed. The dogs went on barking, sometimes louder than before. Nordahl, whose watch it was, went up several times, but could discover no reason for it. As I was lying reading in my berth I heard a peculiar sound; it was like boxes being dragged about on deck, and there was also scraping, like a dog that wanted to get out, scratching violently at a door. I thought of Kvik who was shut up in the chart-room [because she was about to have puppies]. But I called into the saloon to Nordahl that he had better go up again and see what this new noise was.

He did so, but came back saying that there was still nothing to be seen. It was difficult to sleep, and I lay long tossing about. Peter came on watch. I told him to go up and turn the air-sail to the wind, to make the ventilation better. He was a good time on deck doing this and other things, but he also could see no reason for the to-do the dogs were still making. He had to go forward, and then noticed that the three dogs nearest the starboard gangway were missing. He came down and told me, and we agreed that possibly this might be what all the excitement was about; but never before had they taken it so to heart when some of their number had run away. At last I fell asleep, but heard them in my sleep for a long time.

Wednesday, December 13

Before I was rightly awake this morning I heard the dogs at it still, and the noise went on all the time of breakfast, and had, I believe, gone on all night. After breakfast Mogstad and Peter went up to feed the dogs and let them loose on the ice. Three were still missing. Peter came down to get a lantern; he thought he might as well look to see if there were any tracks of animals. Jacobsen called after him that he had better take a gun. No, he did not need one, he said. A little later, I heard a scream at the top of the companion. "Come with a gun!" In a moment I was in the saloon, and there was Peter tumbling in at the door, breathlessly shouting, "A gun! A gun!"

The bear had bitten him in the side. I was thankful it was no worse. Hearing him put on so much dialect, I had thought it was a matter of life and death. I seized one gun, he another, and up we rushed, the mate with his gun after us. There was not much difficulty in knowing in what direction to turn, for from the rail on the starboard side came confused shouts of human voices, and from the ice below the gangway the sound of a frightful uproar of dogs. I tore out the tow-plug at the muzzle of my rifle, then up with the lever and in with a cartridge; it was a case of hurry. But, hang it! There is a plug in at this end too. I poked and poked, but could not get a grip on it. Peter screamed: "Shoot, shoot! Mine won't go off!" He stood clicking and clicking, his lock full of frozen Vaseline again, while the bear lay chewing at a dog just below us at the ship's side. Beside me stood the mate, groping after a tow-plug which he also had shoved down into his gun, but now he flung the gun angrily away and began to look round the deck for a walrus spear to stick the bear with. Our fourth man, Mogstad, was waving an empty rifle (he had shot away his cartridges), and shouting to someone to shoot the bear. Four men, and not one that could shoot, although we could have prodded the bear's back with our gun-barrels. Hansen, making a fifth, was lying in the passage to the chart-room, groping with his arm through a chink in the door for cartridges; he could not get the door to open because of Kvik's kennel.

At last Johansen appeared and sent a ball straight down into the bear's hide. That did some good. The monster let go the dog and gave a growl. Another shot flashed and hissed down on the same spot. One more, and we saw the white dog the bear had under him jump up and run off, while the other dogs stood round, barking. Another shot still, for the animal began to stir a little. At this moment my plug came out, and I gave him a last ball through the head to make sure. The dogs had crowded round barking as long as he moved, but now that he lay still in death they drew back terrified. They probably thought it was some new ruse of the enemy. It was a little thin one-year-old bear that had caused all this terrible commotion.

While it was being flayed, I went off in a northwesterly direction to look for the dogs that were still missing. I had not gone far when I noticed that the dogs that were following me had caught scent of something to the north, and wanted to go that way. Soon they got frightened, and I could not get them to go on;

they kept close in to my side or slunk behind me. I held my gun ready, while I crawled on all fours over the pack ice, which was anything but level. I kept a steady lookout ahead, but my eyes could not pierce far in the darkness. I could only just see the dogs, like black shadows, when they were a few steps away from me. I expected every moment to see a huge form rise among the hummocks ahead, or come rushing towards me. The dogs got more and more cautious. One or two of them sat down, but they probably felt that it would be a shame to let me go on alone, so they got up and followed slowly after. Terrible ice to force one's way over! Crawling along on hands and knees does not put one in a very convenient position to shoot from if the bear should make a sudden rush. But unless he did this, or attacked the dogs, I had no hope of getting him.

We now came out on some flat ice. It was only too evident that there must be something quite near now. I went on, and presently saw a dark object on the ice in front of me. It was not unlike an animal. It was poor "Johansen's Friend," the black dog with the white tip to his tail, in a sad state, and frozen stiff. I bent down again and found the second of the missing dogs, Gammelen. This one was almost whole, only eaten a little about the head, and it was not frozen quite stiff. There seemed to be blood all round on the ice. I looked about in every direction, but there was nothing more to be seen. The dogs stood at a respectful distance, staring and sniffing in the direction of their dead comrades.

Some of us went not long after this to fetch the dogs' carcasses, taking a lantern to look for bear tracks, in case there had been some big fellows along with the little one. We scrambled on over the pack ice. By the light of the lantern we traced the blood-marked path on among the hummocks. We found the dead dogs, but no footprints except small ones, which we all thought must be those of our little bear. Svarten, alias "Johansen's Friend," looked bad in the lantern-light. Flesh and skin and entrails were gone; there was nothing to be seen but a bare breast and backbone, with some stumps of ribs. It was a pity that this fine strong dog should come to such an end. He had just one fault: he was rather bad-tempered. He had a special dislike for Johansen. He barked and showed his teeth whenever Johansen came on deck, or even opened a door, and when Johansen sat whistling in the crow's nest these dark winter days, the "Friend" would answer with a howl of rage from far out on the ice. Johansen bent down with the lantern to look at the remains.

"Are you glad, Johansen, that your enemy is done for?"

"No, I am sorry."

"Why?"

"Because we did not make it up before he died." And we went on to look for more bear tracks, but found none; so we took the dead dogs on our backs and turned homeward.

On the way I asked Peter what had really happened with him and the bear. "Well, you see," said he, "when I came along with the lantern we saw a few drops of blood by the gangway; but that might quite well have been a dog that had cut itself. On the ice below the gangway we saw some bear tracks, and we started away west, the whole pack of dogs with us, running on far ahead. When we had got away a bit from the ship, there was suddenly an awful row in front, and it wasn't long before a great beast came rushing at us, with the whole troop of dogs around it. As soon as we saw what it was, we turned and ran for the ship. Mogstad, you see, had moccasins on, and knew his way better and got there before me. I couldn't get along so fast with my great wooden shoes, and in my confusion I got right onto the big hummock to the west of the ship's bow. I turned there and looked back to see if the bear was behind me, but I saw nothing and pushed on again, and in a minute those slippery wooden shoes had me flat on my back among the hummocks. I was up again quick enough, but when I got down to the flat ice close to the ship, I saw something coming straight for me on the right-hand side. First I thought it was a dog—it's not easy to see in the dark, you know. I had no time for a second thought, for the beast jumped on me and bit me in the side. He growled and hissed as he bit.

"I thought it was all up with me. What was I to do? I had neither gun nor knife. But I took the lantern and gave him such a whack on the head with it that the thing broke, and went flying away over the ice. The moment he felt the blow he sat down and looked at me. I was just taking to my heels when he got up. I don't know whether it was to grip me again or what it was for, but anyhow at that minute he caught sight of a dog coming, and set off after it, and I got on board."

"Did you scream?"

"Scream? I screamed with all my might." And apparently this was true, for he was quite hoarse.

"But where was Mogstad all this time?"

"Well, you see, he had reached the ship before me, but he never thought of running down and giving the alarm, but takes his gun from the round-house wall and thinks he'll manage all right alone, but his gun wouldn't go off and the bear would have had time to eat me up in front of his nose."

We were now near the ship, and Mogstad, who had heard the last part of the story from the deck, corrected it in so far as he had just reached the gangway when Peter began to roar. He jumped up and fell back three times before he got on board, and had no time to do anything then but seize his gun and go to Peter's assistance.

When the bear left Peter and rushed after the dogs, he soon had the whole pack about him again. He would make a spring and get one below him, but then all the rest would set upon him and jump on his back, so that he had to turn to defend himself. Then he would spring upon another dog and the whole pack would be on him again. And so the dance went on, backwards and forwards over the ice, until they were once more close to the ship. A dog stood there, below the gangway, wanting to get on board. The bear made a spring on it and it was there, by the ship's side, that the villain met his fate.

An examination on board showed that the hook of Svarten's leash was pulled out quite straight, and Gammelen's was broken through. But the third dog's was only wrenched a little; it hardly looked as if the bear had done it. I had a slight hope that this dog might still be in life, but though we searched well, we could not find it.

When I went below after this bear affair, Juell said as I passed the galley door, "You'll see that Kvik will have her pups today, for it's always the way here on board that things happen together." And, sure enough, when we were sitting in the saloon in the evening, Mogstad, who generally plays "master of the hounds," came and announced the arrival of the first. Soon there was another, and then one more. This news was a little balsam to our wounds. Kvik has got a good warm box, lined with fur, up in the passage on the starboard. It is so warm there that she is lying sweating, and we hope that the young ones will live.

It seems this evening as if everyone had some hesitation in going out on the ice unarmed. Our bayonet-knives have been brought out, and I am providing myself with one. I must say that I had felt quite certain that we should find no bears as far north as this in the middle of winter; and it never occurred to me, in making long excursions on the ice without so much as a penknife in my pocket, that I was liable to encounters with them. But after Peter's experience it seems as if it might be as well to have, at any rate, a lantern to hit them with. The long bayonet-knife shall accompany me henceforth.

Thursday, December 14

"Well, Mogstad, how many pups have you now?" I asked at breakfast.

"There are five now." But soon after he came down to tell me that there were twelve. Gracious! That is good value for what we have lost. But we were almost as pleased when Johansen came down and said that he heard the missing dog howling on the ice far away to northwest. Several of us went up to listen, and we could all hear him quite well; but it sounded as if he were sitting still, howling in despair. Perhaps he was at an opening in the ice that he could not get across. Blessing had also heard him during the night watch, but then the sound had come more from a southwesterly direction. When Peter went after breakfast to feed the dogs, there was the lost one, standing below the gangway wanting to get on board. Hungry he was—he dashed straight into the food dish—but otherwise hale and hearty.

This evening Peter came and said that he was certain he heard a bear moving about and pawing the ice; he and Pettersen had stood and listened to him scraping at the snow crust. I put on my fur shirt, and got hold of my double-barreled rifle, and went on deck. The whole crew was collected aft, gazing out into the night. We let loose Ulenka and Pan and went in the direction where the bear was said to be. It was pitch-dark, but the dogs would find the tracks, if there was anything there. Hansen thought he had seen something moving about the hummock near the ship, but we found and heard nothing, and, as several of the others had by this time come out on the ice and could also discover nothing, we scrambled on board again. It is extraordinary, all the sounds that one can fancy one hears in this great, still space, mysteriously lighted by the twinkling stars.

A Conversation with Steve Trautman and Sonja Gustafson

I traveled to the North Pole with seventy-seven other passengers on a Russian ship named Yamal. *Steven (Steve) Trautman and I were carrying around copies of the same book, and we struck up a conversation about it—the Modern Library edition of* Farthest North *by Fridtjof Nansen. "Did you know this version of the book is abridged?" Steve asked me. "We have several of the original copies at home. It's in two large volumes."* Farthest North *was first published in 1897. Steve's wife, Sonja Gustafson, collects rare copies of it. Steve and Sonja live in Seattle, where Steve owns and runs a small business helping computer technicians make themselves clear to ordinary people. Sonja works in marketing. In this conversation, we spoke about our trip, about some of the polar explorers of a hundred years or so ago, and, especially, about Nansen.*

STEVE: It really was an amazing trip, but it's almost impossible to explain why. The sun never went down, and we didn't see a single tree from the first day of our trip to the last. Our activities from one hour to the next didn't change much, and what we saw out the window didn't change much either. It was twenty-four hours a day pretty much the same thing. But I never got bored.

Why did you go?

STEVE: Sonja wanted to go, not me.

SONJA: When I came back with the brochure, Steve said, "You are just crazy. Let's go to the tropics, not cold and dismal places." The whole thing—he just couldn't see it.

Steve Trautman Sonja Gustafson

My husband felt the same way. He didn't end up going.

STEVE: Well, I like gardening, and I thought it would be worth going just to see the tundra-type plants on the Arctic islands. We had to forego our usual family vacation. We have two children, ages six and nine, and we left them with relatives.

SONJA: They would have loved the polar bears, but the rest would have been good for about one hour a day.

I'll never forget the bear that tried to climb up the side of the ship. The other bear I saw was in the distance. He ran when he saw us.

SONJA: I heard that they can die from overheating by running, because they have so much insulation. And they don't need to run. All they need to do is catch up with you, and they basically know that they will. Anyone who knows about polar bears knows that if they see you, they will eat you. They think you're meat. That's just what they do.

Polar bears are almost twice as big as their cousins, the black bears.

SONJA: We're a little smaller than a seal, so we would be pretty easy prey. And you can't scare them away with noise or anything.

Even firing a gun in the air doesn't always scare them, because they are so used to the sound of cracking ice. They don't naturally fear anything, and the ones who have had experience with guns are dead. Every time we got off the ship and I saw the guards with guns, I was hoping a bear wouldn't appear. If one had, they probably would have killed it.

SONJA: They would have had to.

Sonja, why did you want to go on the trip?

SONJA: It was a book that got me to the North Pole. A friend gave me *Farthest North* by Fridtjof Nansen about five years ago and said, "You need to read this. It is great story, a great book, by a great hero of Norway." I grew up surrounded by Scandinavian culture, and in college I studied Norwegian. After I read the book, I was hooked. I started going to antiquarian bookstores. I have several copies, different editions, including one in the original Norwegian.

By now, you must feel as if you know Nansen personally.

SONJA: One of the booksellers said to me, "You're a woman. Why do you like Nansen? He was such a womanizer." I hadn't thought about it until then but, you know, Thomas Jefferson had an affair too, and he made such a difference to our country. Nansen had earned the equivalent of a PhD in zoology and done original research in that field before he began his explorations. When he got back from the Arctic, he went into politics. Norway was part of Sweden at the time, and he was instrumental in bringing about its independence without violence. He was the first Norwegian ambassador to Great Britain, and later he was the League of Nations High Commissioner for Refugees. He used his influence to get thousands of prisoners of war repatriated after World War I and to find homes for hundreds of thousands of refugees after the Russian revolution. And he won a Nobel Peace Prize for that work. He tried hard to contribute to the larger picture.

I didn't think he was a womanizer, but you told me he had an affair with the wife of the English explorer, Robert Scott, didn't you?

SONJA: Yes. Scott got to the South Pole just after Roald Amundsen, who was Norwegian, and was the first person to get there.

Scott died on the way back from his South Pole expedition.

SONJA: He's the perfect example of the gentleman English explorer.

One of the books I read quoted from an early book of Scott's to make that point. I copied down the quote: "No journey made with dogs can approach the height of that fine conception which is realized when a party of men go forth to face hardships, dangers, and difficulties by their own unaided efforts." Scott wrote that in 1905.

SONJA: Yes, that's perfect! Scott has been made into a huge tragic hero in Britain. No big deal is made out of Amundsen's achievements.

Scott is *a tragic hero. Not only did he die on his greatest expedition, but also he was idealistic about exploration. Amundsen had an absolutely practical approach. He learned his skills in the Arctic, and by the time he went to the South Pole he had already been the first to get through the Northwest Passage, from the Atlantic to the Pacific. That was in 1905. What was important to Amundsen was winning, not how the game was played. And, unlike Scott, he survived his South Pole expedition, and he got there first.*

SONJA: A lot of Brits feel that Amundsen cheated by not announcing that he was going to the South Pole so Scott would know that it was a race while there was still time to win it.

Amundsen announced he was going to the North Pole, and then secretly went the other direction. That was because in 1909

Frederick Cook and Robert E. Peary claimed to have reached the North Pole, so Amundsen thought it had already been discovered. He knew Scott's expedition to the South Pole was planned for 1911, and he wanted to beat him there.

SONJA: The South Pole doesn't interest me so much. For one thing, it is definitely a place, which the North Pole is not. The South Pole is on land. When Scott arrived there, he found a cairn and in it a message to him from Amundsen. That model wouldn't work for the North Pole.

That's why Cook's and Peary's claims were disputed, even soon after they made them, and can never be proved. It is impossible to leave a record at the North Pole that someone else can find later, because the ice at the North Pole is always drifting. Many people who are very well educated about other things think there is land at the North Pole.

STEVE: For sure. We got a question—someone asked us, "How big is the North Pole?"

I can understand that question. The North Pole is so important, how could it not be a place with a definable size?

STEVE: Our image of it comes from Santa Claus. We picture him up there building toys.

SONJA: What I think about is the absolutely ephemeral nature of where we were. It's always changing but never changing. It was difficult to know when we had actually arrived at the North Pole. When we got close to it, a lot of people crowded around the GPS [Global Positioning System] display, because the only way to know we were there was to see that the reading was 90° north. The ship kept moving in little bursts. It was difficult to get exactly on the spot. It was as if there was a little laser light shining down from the North Star and we were trying to maneuver that big ship to get exactly under the light.

In one of his lectures on the ship, Bob Headland talked about that. Because he is the archivist at the Scott Polar Research Institute in Cambridge, he put it this way: "If you are at the university, you are definitely in Cambridge. But if you are at the grocery store down the street, are you still in Cambridge?" A lot of the controversy about whether Peary reached the pole has to do with making guesses about how close he was. Five miles? Sixty? If he got no closer than a hundred miles to that spot, did he still discover the North Pole?

SONJA: Peary got some of his ideas about how to handle Arctic exploration from Nansen. The Norwegians developed a low-support approach, traveling with very few people and using dog sledges and kayaks like the Arctic natives did. That was part of Nansen's breakthrough. On his ship, the *Fram*, there were only thirteen men, including Nansen. And they took thirty dogs.

That's a big contrast to Sir John Franklin's expedition. Franklin's government-sponsored attempt to go through the Northwest Passage in 1845 started the nineteenth-century wave of Arctic exploration. Franklin took 129 men on two ships, and no dogs. The men hauled the sledges themselves. And they all died.

SONJA: It's interesting that thirty years after Franklin's terrible trip, the British government sent out an expedition to try to go to the North Pole, and it was very similar to Franklin's. George Nares was in charge of that one, and he took 120 people. They did take dogs, I believe, but the dogs died and the men ended up hauling the sledges themselves anyway.

Nares sent home a famous telegram: "North Pole impracticable." He came back a year before he was expected, and he and most of his men stayed alive. Nansen's trip in the Fram *began eighteen years later, 1893, and he had a completely different approach.*

STEVE: Nansen figured out that the pack ice drifts around the North Pole by studying artifacts that drifted in from the wreck of an earlier expedition.

A pair of oilskin trousers was found frozen into an ice floe almost three thousand miles from where it was lost.

STEVE: I didn't know it was oilskin trousers. Imagine somebody finding them and turning them in! And then Nansen heard about it. I really admire him for following through and testing his drift theory. He designed the *Fram* and got it built, and then deliberately got it locked in the ice. Over and over he describes how comfortable he was on the *Fram.* They hardly used any coal. The ship still had coal on it when it returned.

How did they manage not to use it?

SONJA: The drift. They were locked in the ice almost the whole time, for three years.

STEVE: They used kerosene, or what they called coal oil, for heating and cooking. The Primus stove was invented just in time for their trip. And they built a windmill and generated electricity for lights. They were saving the coal in case they needed to fire up their steam engine. But the *Fram* just drifted beautifully.

SONJA: Before we left on the North Pole trip, we saw the *Fram* in Oslo. It's on display. One of the sledges was sitting right there by the ship. It was exciting! I thought, "This is Nansen's sledge!" It was so close, almost touchable. So were the kayaks. All

Nansen's designs are so remarkable.

STEVE: They designed and built the sledges and kayaks on the ship, while they were under way. Of course, now the ship is empty. You can't get a sense of it as a working ship. You can walk around inside it, but all you can see are the cabins. They had a shop with machine tools, and a dining room, kitchen, library, lounges, almost as many amenities as our ship, the *Yamal*.

SONJA: You couldn't see any trace of all the different levels of insulation. I wish there had been a cutaway. Reindeer hide, felt, straw, and wood were incorporated into the structure of the hull. Some of the materials were there to control the condensation. Nansen studied wrecks of earlier ships and learned from them how to keep people warm and dry, as well as to design the shape of the hull so the ship could push up in the ice and not get crushed.

It was an achievement in itself that Nansen's crew spent three years on a ship up there without its being crushed.

STEVE: Even now, conditions have to be right for anyone to stand where we stood. But it wasn't just that our trip was unusual, it was that everything up there is undisturbed—people haven't been there. Nansen talks in his journal about finding a big log on Cape Norway. That log was still there, just lying there, after a hundred years. What serendipity for him to find that log! There were no trees within more than a thousand miles. When I saw that log, what I had read became so vivid: Nansen and Johansen building their hut, using the log for a ridgepole, draping walrus hides over it.

SONJA: Without that log, what would have happened to them?

How long had it been there before they got there? And where did it come from?

STEVE: Wouldn't it be nice to carbon-date it? Because it really must be almost petrified—it's so dry there.

SONJA: When we sighted Cape Norway from our ship, we got very excited. This was the place where Nansen built his hut! It took us an hour to get there after sighting it. It took Nansen fourteen days.

STEVE: He spent the length of our whole trip just to get from seeing land to standing on land. It was fourteen days from the time we left home in Seattle until we arrived back there again.

Yes. The time we spent on the ship was less: ten days. It's absolutely true that Nansen's sense of time was completely different from ours. His trip was like going to the moon.

SONJA: For us, there was still some of that feeling. I know that some of the people in our group came because they had been everywhere else and there weren't any more notches left to put on their belts. But what I loved about it was their surprise and delight in what they were seeing. It was more than a notch. On a deeper level, everyone truly understood the magnitude of where we were. What brought you on this trip, by the way?

I wanted to be someplace I couldn't imagine being. This was different from you. You wanted to see what Nansen saw. I didn't even know about Nansen before I started out, and never thought particularly about the Arctic before. But the North Pole is a truly symbolic place. There is an expression people sometimes use, "my true north," meaning the love of your life, the steady guiding spirit, and true north, in scientific language, means the top point of the axis on which the earth rotates, the North Pole.

CHAPTER TWO
THE SHIP

Journey: the Ship

The *Yamal* is a solitary ship in the summertime. From the air she looks small and self-contained on a cushion of ice that could just as well be clouds stretching as far as it is possible to see. In fact, she is large, a cumbersome giant that in the wintertime shelters freighters against her stern as she clears the way for them on the long trip from Murmansk, Russia, through the Northeast Passage and the frozen Bering Strait to the Pacific Ocean.

In the larger of her two helicopters, we passengers, a dozen at a time, took flight-seeing excursions. Looking down in overcast daylight, I could see a line at the horizon but no difference above or below it. We were given earplugs to mute the helicopter's noise and, dreamily, I saw the ship as if suspended. She was moving, but her rapidly freezing wake was barely visible. Her blunt nose pressed forward, her towers did not smoke, and the flat empty ledge of the helicopter-landing pad sat like a folded wing at her rear. She was completely alone in the expanse of white. We banked and dropped to see her wide bridge and the ice-eating grin painted on her face, and at close range we saw at her side a great blue shape emerging. A piece of ice six feet thick and three times as high glided gracefully into the air and then submerged under the dark hull. I could grasp the size of the ice shape only by thinking about it in relationship to the size of the ship; from the air everything was toylike.

On the ship, understanding size was even more difficult. In the space around us, there was nothing familiar, only ice stretching to the horizon, so we could not make comparisons of scale. And as we were twenty feet above the ice on the *Yamal*'s lowest deck, the ice fragments rising and falling at our sides seemed smaller than they were. In our bodies, however, we felt the size of the chunks that we were displacing. The ship rammed against the ice sheet with a great shuddering. Then it stopped, backed up with a sustained grinding noise, and rammed again. A glistening pale blue shape appeared followed by another and another, dripping icicles, and finally subsiding underneath us.

"Those ice blocks are the size of SUVs," someone shouted over the noise.

"Most of them are bigger," someone else replied. The grinding and banging were punctuated by the sharp cracking sound of splitting ice as deep blue fissures opened at our sides. Some of these split delicately with an almost tuneful sound, and others opened quickly with a sound like a rifle shot. The ship rammed and retreated, rammed and retreated. In the dining room, stacked plates jiggled with a high-pitched stuttering and silverware rattled of its own accord, snare-drum-like against the table. Our top speed, in open water, was twenty-two knots, about twenty-five miles an hour, but in the permanent ice pack close to the pole we moved at barely three knots, three and a half miles an hour.

In my cabin, I climbed up onto a narrow ledge with my camera and pushed my head and arms out the open window, pulling in after each photo to warm myself and keep the camera from freezing. I calculated that my cabin was at about the height of an eight- or nine-story building above the ice, but fine frozen spray sometimes would hit me in the face. Hours passed.

When I became stiff from the effort of maintaining my cramped position, I would climb two flights of stairs to the bridge. Here there were always people, ship's officers and passengers, scattered along the row of windows that stretches nearly the ship's full width of ninety-eight feet. A working icebreaker must be wider than any ship that she escorts. In winter, especially, when the sun does not come up for months, she needs a tall bridge and high-intensity lights. *Yamal* is a Siberian Nenets word meaning "end of the earth."

The *Yamal* has an ice knife seventy-five feet behind the tip of the prow, just where the keel first touches the water. The ice knife works passively, cutting ice like glass by nicking it and then riding up on it until it shears of its own accord. The *Yamal*'s keel, like that of Nansen's *Fram*, is deeply sloped so if she is "nipped" by ice, she will rise up and not be crushed.

The *Yamal* is 492 feet long, a football field and a half. She was launched in 1992 and is the newest of a group of five Arktika class nuclear icebreakers leased by the Russian government to the Murmansk Shipping Company. The first of these, named *Arktika* and launched in 1975, traveled to the North Pole in 1977. It was the first surface vessel to succeed in reaching it.

On the *Yamal* we felt safe, except perhaps at the lifeboat drill on our first day at sea. We were given full-body dry suits, one for each of us. Anyone in the water for more than fifteen minutes without one, we were told, would not survive. We imagined crowding into an inflatable lifeboat in our suits, huddling against one another to keep warm, great ice shapes pressing against our vulnerable craft.

But this was fantasy. Deep down, we regarded the *Yamal* as invulnerable. The hull is made of double steel layers, each two inches thick at its thinnest spot, with water ballast in between. There are nine watertight compartments. A large helicopter, used to check ice conditions, is backed up, in case of emergency, by a second, smaller one. There is a complete machine shop, and machinists in the crew are trained to manufacture parts that might become damaged. There are four extra blades for the propellers, and the crew includes divers skillful enough to install them beneath the ice.

Russia has one diesel and five nuclear-powered icebreakers. After the *Yamal* finished our trip, the Russian ships collectively had made thirty-one trips to the North Pole. Our trip was the twentieth for the *Yamal*. Ships from countries other than Russia, all together, have made eight. Someone asked the chief engineer if the *Yamal* could make it to the pole without using nuclear power. "With *Yamal*, so strongly made, perhaps it could be done with coal," he replied. "But you'd have to have two other ships following along behind to hold enough coal, and it would be very dirty." I imagined three ships piled with coal spewing black smoke into this white place."If it ever becomes illegal to operate nuclear ships," the engineer continued, "we can park *Yamal* offshore by a medium-sized city and supply it with power for four and a half years before we would need to replace the fuel."

We climbed down narrow green stairways and walked single file through corridors lined with pipes into *Yamal*'s hull. We saw massive hot-water tanks linked by fat twisting pipes to steam turbines. Then a door opened and we were in another place entirely, a science-fiction place full of dials and glowing lights, the control room for the reactors. Just behind this room we looked through thick, clouded glass at the reactors themselves, two large, red tanks. "They hold 245 enriched uranium rods, shielded by pressurized water, high-density concrete, and steel," the engineer explained. "It's not dangerous to go near them—we used to take passengers into the compartment. But now it is forbidden." He laughed. I learned later that it was forbidden because of terrorism fears, not because of danger. Radiation in the compartment is within established limits for reactor operation. In the passenger areas of the ship, eighty-six sensors monitor constantly and radiation levels are about the same as ordinary radiation in the *Yamal*'s homeport of Murmansk, about the same as most cities around the world.

The *Yamal*'s smokestack does not smoke, but her powerful nuclear heartbeat sends a great quantity of heat into the air. Heat poured from every opening. Windows were not closed, and here and there around the deck were louvers leaking heat, cozy for us to press against as we stood outside. Inside, we wore lightweight clothes.

ВХОД

RA-25394
СПАРК SPARC

MCO
MSC

ГТГ-1

From the Journal of Fridtjof Nansen
September 23 to November 18, 1894

Sunday, September 23

It was a year yesterday since we made fast for the first time to the great hummock in the ice. Hansen improved the occasion by making a chart of our drift for the year. It does not look so very bad, though the distance is not great; the direction is almost exactly what I had expected. But more of this tomorrow; it is so late that I cannot write about it now. The nights are turning darker and darker; winter is settling down upon us.

Tuesday, September 25

Everything has come right so far; the direction of our drift is exactly parallel with the course which I conjectured to have been taken by the floe with the *Jeannette* relics, and which I pricked out on the chart prepared for my London address. This course touched about latitude 87.5° north. I have no right to expect a more northerly drift than parallel to this, and have no right to be anything but happy if I get as far. Our aim, as I have so often tried to make clear, is not so much to reach the point in which the earth's axis terminates, as to traverse and explore the unknown Polar Sea; and yet I should like to get to the Pole, too, and hope that it will be possible to do so, if only we can reach 84° or 85° by March. And why should we not?

Thursday, October 4

Life goes on in the regular routine; there is always some little piece of work turning up to be done. Yesterday the breaking in of the young dogs began. These were the puppies born on December 13, 1893. They were unmanageable at first, and rushed about in all directions; but in a little while they drew like old dogs, and were altogether better than we expected.

Kvik, of course, set them a noble example. It fell to Mogstad's lot to begin the training, as it was his week for looking after the dogs. This duty is taken in turns now; each man has his week of attending to them, both morning and afternoon.

It seems to me that a very satisfactory state of feeling prevails on board at present, when we are just entering our second Arctic night, which we expect is to be a longer, and probably also a colder, one than any people before us have experienced. There is appreciably less light every day; soon there will be none; but the good spirits do not wane with the light. It seems to me that we are more uniformly cheerful than we have ever been. What the reason of this is I cannot tell; perhaps just custom. But certainly, too, we are well off—in clover, as the saying is. We are drifting gently, but it is to be hoped surely, on through the dark unknown, where terrified fancy has pictured all possible horrors. Yet we are living a life of luxury and plenty, surrounded by all the comforts of civilization. I think we shall be better off this winter than last.

The firing apparatus [Primus stove] in the galley is working splendidly, and the cook himself is now of the opinion that it is an invention which approaches perfection. So we shall burn nothing but coal-oil there now; it warms the place well, and a good deal of the heat comes up here into the workroom, where I sometimes sit and perspire until I have to take off one garment after another, although the window is open and there are 30 odd degrees of cold outside.

Wednesday, October 10

Exactly thirty-three years old, then. There is nothing to be said to that, except that life is moving on, and will never turn back. They have all been touchingly nice to me today, and we have held fête. The thermometer is down to 24° below zero this evening; this is certainly the coldest birthday I have had yet.

A sumptuous dinner: 1. Fish-pudding. 2. Sausages and tongue, with potatoes, haricot beans, and peas. 3. Preserved strawberries with rice and cream; Crown extract of malt. But when one has said goodnight and sits here alone, sadness comes; and if one goes on deck there are the stars high overhead in the clear sky. In the south is a smoldering aurora arch, which from time to time sends up streamers, a constant, restless flickering.

We have been talking a little about this expedition, [ship's captain] Sverdrup and I. When we were out on the ice in the afternoon he suddenly said, "Yes, next October you will, perhaps, not be on board the *Fram.*" To which I had to answer that, unless the winter turned out badly, I probably should not. But still I cannot believe in this rightly myself.

Tuesday, November 13

Thermometer minus 36.4°F. The ice is packing in several quarters during the day, and the roar is pretty loud, now that the ice has become colder. It can be heard from afar—a strange roar, which would sound uncanny to anyone who did not know what it was.

A delightful snowshoe run in the light of the full moon. Is life a vale of tears? Is it such a deplorable fate to dash off like the wind, with all the dogs skipping around one, over the boundless expanse of ice, through a night like this, in the fresh, crackling frost, while the snowshoes glide over the smooth surface, so that you scarcely know you are touching the earth, and the stars hang high in the blue vault above? This is more, indeed, than one has any right to expect of life; it is a fairy tale from another world, from a life to come.

And then to return home to one's cozy study-cabin, kindle the stove, light the lamp, fill a pipe, stretch oneself on the sofa, and send dreams out into the world with the curling clouds of smoke—is that a dire infliction? Thus I catch myself sitting staring at the fire for hours together, dreaming myself away—

a useful way of employing the time. But at least it makes it slip unnoticed by, until the dreams are swept away in an ice-blast of reality, and I sit here in the midst of desolation, and nervously set to work again.

Friday, November 16

In the forenoon I went out with Sverdrup on snowshoes in the moonlight, and we talked seriously of the prospects of our drift and of the proposed expedition northward over the ice in the spring. In the evening we went into the matter more thoroughly in his cabin. I stated my views, in which he entirely coincided. I have of late been meditating a great deal on what is the proper course to pursue, supposing the drift does not take us so far north by the month of March as I had anticipated. But the more I think of it, the more firmly am I persuaded that it is the thing to do. For if it is right to set out at 85°, it must be no less right to set out at 82° or 83°. In either case we should penetrate into more northerly regions than we should otherwise reach, and this becomes all the more desirable if the *Fram* herself does not get so far north as we had hoped. If we cannot actually reach the Pole, we must turn back before reaching it.

But now, for the expedition itself. It will consist of twenty-eight dogs, two men, and 2,100 pounds of provisions and equipments. The distance to the pole from 83° is 483 miles. Is it too much to calculate that we may be able to accomplish that distance in fifty days? In fifty days we shall have consumed a pound of pemmican [dried meat with bone marrow grease] a day for each dog—that is, 1,400 pounds altogether; and two pounds of provisions for each man daily is two hundred pounds. As some fuel also will have been consumed during this time, the freight on the sledges will have diminished to less than five hundred pounds; but a burden like this is nothing for twenty-eight dogs to draw, so that they ought to go ahead like a gale of wind during the latter part of the time, and thus do it in less than the fifty days.

There is yet another question that must be taken into consideration. Have I the right to deprive the ship and those who remain behind of the resources such an expedition entails? The fact that there will be two men less is of little importance, for the *Fram* can be handled quite as well with eleven men. A more important point is that we shall have to take with us all the dogs. But there are ample sledge provisions and first-class sledge equipments on board, and it is inconceivable that in case anything happened to the *Fram* they should be unable to reach Franz Josef Land or Spitsbergen.

Now, as before, I am of the opinion that the *Fram* will in all probability drift right across the polar basin and out on the other side without being stopped, and without being destroyed. But even if any accident should occur, I do not see why the crew should not be able to make their way home in safety, provided due measures of precaution are observed. Consequently, I think there is no reason why a sledge expedition should not leave the *Fram*, and I feel that as it promises such good results it ought certainly to be attempted.

I have chosen Johansen to be my companion, and he is in all respects well qualified for that work. He is an accomplished snowshoer, and few can equal his powers of endurance—a fine fellow, physically and mentally. I have not yet asked him, but think of doing so soon, in order that he may be prepared. Blessing and Hansen also would certainly be all eagerness to accompany me; but Hansen must remain behind to take charge of the observations, and Blessing cannot desert his post as doctor. Several of the others, too, would do quite well, and would, I doubt not, be willing enough.

Sunday, November 18

It seems as if I could not properly realize the idea that I am really to set out, and that in three months' time. Sometimes I delude myself with charming dreams of my return home after toil and victory, and then all is clear and bright. Then these are succeeded by thoughts of the uncertainty and deceptiveness of the future and what may be lurking in it, and my dreams fade away like the northern lights, pale and colorless.

Ugh! These everlasting cold fits of doubt! Before every decisive resolution the dice of death must be thrown. Is there too much to venture, and too little to gain? There is more to be gained, at all events, than there is here. Then is it not my duty? Besides, there is only one to whom I am responsible, and she—? I shall come back, I know it. I have strength enough for the task. "Be thou true unto death, and thou shalt inherit the crown of life."

A Conversation with Larry Braden and Janet Landfried

On the Yamal, *I thought that passengers Lawrence (Larry) Braden and Janet Landfried had especially independent frames of mind. Both are high school teachers and licensed pilots. Larry teaches mathematics and science at St. Paul's School, an Episcopal residential college preparatory school in New Hampshire. Janet recently retired from thirty-seven years of teaching history, government, and economics in the public high schools of Redlands, California. We spoke about the* Yamal *and its Russian crew, Peary's North Pole claim, and attitudes toward global warming.*

LARRY: We traveled seven hundred miles from Spitsbergen to the North Pole on the *Yamal*, and a little more than that on the way back, since we detoured to Franz Josef Land. This was the eighth trip for our captain, and he said the ice conditions were as bad as he had ever seen them this time of year.

I was delighted that we saw so much ice. I had read that the ice at the North Pole is melting, and I was afraid we would not see very much of it.

JANET: The ice is melting overall. But it seems to vary on different routes in different years. I thought the motion of the ship when it was breaking ice would be rhythmic, like being on a train. But it wasn't. There was booming and grinding and the ice was rolling out from under us. The ship jolted and shuddered, but it didn't sway, the way normal ships do.

LARRY: Ice chunks as big as football fields were getting pushed aside; pieces bigger than my living room were erupting from the sides of the ship; shards the size of your head traced parabolic arcs through the sky! But in terms of all the ice on earth, only a

Janet Landfried

Larry Braden

small amount is around the North Pole. Ninety percent of the earth's ice is in Antarctica, nine percent in Greenland, and only one percent everywhere else.

The Arctic Ocean is small, isn't it?

LARRY: It's the smallest of the five oceans of the world, about eight and a half million square miles. About 50 percent of it is permanently covered by sea ice. I was glad to be up there! If I hadn't picked up a copy of *New York* magazine at Boston's South Station, I wouldn't have even known about the trip. There was a picture of the *Yamal* at the North Pole. Wowee, I thought, You can go there on that? When I got to New York, I called and reserved the very last cabin aboard the ship.

That was a quick decision. Why did you want to go?

LARRY: When my daughter was a little girl, I took her up to the top of the World Trade Center and said, "Look, Abbey, we're the highest-up people in New York!" I always wanted to be the highest, go the farthest. On the Big Island of Hawaii, at South Point, it thrilled me to be the southernmost person in the United States. I grew up in the oil fields north of Bakersfield. My entire world stretched from Los Angeles to San Francisco. I couldn't wait to get out.

Did you tell me that you dropped out of high school?

LARRY: Actually, I flunked out of high school. I developed a lifelong hatred of sports and was totally indifferent to all the things lauded by high schools. Then somebody showed me a calculus book, and I thought, I can understand this! Mathematics has an eternal beauty. Paintings and sculpture will decay over the millennia, but the stark beauty and logic of Euclid's proof of the infinitude of primes is just as fresh as when he proved it twenty-three hundred years ago. Mathematics is the one certain thing.

Does this have anything to do with the North Pole? Is the North Pole actually an abstraction? It is a mathematically determined point.

JANET: The pole is a certainty. It is definitely there. It is an exact location.

LARRY: The poles and the equator are real enough, therefore not abstractions. But the longitudes and latitudes are abstractions. Lewis Carroll wrote in 1876:

> "'What's the good of Mercator's North Poles and Equators,
> Tropics, Zones, and Meridian Lines?'
> So the Bellman would cry: and the crew would reply,
> 'They are merely conventional signs!'"

I disagree with him about the poles and the equator. But the meridian lines are abstractions.

Despite flunking out of high school, you're a high school teacher now, aren't you?

LARRY: Yes. I've also worked as a dishwasher, oil-field roustabout, bodyguard, and statistician. My first job after graduating from Berkeley and Harvard was teaching math and science at Iolani School, a private Episcopal school in Honolulu. I was also a commercial pilot and parachute rigger in those years.

Janet, you're originally from Hawaii, aren't you?

JANET: Yes. That's how Larry and I became acquainted on the *Yamal*, talking about Hawaii. I grew up on Kauai. My mother's father was a contract laborer who came from China to work in the sugar fields there. On my father's side there is missionary background, along with Hawaiian, French, Portuguese, and German ancestry. I was part of the last graduating class in the Territory of Hawaii—it became a state that August. I spoke mostly Pidgin English among my friends when I was growing up.

Could you say something in Pidgin? I don't know what it sounds like.

JANET: Eh you guys, stay come heah. I goin' show you one akami dog. One poi dog, but oh, da cute. She fo' real. Eh? Pidgin is really a spoken language and depends on inflections in speech and a mixture of words from various ethnic groups. It began primarily as a way for the different groups to communicate on the sugar plantations. Although I left Hawaii to go to college on the mainland, and stayed there to teach, I still consider Hawaii my home and I go back often.

Larry, you lived in Russia for a while. When was that?

LARRY: I was there in 1969-70, the Brezhnev years.

Both of you got to know some of the Russian crew members on our trip.

JANET: I was traveling with a friend who is an airline pilot, and we became friends with one of the electrical engineers, Vadim. The crew of the *Yamal* works four months on and four months off, and Vadim invited us to visit him in St. Petersburg during one of his times off. The Russians are very hospitable, and we were honored by the invitation. We visited him several months later, and he drove us all over the city. We had a great time! Soon after we saw him, he went back to work on the *Yamal* breaking ice for the cargo ships. When Arnold Schwarzenegger was elected governor of California, my Russian friend e-mailed me. Vadim is into weight lifting. They receive live news broadcasts by satellite.

LARRY: I speak a little Russian, and I got into some conversations with Alexander, a crew member I met by hanging out on the stern, away from the other passengers. He said that he had once served on a Soviet submarine and had been underneath the pole. He asked if I had been in the American navy. I said I hadn't, but that I once shipped out as a guest on a fast frigate from Pearl Harbor, looking for Soviet submarines. "I guess you could say that we were looking for you," I told him. We both thought this was terribly funny. He showed me a picture of his wife and his three sons, all of them in medical school. I gave him an 82nd Airborne patch. He gave me a Russian naval calendar for my wallet.

There was a lot of activity around the pole during the Cold War. In the late 1940s we discovered that the Soviets had bombers capable of reaching us by that route, and in the late 1950s there was the threat of submarines that could fire missiles.

LARRY: That was the shortest distance for them to shoot a missile headed for us. They were out there, and we were watching them.

The Russians developed their fleet of nuclear icebreakers in the 1980s. Was that for military purposes?

JANET: The icebreakers were developed to break ice for commercial ships traveling through the Northeast Passage. The Russians have a long coastline along the Northeast Passage, which is a short cut from the Barents Sea to the Bering Sea and America and Asia. It is usually full of ice except for Murmansk, the Russian port on the Barents Sea; the Gulf Stream keeps Murmansk open, and that's where the icebreaker fleet is based.

We really knew we were on a nuclear ship. It was so warm, for one thing. And there was plenty of electricity, and plenty of fresh water.

LARRY: The evaporators gave us five tons of fresh water every hour. So what if we took hour-long hot showers, or left the windows open or the lights on? The reactors were generating more energy than we could possibly use.

I swam every day in the little pool down below the decks, by the engine room, until I heard that the pool was filled with secondary cooling water from the reactors.

LARRY: That couldn't be correct. The pool is saltwater. The secondary water is very pure distilled water. Hot salt water would cause terrible problems in the turbines. The *Yamal* is run by a steam engine that uses unconventional fuel. The reactors heat water to turn it into 660°F steam, superheated steam, not the tame stuff on locomotives and riverboats. On the *Yamal,* there's a heat interchange system. The hot water tanks we saw are not storage tanks as such. They hold the extremely hot water from the reactors that immediately goes out in tubes to heat the secondary water, which is what creates the steam that goes into the turbines.

Where does the water in the swimming pool come from?

LARRY: The steam needs to be cooled to condense it into water again, and seawater is used. That must be the water that later goes in the pool. It's two closed systems. The distilled water is in pipes with the seawater going over them.

So the water in the pool wasn't even near the reactor. I'm relieved. I stopped swimming for a couple of days, but the warm salt water was so wonderful, I went back to it. I usually had the pool to myself, and it was strange to be swimming deep down in the ship, knowing it was in the middle of all that ice.

JANET: When the ship was breaking ice, the waves in the pool were violent. If we had been on an American ship, I don't know that swimming would have been allowed.

Do you think the Yamal *was absolutely safe in regard to the nuclear power?*

LARRY: Yes, it was perfectly safe. It is perfectly safe to live next door to Three Mile Island. Radiation is part of nature, and in New Hampshire where I live we have radon in our cellars from the uranium in granite decomposing into radium and then radon. Of course, nuclear radiation from the sun keeps us alive. Not that the reactors on the *Yamal* weren't potentially dangerous. Mishandled, I am sure they could have killed us all. But a boiler blowing up on a ship of any kind would kill people.

JANET: The reactors didn't really bother me. I guess I just optimistically think that most people will not do anything that will put them in jeopardy. And these ships have been around for a few years.

Do you think the Russians are less cautious than we are?

LARRY: Absolutely, the Russians are less cautious! But they are very good technicians.

Janet, you and Larry are both pilots, and Larry is a parachutist. I was wondering if you see danger as a kind of sport? That was something the explorers were familiar with.

JANET: As I said, I don't think most people put themselves in situations that are going to be dangerous. I learned to fly when my former husband wanted to learn. We got our licenses within a month of each other and flew our own plane all over the states. I even taught private ground school for three years. It took most of the mystery out of flying. I don't think I'm a risk-taker but I do like to do unusual things.

Larry, you told me you have been flying since you were a teenager. When did you begin parachuting?

LARRY: I jumped off the garage twenty or thirty times when my father forbade me to take parachuting lessons at the age of fifteen. He said that I could learn to fly instead. I know "fun jumping" is an oxymoron for most people, but not for me. I started parachuting as soon as I graduated from college. I'm very much the coward, though. When jumping out of airplanes, for instance, I always pack my own parachute so I know it will open. If there is any sight more beautiful than a freshly opened parachute canopy above your head, I have yet to experience it.

Have you ever thought about parachuting over the North Pole? There's a base, called Borneo, on the drift ice, and planes take parachutists from there. I think it's run mainly by Russians.

LARRY: I have American and Indian friends who have parachuted onto the pole in essentially suicidal conditions—forty-knot winds, for starters. Nowadays, Russians are actually more concerned about loss of life. I tried to get onto the pole by parachute. I could have gone with a military group—I've done some work for the military as a rigger and parachute instructor. But my teaching schedule precluded that trip.

Adventurers who go to the North Pole now by walking, or dogsled, or skiing can be looked after by Borneo. The people at the base keep track of them using Global Positioning Systems. And rescue helicopters fly from there. Of course, if you fall into a lead opening up underneath you, no one at Borneo can save you. Still, it's different traveling now from when Nansen was out there, or Peary, trying to be the first to set eyes on the North Pole.

JANET: Most expeditions today seem to start from Ellesmere Island, in Canada, or from Greenland. Didn't Peary start out from that direction?

LARRY: Peary tried to reach the pole by a route through Smith Sound, between Canada and Greenland, with Polar Eskimos from Greenland. But he failed. And then he lied about it. All the authorities think that now.

JANET: I recently read an article that makes a case for Peary having got there.

LARRY: Oh, really? I thought everybody was in agreement now that he didn't.

JANET: There've been two or three books that I know of published in the past few years that argue that he didn't. History is constantly being re-examined. If I could go back, I would major in science instead of history; the answers there are so much more definite. But in history, you have to look at the social and political climate of any event. It seems that the arguments now about whether Peary made it to the pole have something to do with race. Peary didn't take a white man with him on the last leg of his trip. He took Matthew Henson, who was black, and four Eskimos. If you dismiss Peary's claim, you also have to dismiss them. Henson's word was not given credibility in 1909 because he was black. But now we know that he was professional as an explorer and truthful as a person. And he always maintained, to his death, that he and Peary had reached the pole.

It's not surprising that Henson would be ignored in 1909. And Peary didn't help any. He was very patronizing to Henson.

JANET: Peary couldn't have gotten as far as he did without him. Henson was the best sledge-dog driver Peary had in the big party that started out with him. And he spoke the Eskimos' language; he was the only one who could communicate with them. He had to convince them to venture so far onto the sea ice, something they wouldn't ordinarily do. The article I read makes a very good case about it.

This controversy is complicated by all the strong personalities involved. Peary strikes me as driven by ambition. Maybe he did lie. There is a serious question about whether he could have made it to the pole in the time he said he did. But, I remember reading a comment by someone who knew both Cook and Peary: "Cook is a gentleman and a liar, and Peary is neither."

LARRY: Congress debated whether Cook or Peary reached the

pole and decided Peary did and Cook didn't! Congress! How could they decide?

I guess it needed resolution. The public had been reading books by explorers and getting excited about the North Pole since the mid-1800s. Two years after Cook and Peary claimed the North Pole, Amundsen and Scott competed in getting to the South Pole. That was in 1911. In 1914, the Great War, as it was called then, came along and replaced exploration as a news focus. The explorers never regained much popular interest, although lately there has been some excitement about Antarctic exploration with the retelling on television of the story of Ernest Shackleton's 1914-17 expedition there. The Arctic seems to be mentioned in the newspapers now only once in a while, usually in connection with global warming.

LARRY: There's a lot of gloom and doom about global warming, but I just read a newspaper story about a research institute in Montreal that basically points out the good things: we live twice as long as our great-grandparents, our environment is improving, and our forests are healthy.

In Alaska, I saw an unhealthy forest that was destroyed by beetles that had never been able to live there before, but had moved in because of warming.

LARRY: What I meant by healthy forests was that carbon dioxide, CO_2, in the atmosphere is partly carbon, and it fertilizes plants. The carbon cycle keeps things in balance. Topsoil is improved and plants grow stronger in an atmosphere with more CO_2. The growing plants absorb and use some of the CO_2 that we're putting into the atmosphere.

That's true, but it can only go to a point, since plants can only use a certain amount of fertilizer. Too much, and they die. But we could keep global warming from being all gloom and doom if we managed the carbon cycle better in regard to plants.

JANET: I read recently that native Canadian tribes, environmental groups, and energy and forestry companies in Canada are forming a coalition to conserve and manage the boreal forest there. This is unprecedented cooperation among those groups. The boreal forest in Canada is one of the largest unspoiled woodlands in the world.

The boreal forest is the forest just south of the area of permafrost, the permanently frozen soil. However, the permafrost is no longer permanently frozen in a lot of places. Warming temperatures in the Arctic are not in dispute—they are documented. And more heat means more moisture in the air, which makes the storms generated in the Arctic more extreme, and causes damage around the world from floods, among other things. Have you ever heard of an organization called the Global Climate Coalition?

JANET: No, I haven't.

It's an organization that was founded in the early 1990s by major corporations, mostly oil companies and auto manufacturers. It produces publications, and hires publicists to influence journalists toward the view that there is nothing alarming in global warming. The interesting thing is that several insurance companies have just quit the Global Climate Coalition. They have had huge losses lately from storms and floods.

LARRY: I recently read a book, *The Skeptical Environmentalist,* written by Bjorn Lomberg, a mathematician and Greenpeace activist, telling how environmental groups twist statistics and scare people for their own purposes.

In the subject of global warming, science and politics are mixed together. We live in a world of manipulators. You have to decide whom to trust.

CHAPTER THREE
THE WEATHER

Journey: the Weather

Day and night the sun was visible in the sky, but for four days and nights it stayed behind clouds and leaked through them to glare against the ice in streaks or flares. Blue pools became light-reflecting mirrors and rubble ice flashed startling blue dots and dashes from nicks in its surface snow.

Snow in the Arctic is not the soft, fluffy stuff of romantic movies. Matthew Henson, Peary's companion on his attempts to reach the North Pole, likened Arctic snow to granulated sugar: dry, hard, and crystalline. He pointed out in his journal that igloos are made from it—not from ice, which would be impossibly hard to cut. A hundred years ago when Henson was in the Arctic, the snow was deeper than it is now, but in general the air near the pole is too cold and dry to produce a lot of snow. In winter, with temperatures 20°F or more below zero, the snow cover is less than a foot deep, and in summer, which is barely freezing, there is only just enough snow in the highest latitudes to turn everything white.

The snow that does fall doesn't quickly melt, nor does it stick well to the ice. It blows around. Standing on the deck of the *Yamal,* I saw it being picked up by wind and imagined the whiteouts dreaded by explorers when nothing is visible and movement is nearly impossible. Suspended snow crystals often formed halos from ground to air like colorless rainbows when the sun appeared.

The ship's cabins were bright at night, so I slept wearing an eyeshade. During the fourth night we were on the *Yamal,* I woke and pulled off the shade to see the time. The clock said 3 a.m. I thought, "It can't be." A sunbeam was full in my eyes, as if it were a bright morning at home. I got out of bed and stuck my head out the open window, feeling the cold air on my face. The sun was fully visible, in blue sky above dazzling ice. I put on my coat and walked around the ship's decks taking pictures, thinking this might be the only blue sky I would see, and not meeting another soul. The next day, however, the sun was still free of clouds when we arrived at the pole. This was unusual for July.

Summer in the high Arctic is almost always cloudy. There are many open-water leads then, and clouds are formed by evaporation; explorers call low distant clouds "water-sky," a warning of water ahead. Because of the angle of the tilt of the earth, the sun stays low in the sky at high latitudes, and its rays fall to the ground obliquely and do not provide much heat. That, essentially, is why the polar regions are cold. If there is a lot of ice, some heat from the sun is reflected back into the atmosphere, and the air stays cold. But if there is a lot of water instead of ice, the heat is absorbed into the water, warming the air above it, increasing the clouds, and further melting the ice.

In winter, when the sun does not appear at the pole for six months, it can be inconceivably cold, and when it is that cold, it is also clear. Very cold air cannot carry much water vapor. But in the earth's high atmosphere, warm air from the equatorial region is always circulating, meeting cold air from polar regions at what are called weather fronts. Storms often result that affect weather throughout the world. Warm air from the equator that reaches the North Pole brings water vapor that is released as clouds and snow, and it mitigates the temperature, but not enough to significantly melt the ice.

The permanent pack, the sea ice that does not melt in summer, has a boundary stable enough to be shown on maps. It runs irregularly around the pole and passes the north side of the islands of Franz Josef Land and the Svalbard archipelago, which includes the island of Spitsbergen. It continues on at nearly the same latitude to almost touch Greenland at Pearyland (its northernmost tip), and then drops to a slightly lower latitude in the vicinity of Alaska. The permanent pack is almost as large in area as the United States.

In 2002 our group found the ice pack thick and hard to penetrate, and the leads we saw near the pole were small. But in 2000 when the *Yamal* made the trip at the same time of year, it found a lead ten miles long and three miles wide at the pole, and many more leads everywhere, the ice easy to penetrate. The *New York Times* interviewed two scientists who had been on that trip. They were alarmed. The polar regions, they said, would be among the first to respond to a global warming trend.

Clearly the quantity of ice that melts in summer varies from year to year, and if the two scientists had been on our trip they would not have been so shocked. But there is cause for worry. In the big picture, Arctic ice is shrinking, both in thickness and in area. Ice thickness has been measured since 1958 by submarines using upward-looking sonar, and the ice indisputably has thinned by roughly 40 percent in that forty-five-year period, dropping from ten to six feet on average at the pole.

Measurements of ice area also show decline. The maximum extent of winter ice decreased by about 3 percent in the 1980s and an additional 3 percent in the 1990s. Summer ice decreased in extent by 9 percent per decade in the same time period. Accurate figures are available from unmanned land and sea stations and from weather satellites.

Science, as it is practiced today, requires massive quantities of detailed measurements, and satellites are increasingly able to provide them in abundance. Radarsat-2, for example, is an orbiting radar satellite launched by Canada in the year 2000. Every three days the satellite provides a complete picture of the ice cover of the Arctic. Because it uses radar rather than photography to generate its information, it can create detailed images in all weather, day and night, and it can reveal information on both ice area and ice thickness. We have only to wait for this and other satellites to accumulate statistics that will provide convincing corrections or irrefutable corroborations for theories of global warming.

How long will we have to wait? Statistics deal in probability. They show trends, not certainties. They incorporate every possible discontinuity and tabulate enough information to show its significance or insignificance. The more certainty is demanded, the longer this takes. Maybe it will take decades, maybe centuries.

It seems wise, however, not to wait that long. Even though some details remain unclear, it is certain that human activities are creating quantities of extra heat in the atmosphere, and the least of many possible consequences is an increase in the number and severity of storms that cause extremes in global weather. Nearly twice as many weather disasters were reported around the world in the 1990s as in the 1980s.

Alarm bells are going off about global warming, and an enormous field of scientists is working on projects related to it. Students in universities use textbooks thick with citations and data, and they must learn a language that is understood only by people in the field. At the same time, new data pours in constantly. Theorists sometimes contradict one another, and other theorists try to reconcile conflicting ideas. The picture will never be crystal clear.

Nevertheless, by using computer modeling based on information about the past, it is possible to create a reasonably clear picture of expected future climate changes, and perhaps even to find a course of action. As we all know, however, computers are only as good as the information put into them. Tested information takes time to develop; the work of each individual is slow. But the work overall is moving quickly. As each small group of scientists develops information in its own narrow field, that information is tested against the work of others in other fields, and the picture comes closer to being formed. The biggest problem now, according to Paul Mayewski, who directed a team that drilled ice cores in the Greenland Ice Sheet, is "creating and holding together teams of people with specialized capabilities over time."

Global warming is extremely complex. Everyone knowledgeable about it agrees it exists, and there is wide agreement on why it exists. But everyone does not agree on what can be done about it, or if something should be done. What scientists are doing now is discovering information and testing it in different frameworks. The Greenland Ice Sheet Project Two, for example, has worked under the auspices of the U.S. National Science Foundation since 1989 to drill ice cores from which its team members (from twenty-five universities) can date large-scale weather events that have happened over the past 110,000 years. An ice core drilled in 1993 by this project and another drilled seventeen miles away by European scientists reinforce each other and have been enormously influential. Information from the cores is being compared to records made by geologists, paleontologists, historians, and others. An assembled puzzle picture is beginning to emerge.

A picture of climate change over more than one hundred thousand years seems like a big picture, but it is only the foreground of an even bigger one. Behind the foreground, stretching back in deep perspective, are more than two million years during which glacial ages have alternated with warm periods, called interglacials. Climate change is caused by several overlapping mechanisms, one of which is the slow movement of continents due to the shifting of the tectonic plates that form the structure of the earth's crust. At present, the arrangement of continents keeps warm equatorial ocean currents from reaching into the highest latitudes, and this encourages ice and snow to accumulate around the poles. As snow accumulates without melting, it forms glaciers.

In a glacial age (also called an ice age), ice sheets cover much of the earth, and the climate is characterized overall by paralyzing cold. Major ice ages in the past have lasted about ninety thousand years and have been separated by warm interglacial periods lasting about ten thousand years. Together, a glacial age and an interglacial make up a cycle of one hundred thousand years. That's oversimplified, of course, but in general it describes the effects of what are called Milankovitch cycles after the Serbian scientist who discovered them in 1912 (they were corroborated by data from other sources in the 1970s). Milankovitch cycles derive from astronomy and mathematics and concern subtle ongoing changes in the behavior of the earth as it orbits the sun: variations in the tilt of its axis, the shape of its orbit, and the direction in which its axis points.

The earth is presently in an interglacial period that has lasted about ten thousand years and, according to Milankovitch cycles, is due to enter an ice age soon. Since our situation at present, so far as Milankovitch cycles are concerned, is that of entering an ice age rather than leaving one, information that tracks the earth's transition from the previous interglacial into the time of the Great Ice Age would be especially useful. The Greenland Ice Sheet was formed in that transition and is only a little more than one hundred thousand years old, but the Antarctic Ice Sheet is much older. In the late 1980s, Russian and French scientists at the Vostok Base, about six hundred miles from the South Pole, succeeded in extracting a core that has been proven to be four hundred thousand years old. This core showed definitively that CO_2 plays a central role in climate change. A second core was drilled in 1995 with American scientists added to the Russian-French team, and both cores are still being analyzed. In the early years of the twenty-first century, we can expect many scientific papers of value to scientists who are contemplating connections between CO_2 in the atmosphere and Milankovitch cycles.

Hundreds of papers have been published since 1993 using data from the one-hundred-thousand-year-old cores pulled from the Greenland ice cap in that year. Many of those papers focus on rapid climate change events that had been postulated from earlier climate data sources and were confirmed by the 1993 Greenland core. Scientists use the acronym RCCE to describe rapid climate change events, and call them "Rickies." That codification masks, in a way, the shock of their meaning. It has been proved, beyond question, that in the distant past severe climate changes frequently have happened very quickly. It is possible for the earth to move from temperate conditions to those of an ice age within a hundred years, possibly even within as short a time as a decade.

A clear example of a rapid climate change event is the Younger Dryas period, which was part of the transition from the Great Ice Age to the interglacial period we are in now. Fourteen thousand five hundred years ago, sea ice in the Arctic decreased suddenly and significantly. At that time, the earth's climate warmed at a dramatic pace. In the previous fifteen hundred years, earth had been sliding gently out of the Great Ice Age, moving toward our present interglacial. Fossils show that forests had returned to northern Europe, and warm-blooded animals, including hunter-gatherer human beings, were living there. Then, warming gathered speed, the sea ice and the glaciers diminished, and in a very short time, possibly only ten years, some parts of the world reversed back into glaciation. Summer temperatures dropped by about 10°F in northern Europe and there is some evidence that mean annual temperatures may have fallen by as much as 20°F. The vegetation changed. The dominant plant became a member of the rose family, the Arctic dryad (*Dryas integrifolia*), and the period—which lasted a thousand years—is named for it.

The most influential current theory of climate change, the theory of the Great Ocean Conveyer Belt, suggests a mechanism other than Milankovitch cycles that could cause an ice age. The Great Ocean Conveyer Belt theory was put forward by geochemist Wallace Broecker in 1985, and Broecker and others are still developing it. Broecker began his research by tracking ocean currents using radioactive isotopes and then connected that knowledge to information about rapid climate shifts gained from ice core samples.

When I read about Broecker's theory, I remembered leaning over the railing of the *Yamal*, watching the polar bear drink fresh water from a melted pool in the saltwater pack ice. Cold and salt make water dense, and dense water sinks. There is more salt in the northern Atlantic Ocean than in any other ocean on earth, and salt hinders freezing, so this ocean freezes at a temperature that is lower by about 7°F than the average. In the Atlantic Ocean, freezing begins at around 25°F. The salt water congeals into a thick layer of ice that contains air-filled bubbles, and the mixture freezes without incorporating much of the salt; the salt sinks. As pack ice gets older, it constantly melts and refreezes. Brine channels develop in the melting process and, in time, most of the remaining salt gradually passes through them into the ocean. "First-year ice will do for washing," Bob Headland, our leader on the *Yamal*, told us. "Second-year ice is for cooking, and third-year ice is best for tea."

Polar explorers have always gotten their drinking water from the top layers of multiyear pack ice, and some, in diaries and books, mention the brine that drips from the undersides of dislodged ice chunks. As salt builds up in the water under the ice, that water becomes very dense and sinks below the warm current arriving from the south. The warm current is about 50°F when it arrives; some of it creates leads, and some is frozen into new ice. Some moves in under the pack ice and is cooled and frozen to the underside, compensating for ice lost as the topside melts. In the course of this cycle, heat is released that warms the air and the water that flows alongside Europe, which would be about 30 percent colder if the ocean did not supply it with warmth. Meanwhile, the dense cold salty water sinks to the bottom, where it becomes a forceful part of the Great Ocean Conveyor Belt.

The Conveyor Belt doesn't reach all the way to the North Pole. It loops back on itself near Greenland and moves south to Antarctica where it mixes with deep water from that area. It rises to become a warm shallow current that passes tropical lands above Australia and then winds around the tip of Africa. Finally, the warm shallow current moves back to Greenland, where it is cooled and becomes deep water that repeats the cycle again.

The Arctic portion of the Conveyor Belt moves especially fast because the extra saltiness of the water makes it sink so deep. Broecker says that Conveyor Belt movement at the Arctic is twenty times more forceful than all the world's great rivers put together. But this movement could slow or even stop if excess freshwater mixes with the salt water while it is being cooled. Broecker speaks of a "salt oscillator" or an "on/off conveyor switch" that could be triggered by something that produces large-magnitude freshening: the melting of a very large glacier, for example, or unusual quantities of snow and rain above the Arctic Circle. Ice core samples from Greenland—and, over a longer period, from Vostok in Antarctica—definitively link warming and freshening events to periods of high levels of carbon dioxide in the atmosphere. Of course, in prehistory, the amount of CO_2 in the atmosphere had nothing to do with human activities. To consider human intervention as a source of global warming, we must return to the foreground of our picture, the interglacial period that began ten thousand years ago. It is in that time period that human beings have gradually created the culture in which we live.

The years from 1300 to 1850 loosely compose what climatologists call the Little Ice Age, a short cold period within that ten-thousand-year time. During what is called the Medieval Warm Period, just before the Little Ice Age, the weather was beautiful worldwide. Consistently warm summers and mild winters were the norm, harvests were abundant, and farming was successful farther north than it can be now. There were vineyards in Wales. The ancestors of the Cree grew corn in Canada near Winnipeg. In Europe, this was the time of the building of the great cathedrals, a wealthy and stable time.

Then, sometime in the thirteenth century, existing glaciers began to grow and new ones appeared. In the Rocky Mountains, ice pushed its way down the slopes, bending and breaking trees in its path; the stumps are still there and can be dated. On Ellesmere Island, in spots where Little Ice Age glaciers have receded, scientists have found mats of smashed but recognizable seven-hundred-year-old plants, the same plants that live in the Arctic now: white dryad, saxifrage, Arctic poppy. When these plants were being frozen into the glaciers on Ellesmere, Europe was becoming exceptionally cold. In 1310 the Thames iced over, and people made bonfires and held foxhunts on its surface. Shipping was disrupted. Then came exceptional rains. In 1315 an invading French cavalry was stopped in Flanders by rain so unremitting that the horses sank into the mud up to their saddles and the foot soldiers up to their knees. Calamitous rain throughout Europe caused crop failures and famine.

In the previous centuries of stable weather and reliable crops, population had increased and people had cut down forests to create farms. Now there was nothing to stop the rain from destroying the land. Real estate records of the time show huge increases in sales of small farms to large landowners, and literature describes bands of rural beggars that roamed from village to village. The early 1320s was called the time of the "Great Dying of the Beasts" by a contemporary chronicle. Farmers, unable to feed their animals, turned them out to forage for themselves; their bodies lay dead around the countryside. A writer in Flanders described city life: "The people were in such great need that it cannot be expressed. The cries that were heard from the poor would move a stone, as they lay in the street with woe and great complain, swollen with hunger."

That was the beginning of five hundred years of wildly fluctuating weather, extreme heat as well as extreme cold, drought as well as deluge. The fluctuations cannot be explained by any single cause. We know that the period included a series of volcanic eruptions (in the seventeenth century alone there were six), and each eruption produced major cold episodes around the world, during which the sun was dimmed for months and sulfur and dust were held in the atmosphere for as long as three years. Sulfur, a component of smog as well as of volcano emissions, causes cooling. Other causes of the radical weather shifts of the Little Ice Age are the subjects of studies and speculations. Some suggest a change in the energy output of the sun. Some suggest that the Little Ice Age was the beginning of the next glacial age. In this line of thought, the Little Ice Age is not over: it only seems so because human activities have forced unnatural heat upon us. There is more work to be done before anyone claims certainty about these theories.

One thing is certain, however: the ocean and the atmosphere work together to produce the weather and climate conditions that affect us. As polar ice caps expanded during the Little Ice Age, atmospheric weather patterns over Europe and North America changed. An excessive number of storm fronts developed, blown from the vicinity of the North Pole by northeasterly winds that largely replaced the southwesterlies that had favored the Vikings in their explorations during the Medieval Warm Period.

When Erik the Red discovered Greenland, named it, and colonized it in the late tenth century, more of it was green than is the case today. It was then, as it is now, glacier covered at the center, but a sizable belt of fertile land existed along the coast. The Viking Greenlanders traded in furs and walrus ivory and also in wool from the sheep that they raised. They traveled frequently to North America, making their way around the lower tip of Greenland. They went routinely to Norway and Iceland. In 1075 a Greenland merchant made a gift of a live polar bear to the king of Denmark. He sent the bear by sailing ship through seas evidently calm enough that the sailors didn't fear the bear's accidental release among them. But by the mid-1500s Greenland's surrounding sea was so turbulent and ice filled that the Viking settlers could no longer conduct lucrative trade. They abandoned Greenland. Its glacier had expanded so that only slim areas at the edges of Greenland were green.

Around 1850, glaciers that had expanded everywhere (in the Alps, the Rockies, and Antarctica as well as the Arctic) began to melt. In 1846, a Russian ship captain recorded a trip in Siberia down a river that had brought him to a flooded landscape. Huge chunks of earth rushed past as he struggled to stay in the main channel. He and the crew were stunned when they saw that one of the chunks was not earth but the monstrous head of an ice age mammoth that had been preserved in permafrost thousands of years earlier.

Those who believe that the Little Ice Age is not over despite the melting of glaciers and general warming make a point of noticing that 1850 marks the approximate beginning of serious human interference with climate. At that time there was a great immigration of European settlers to virgin lands in Australia, New Zealand, and the Americas, and they created farms and grazing lands by cutting and burning forests. Cities throughout Europe and America burned coal; railroads and factories depended on it for energy. The Industrial Revolution had begun, and with it the global warming that concerns us now.

The principle of global warming is faster in its measurable consequences than other principles of climate change. That principle is basically that living plants absorb carbon dioxide, and dead ones release it, especially if burned. Carbon dioxide, along with other greenhouse gases (methane, for example), hangs in the atmosphere like glass, trapping heat. Since coal, oil, and gas were once plants, the burning of forests and coal a hundred years ago and the burning of oil and gas in our own time are part of the same puzzle piece. As scientists attempt to interlock it with the other pieces, they are finding that it alters the picture entirely.

One alteration, some scientists say, could be a delay or interruption of Milankovitch cycles poised to bring on an ice age. In that case, we would see the Little Ice Age as the beginning of the glacial age that normally should have cycled in after ten thousand years of mild interglacial climate. The glacial age was stopped or delayed because of the discovery of coal and oil. By burning those fossil fuels, we began a warming period that has so far kept us from the freezing that was otherwise in store for us.

This would be a good thing if only we could control the weather events that we are creating. We cannot do that, however, and it doesn't seem likely that we will be able to do it in the near future. In the meantime, scientists are projecting long-term dangerous consequences to global warming, and it seems that the only way we will be able to understand those consequences is to experience them. I wonder how much extreme weather we will need to experience before we begin to think about what we are doing. This is the first time in the history of the world that weather and climate are being altered by people. If we continue in the direction we are going, carbon dioxide in the atmosphere will double in as little as seventy years.

Someone recently asked Wallace Broecker how increased carbon dioxide in the atmosphere will affect the Conveyor Belt. "Scientists don't yet have the foggiest idea whether what we are doing to our planet threatens to change the behavior of the Conveyor," he answered. "All we know at this point is that we're giving the system the biggest jolt imaginable. The effect of CO_2

doubling is as big as a Milankovitch cycle—as big as any of the great events that have precipitated radical climate changes in the past."

Here we are in the foreground of the picture, and suddenly we must look back again into its deep perspective, farther back than the Little Ice Age, back to the time when mammoths were alive. Could humans survive if the world were plunged into that kind of climate? Standing at the railing of the *Yamal* and looking at the expanse of ice before me, I thought of Nansen and Johansen with their "courage and confidence," and of Peary, Henson, and the four Eskimos, all dressed in animal furs, making a dash for the pole. "The temperature during this march dropped from minus 30° to minus 40°," Peary wrote. "There was a biting northeasterly breeze, and the dogs traveled forward in their own white cloud of steam."

Dogs were lifelines for the explorers, but even the ones born and bred in icy places are not well adapted to this land. A few kinds of birds are adapted, as are seals, whales, and the two large land/marine mammals: polar bear and walrus. Walruses and polar bears are too large for our civilized world, but they are perfectly scaled in this place. If human beings ever have to adapt to a new ice age, it will probably be necessary for us to grow very much larger.

From the Journal of Fridtjof Nansen
February 26 to March 31, 1895

Tuesday, February 26

At last the day has arrived, the great day, when the journey is to commence. The week has passed in untiring work to get everything ready. We should have started on the 20th, but it has been postponed from day to day; there was always something still to do. My head has been full night and day, with all that was to be done and that must not be forgotten. Oh, this unceasing mental strain, which does not allow a minute's rest in which to throw off the responsibility, to give loose rein to the thoughts, and let the dreams have full sway; the nerves are in a state of tension from the moment of awakening in the morning till the eyes close late at night. Ah! How well I know this state, which I have experienced each time I have been about to set out and retreat was to be cut off—never, I believe, more effectually than now. The last few nights I did not get to bed before half-past three or half-past four o'clock in the morning. It is not only what we ought to take with us that has to be taken care of, but we have to leave the vessel. Its command and responsibility have to be placed in other hands, and care must be taken that nothing is forgotten in the way of instructions to the men who remain, for the scientific observations will have to be continued on the same lines as they have been carried on hitherto.

The last night we were to spend on board the *Fram* eventually arrived, and we had a farewell party. In a strange, sad way, reminiscences were revived of all that had befallen us here on board, mingled with hope and trust in what the future would bring. I remained up till far into the night. Letters and remembrances had to be prepared for those at home in case the unforeseen should happen.

At last the brain was to get some rest, and the work for the legs and arms to commence. Everything was got ready for the start this morning. Five of our comrades, Sverdrup, Hansen, Blessing, Henriksen, and Mogstad, were to see us off on our way, bringing a sledge and a tent with them. The four sledges were got ready, the dogs harnessed to them. Lunch, with a bottle of malt extract per man, was taken just before starting, and then we bade the last hearty farewell to those left behind. We were off into the drifting snow. I myself took the lead with Kvik as leading dog, in the first sledge, and then sledge after sledge followed amid cheers, accompanied by the cracking of whips and the barking of dogs.

At the same time a salute was fired from the quarterdeck, shot after shot, into the whirling drift. The sledges moved heavily forward; it was slow traveling uphill, and they came to a dead stop where the ascent was too steep, and we all had to help them along—one man alone could not do it. But over level ground we flew along like a whirlwind, and those on snowshoes found it difficult enough to keep pace with the sledges. I had to strike out as best I could when they came up to me to avoid getting my legs entangled in the line.

A man is beckoning with his staff far in the rear. It is Mogstad, who comes tearing along and shouting that three crossbars had been torn off a sledge in driving. The sledge, with its heavy load, had lurched forward over an upright piece of ice, which struck the crossbars, breaking all three of them, one after the other; one or two of the perpendicular supports of the runners were also smashed. There was nothing for it but to return to the ship to get it repaired and have the sledges made stronger. Such a thing ought not to happen again. During the return, one of the sledges lurched up against another, and a cane in the bow snapped. The bows would, therefore, also have to be made stronger.

The sledges have again been unloaded and brought on board

in order that this may be done, and here we are again tonight. I am glad, however, that this happened when it did; it would have been worse to have had such an experience a few days later. I will now take six sledges instead of four, so that the load on each may be less, and so that it will be easier to lift them over the irregularities of the ground. We shall not be ready to start before day-after-tomorrow. It seemed strange to be on board again after having said goodbye, as I thought, forever, to these surroundings. When I came up on the afterdeck, I found the guns lying there in the snow, one of them turned over on its back, the other had recoiled a long way aft when saluting us. From the mizzentop the red and black flag was still waving.

I am in wonderfully high spirits, and feel confident of success; the sledges seemed to glide so easily, although carrying 200 pounds more than was originally intended (about 2,200 pounds altogether), and everything looks very promising. We shall have to wait a couple of days, but as we are having a southeasterly wind all day long, we are no doubt getting on towards the north, all the same. Yesterday we were at 83°47′. Today, I suppose we are at least at 83°50′.

Wednesday, March 6

We are again on board the *Fram* to make a fresh start, for the third time, and then, I suppose, it will be in earnest. On Saturday March 2nd, we proceeded with the six sledges after I had been on a trip to the northward and found it passable. Progress was slow, and we had to do nearly six turns each, as the sledges stopped everywhere and had to be helped along. I saw now too clearly that we should never get on in this manner; a change would have to be made, and I decided to camp in order to have a look at the ice northward and consider the matter. Having tied up the dogs, I set out, while Johansen was to feed the dogs and put up the tent. They were fed once in every

24 hours, at night, when the day's march was done.

I had not gone far when I came upon excellent spacious plains; good progress could be made, and so far everything was all right; but the load had to be diminished and number of sledges reduced. Undoubtedly, therefore, it would be best to return to the *Fram* to make the necessary alterations on board, and get the sledges we were to take with us further strengthened, so as to have perfect confidence in their durability.

We might, of course, have dragged along, somehow, towards the north for a while, and the load would gradually have decreased. But it would have been slow work, and before the load would be sufficiently lightened the dogs would perhaps be worn out. It was cold for them at night; we heard many of them howling most of the night. If, however, we diminished the load, and consequently allowed a shorter time for the journey, it would be preferable to wait, and not start till a little later in the month when we could make more out of the time as the days would be lighter and not so cold. Having spent another night in the tent dressed in fur that was stiff with frost, in a bag that was also hard frozen, I decided the next morning to return to the *Fram*.

I harnessed a double team of dogs to one of the sledges, and off they went over pressure ridges and all the other obstacles so rapidly that I could hardly keep up with them. In a few hours I covered the same distance that had taken us three days when we started out. The advantage of a lighter load was only too apparent.

As I approached the *Fram* I saw, to my surprise, the upper edge of the sun above the ice in the south. It was the first time this year, but I had not expected it as yet. It was the refraction caused by the low temperature that made it visible so soon. The first news I heard from those who came to meet me was that Hansen had the previous afternoon taken an observation, which gave 84°4′ north latitude.

It was undoubtedly very pleasant once more to stretch my

limbs on the sofa in the *Fram's* saloon, to quench my thirst in delicious lime juice with sugar, and again to dine in a civilized manner. In the afternoon Hansen and Nordahl went back to Johansen with my team of dogs, to keep him company overnight.

The next morning three of us went off and fetched the sledges back. Now, when we made for the ship, the dogs dragged much better, and in a short time we should have been on board had it not been for a long lead in the ice which we could see no end to, and which stopped us. Finally we left the sledges and, together with the dogs, managed to cross over on some loose pieces of ice, and got on board. Yesterday, we tried to fetch the sledges, but there had evidently been some movement in the lead, and the new ice was still so thin that we dared not trust it. We have, however, today got them on board, and we will now for the last time, it is to be hoped, prepare ourselves for the journey. I will now plan out the journey so as to take the shortest possible time, using light sledges and tearing along as fast as legs and snowshoes will carry us. We shall be none the worse for this delay, provided we do not meet too much pack ice or too many openings in the ice.

I have weighed all the dogs, and have come to the conclusion that we can feed them on each other and keep going for about fifty days; having, in addition to this, dog provisions for about thirty days, we ought to be able to travel with dogs for eighty days, and in that time it seems to me we should have arrived somewhere. And besides, we have provisions for ourselves for one hundred days. This will be about 440 pounds on each sledge if we take three, and with nine dogs per sledge we ought to manage it.

Wednesday, March 13

The days have passed, working again at the equipment. Everything is now in order. Three sledges are standing ready out on the ice, properly strengthened in every way, with iron fastenings between uprights and crossbars. This afternoon we tried the dogs with sledges loaded, and they went as easily as could be, and tomorrow we start again for the last time, full of courage and confidence and with the sun up, in the assurance that we are going towards ever-brighter days. Tonight there has been a great farewell feast, with many hearty speeches, and early tomorrow we depart as early as possible, provided our dissipation has not delayed us.

Wednesday, March 20

Beautiful weather for traveling in, with fine sunsets; but somewhat cold, particularly in the bag at nights (it was minus 41.8°F). The ice appears to be getting more even the farther we advance. If this goes on, the whole thing will be done in no time. One of the dogs, Livjaegeren, has become so ill that he cannot be driven any longer, and we had to let him go loose. It was late in the day before we discovered that he was not with us. He had stopped behind at our camping ground when we broke up in the morning, and I had to go back after him on snowshoes, which caused a long delay.

Friday, March 22

Splendid ice for getting over; things go better and better. Wide expanses, with a few pressure ridges now and then, but passable everywhere. Kept at it yesterday from about half-past eleven in the morning to half-past eight at night; did a good twenty-one miles, I hope. We should be in latitude 85°. The only disagreeable thing about it now is the cold. Our clothes are transformed more and more into a cuirass of ice during the day, and wet bandages at night. The blankets likewise. The sleeping bag gets heavier and heavier from the moisture that freezes on the fur lining inside. The same clear settled weather every day. We are both longing now for a change; a few clouds and a little more mildness would be welcome.

Saturday, March 23

We have had the same brilliant sunshine, but yesterday afternoon a wind from the northeast made it rather raw. We killed Livjaegeren yesterday evening and hard work it was skinning him. This was the first dog that had to be killed. When the carcass was dismembered and given to the others, many of them went supperless the whole night in preference to touching the meat.

Friday, March 29

We are grinding on, but very slowly. The dogs are growing rather slow and slack, and it is almost impossible to get them on. And then this endless disentangling of the hauling ropes, with their infernal twists and knots which get worse and worse to undo. The dogs jump over and in between one another incessantly, and no sooner have we carefully cleared the hauling ropes than they are twisted into a veritable skein again. The dogs howl impatiently to follow their companions in front; then one bites through a trace and starts off on his own account, perhaps followed by one or two others, and these must be caught, and the traces knotted. There is no time to splice them properly, nor would it be a very congenial task in this cold.

Saturday, March 30

At first we found much uneven ice, and had to strike a devious route to get through it, so that our day's march did not amount to much, although we kept at it a long time. At the end of it, however, and after considerable toil, we found ourselves on splendid flat ice, more level than it had been for a long time. At last, then, we had come on some more of the good old kind, and could not complain of some rubble and snowdrifts here and there; but then we were stopped by some ugly pressure ridges of the worst kind, formed by the packing of enormous blocks. The last ridge was the worst of all, and before it yawned a crack in the thick ice about twelve feet deep.

When the first sledge was going over, all the dogs fell in and had to be hauled up again. One of them—Klapperslangen—slipped his harness and ran away. As the next sledge was going over, it fell in bodily, but happily was not smashed to atoms, as it might have been. We had to unload it entirely in order to get it up again, and then reload, all of which took up a great deal of time. Then, too, the dogs had to be thrown down and dragged up on the other side.

With the third sledge we managed better, and after we had gone a little way farther the runaway dog came back. At last we reached a camping ground, pitched our tent, and found that the thermometer showed minus 45.4°F. Disentangling dog-traces in this temperature with one's bare, frostbitten, almost skinless hands is desperate work. But finally we were in our dear bag.

Sunday, March 31

Yesterday, at last, came the long-wished-for change of weather, with southerly wind and rising temperature. Early this morning the thermometer showed minus 22°F, regular summer weather, in fact. It was, therefore, with lightened hearts that we set off over good ice and with the wind at our backs. On we went at a very fair pace, and everything was going well, when a lead suddenly opened just in front of the first sledge. We managed to get over this by the skin of our teeth; but just as we were going to cross the lead again with the other sledges, a large piece of ice broke under Johansen, and he fell in, wetting both legs—a deplorable incident.

While the lead was gradually opening more and more, I went up and down it to find a way over, but without success. Here we were, with one man and a sledge on one side, two sledges and a wet man on the other, and an ever-widening lead in between. The kayaks could not be launched, as through frequent capsizing of the sledges they had got holes in them, and for the time being were useless. This was a cheerful prospect for the night, I on one side with the tent, Johansen, probably frozen stiff, on the other. At last, after a long detour, I found a way over; and the sledges were conveyed across. It was out of the question, however, to attempt to go on, as Johansen's nether extremities were a mass of ice and his overalls so torn that extensive repairs were necessary.

Gunter Weller

Yar Petryszyn

A Conversation with Gunter Weller and Yar Petryszyn

Gunter Weller is director of the Cooperative Institute for Arctic Research at the University of Alaska, Fairbanks, and executive director of a research project called Arctic Climate Impact Assessment being conducted under the auspices of the Arctic Council, an intergovernmental forum established in 1996 by Canada, Denmark, Norway, Finland, Russia, Sweden, and the United States. Yar Petryszyn gave several lectures on the Yamal *about weather and wildlife. He is curator of mammals at the University of Arizona Museum, and for more than twenty years has been conducting research on the relationship of weather to wildlife populations in desert areas. We met in Portland, Oregon, a middle ground for all of us. Gunter had given a talk at a conference of the Marine Mammal Commission, a forum created by the U.S. government in conjunction with the Marine Mammal Protection Act of 1972.*

GUNTER: At the conference I just attended, there was a lot of discussion about pollutants. The pollutants move up the food chain from the marine mammals to the Alaskan natives who eat seals and whales. But nobody has died yet from that, and the commission is having a hard time trying to sell Congress on the idea of doing something about it. It was interesting. I was an outsider.

You were an outsider?

GUNTER: They asked me to give them some information on climate change. I'm a geophysicist, not a marine mammal biologist. I've seen a few marine mammals, but—

Have you gone to the North Pole?

GUNTER: I've worked professionally doing research on ice islands. I was on one of them when it floated past the pole. I've never been there on a trip like the one you were on.

Yar, how many times have you been a lecturer on the Yamal *trip?*

YAR: Five times. I just did a trip to the Amazon as a lecturer. It seems to be impossible to stop the cutting of the Amazon forest, or even just to slow it down.

And once the Amazon forest is gone we've lost a big carbon sink that absorbs carbon dioxide from the atmosphere. There is the scenario now that we are wrecking the world for future generations.

GUNTER: It's always in the back of our minds. We have a good chance to do it, actually. People in developing countries use the resources that they have. In the Amazon, it's wood; in China, it's coal. The great industrial development in China relies heavily on their coal resources, and coal is very bad. Burning it produces a lot of carbon dioxide. And the Chinese say, to some extent rightly, "You guys in the West have screwed up the environment already and now it's our turn to become prosperous, and we're going to do it whether you like it or not." There are a lot of people who want to make a better living for themselves, not just in China and the Amazon. "What's the environment, and its needs, compared with my need to send my kids to school and have a car and live a decent life?" That's what is really important for people. Everything else is an abstract idea. But in a developed society like ours where there is money and leisure, we can afford to think about these issues more than the people in China or the Amazon.

Look at this weather map from the newspaper. It's all red and orange. Europe is sweltering. It's the hottest summer on record. At the same time, there's tremendous ice at the pole. I've recently been in touch with someone at TCS Expeditions, which sponsored our trip to the pole, and I found out that the Yamal *wasn't able to make it to the pole on the first trip she took this year. There was too much ice.*

YAR: Oh, really? The *Yamal* couldn't make it?

It would have taken three days longer than they had. They hardly even had time to stop at the islands. They were just banging and banging the ice.

YAR: One of my trips was like that, just constant banging away. We went directly and made it, but only barely, and came straight back. We didn't stop at Franz Josef Land at all.

We had the most beautiful trip. Big ice, a real experience of big ice, but we also had time to stop. Five years ago, however, there was a trip where they saw very little ice. And now it's too hot everywhere except the Arctic, where there is tremendous ice. What's going on?

YAR: A few years ago I did trips to the pole two years in a row. On one of them there wasn't much ice. We had to go a good six miles to find a floe where we could get off near the pole. I thought, whoa, what's this? But then the next year was the one I just mentioned where we barely made it. So when I heard about the guys who were worried by the ten-mile lead, saying it was a sign of global warming, I thought, well, that's bull. It changes dramatically from one year to the next.

GUNTER: Of course it does. Climate change is measured over long intervals and big areas. What happens in a particular place in a particular year is weather, not climate. To jump to the conclusion that global warming is here because one year there is less ice at the pole is nonsense. Climate is an integration over very long periods. There are many factors in the short term. Wind shifts things around. In the circulation in the atmosphere, there are low pressures and highs, cyclones and anticyclones that shunt the ice from one place to another. This year when there was a lot of ice at the pole, there was an ice-free area along the Siberian coast, for example.

YAR: On our trip last summer, it was mostly one- and two-year ice. We had only a little multiyear ice. A slight change in the Arctic Ocean gyre, and all of a sudden you have all this very thick multiyear ice to get through.

I thought we had a lot of multiyear ice. It seemed very thick to me.

YAR: I think 70 or 80 percent of the ice we saw last summer was one or two years old. We didn't see that much massiveness. To get through a really massive pressure ridge takes the *Yamal* maybe three hours: boom, boom. Actually, you're cutting a slot maybe twenty feet deep through ice that is that thick. Ride up on top and basically wallow yourself through it like a seal. That's why the ship has hydraulic pumps to shift water around inside the hull. Get up there, wiggle yourself, change the angle, and hit it again.

GUNTER: In the past, they had the seamen run from one side to the other.

YAR: I could see it on the *Yamal*: "Run over there!"

GUNTER: "Everybody to port! Everybody to starboard!" At least you'd get some exercise. Overall, though, the ice really is diminishing. There are lots of nuclear subs cruising around under the ice, and their sonar records give you an indication of the canopy. They show that over the last forty to fifty years there's been a 40 percent reduction in thickness. But it's limited U.S. Navy data, and they only let it out in short bursts. It would be nice to have more.

Why wouldn't the navy want you to have that data?

GUNTER: It's tracks, you know. Where were the submarines? When? And the next question is what did they do? The Russians have a lot of nuclear submarines under there too, and they haven't released any data. Only U.S. and British submarines provide it.

YAR: On one of the trips I was on we had a lecturer who was a submarine captain. This was his first time going to the North Pole on the surface; he had been five times before underneath. He remembered the early days when in some areas there was very little space between the bottom of the ice and the ocean bottom.

GUNTER: In the Bering Strait, probably. The ocean is shallow there.

I have something here I printed from a website. The headline is "Baltic Sea Gives Cold Shoulder to Global Warming Theorists." It comes from an organization called the Greening Earth Society and says that five hundred years of Baltic Sea ice data shows no evidence of any warming. Does this relate to what we are talking about?

GUNTER: Regional climates are dictated by regional factors. It is an observation, if it's correct, and I have no reason to think it's not correct. But it really doesn't say much about global climate change.

I think this website keeps bringing up things that seem to refute the urgency of global warming.

GUNTER: They're collecting evidence only from one side?

I got that impression from reading a few of their releases. President Bush's staff probably reads this website.

GUNTER: [Holds up a graph.] Here's the record of sea ice extent on the Arctic Ocean. Data from satellites is in color; the earlier data, primarily Russian, is in black and white. You can easily see a downward trend since 1850. That's for the entire Arctic, not just for a little sea like the Baltic. I can also show you similar material illustrating the decline in sea ice thickness—a 40 percent decline observed since the 1950s. That's over a huge area.

YAR: The Baltic is affected by the Gulf Stream.

GUNTER: And by pollution and other anthropogenic conditions. Who knows? There are some areas of the world that are cooling. [Holds up a map.] Look at this: The huge red area is warming on the order of 1.8°F per decade, 5.4°F over the last thirty years. See that small green area in the southern part of Greenland, near Baffin Island? That is cooling. So it's patchy, not uniform. But you can see that there's no doubt that the Arctic is warming overall. You can't think of global greenhouse warming as a uniform thing across the entire globe. It's not so.

We are used to examining arguments on both sides of issues, then making up our minds. When nonscientists put out what they call "the other side" to scientific arguments, it's very confusing. For example, Senator James M. Inhofe, from Oklahoma, made a speech on the floor of the U.S. Senate in which he called "man-made global warming the greatest hoax ever perpetrated on the American people." Senator Inhofe is the chairman of the Senate's Environmental and Public Works Committee.

GUNTER: The Bush administration is not all that keen on the idea of global greenhouse warming. They're skeptics. They put together what they called a strategy on global climate change. More studies. You can always do more studies. In science there's never absolute certainty. If politicians are waiting for certainty, they are talking nonsense. There's enough evidence already in all areas. If you wait very much longer—well, I don't think it's a very good idea.

A man goes to the doctor, and the doctor says, "I'm sorry to tell you that you have a heart condition." The man says, "Doctor, I want to know exactly when I'm going to have a heart attack and how bad it will be. Until I know that, I'm not going to do anything."

GUNTER: That's a good analogy. In that two-hour speech you mentioned of Senator Inhofe's to the Senate, he quoted only sources that doubted global greenhouse warming exists. Almost the entire scientific community of the United States is of the opposite opinion. So are the academies of science of every developed country and two hundred Nobel prizewinners. None of them were quoted. But this is typical political stuff, a guy quoting evidence that favors his point of view and nothing else.

I think that's the way senators are used to behaving, especially now when politics is so polarized. There's no room for evidence on both sides.

GUNTER: Our Alaskan senior senator Ted Stevens is generally conservative, like Senator Inhofe, but he is convinced now that the climate is changing in Alaska. Of course, what he is willing to do about it is a different matter. I think city planners and people concerned with sea-level rise and coastal erosion are taking this a lot more seriously than Congress or the White House.

I read in the New York Times *that a strategist for the Bush administration has advised using the term "climate change" instead of "global warming" because global warming connotes something catastrophic and climate change sounds more gradual and natural. At this point it is hard to deny that something is happening, so the strategy seems to be to characterize it in a way that doesn't imply urgency.*

GUNTER: That's politics. We've always had climate change, you know. We've had ice ages. There have been catastrophic climate events in the past. But one hundred thousand years ago what did it matter if there was a sea-level rise of several feet? There were no coastal cities; there were no ports. It didn't make any difference. But now that 70 to 80 percent of humanity lives in the coastal zones, and we have infrastructure in those areas, a sea-level rise, even of less than a foot, is a disaster.

The sea level is definitely rising?

GUNTER: Oh yes. Over the last one hundred years it has risen by a bit more than nine inches. The Greenland ice cap is melting around its periphery, and that contributes a lot of water to the ocean, not to mention melting in Antarctica. The oceans are getting warmer so they are expanding. Together, glacial effects and ocean expansion are causing the sea level to rise. It's beginning to worry people in low-lying areas, the South Pacific islands, for example. They are really worried. One of those countries already has come to Australia and said, "If our country disappears, can you take us in?" The Australians said, "Forget it."

YAR: It's not going to take much for the coral atolls. Nine-plus inches of increase over a hundred years sounds small, but that's almost a tenth of an inch a year, an inch in ten years, and that is massive because of the differences that storms contribute. I read an article that was trying to estimate how much a two-inch increase would cost in damages along coastlines. Billions of dollars around the world.

GUNTER: Of course, it's hard on wildlife like polar bears. If their habitat disappears, they will become extinct.

Walruses, too, I suppose.

GUNTER: Walruses are in very bad shape already. They need ice over relatively shallow water because the distance they can dive to get to their food source is limited. All the ice-inhabiting animals are in bad shape—the ringed seals along the Alaskan coast, for example. Models vary in their projections, but some show that there will be a seasonal disappearance of sea ice in as little as fifty years' time. It could be pretty dramatic if there is an ice-free ocean in summer. You know, on the Alaskan coast last fall the sea ice didn't form quickly enough and there was an accumulation of twenty to thirty polar bears in Barrow—never had been seen there before. So many bears, just piled up, couldn't get out on the ice, just hanging around. Like in Churchill, Canada, on the Hudson Bay. There was a television program made about that. The bears hang out there until the ice comes in and they can move out.

They don't like to be in groups.

GUNTER: No, they don't. They can get very aggressive.

That can be a big problem.

GUNTER: A bigger problem in Alaska is permafrost. Very much of it is close to the melting point. The annual mean temperature in Fairbanks, where I live, is 28°F. A rise of 4°F begins to melt the stuff, and this much change we have already seen. Most of the roads in Alaska—and also in Siberia where it's even a bigger problem—are built on permafrost. So are houses, so are the trans-Alaska pipeline and oil facilities. Everything sits on permafrost. Permafrost is anything permanently frozen, including rocks and soil. It doesn't make any difference if rocks get warmer, and not as much with soil, but in many places there are big ice masses under there, and they melt. This makes holes in the ground. Buildings collapse into them. Half of the Alaska pipeline is below ground in areas free of permafrost, and the other half is on so-called vertical support members aboveground in permafrost areas. The ground there is kept artificially frozen. Cooling pumps remove the heat so the bottoms of the support members will remain frozen into the ground. As the climate gets warmer, it is hard for the system to cope. The supports begin to sink and have to be replaced at a pretty steady rate now. This is not something that the engineers can't handle, but it costs money and that cost will show up eventually at the gas pumps. It is an economic impact of climate change.

YAR: There's another consequence of permafrost melting, too. As it melts, you get decomposition of plant matter trapped in it, and then more greenhouse gases, methane and CO_2, are released.

The CO_2 in the air causes warming, and then warming causes more CO_2 to be released by decomposition?

YAR: Yes. CO_2 and methane, which is worse.

In a lecture you gave on the Yamal, *you said that methane is a very powerful greenhouse gas released in large quantities by cow flatulence.*

GUNTER: There is an effort being made to develop food that will make cows less flatulent. The cows are a fairly minor contribution, but there is a major contribution in terms of methane and it comes from rice paddies in Asia. And ants. Ants, also.

Ants?

YAR: Ants, termites, yes. They take plant material and grow fungus on it so you have a lot of decomposition going on. You get three million ants in a mound, and scatter hundreds of thousands of mounds across a landscape in Africa, and a lot of material is being processed that releases a lot of gas.

Can we blame the cows and the ants and keep our SUVs*?*

GUNTER: No, no. It doesn't let humans off the hook.

YAR: Up to now, we've had a balanced system, and part of it is the natural release of greenhouse gases. But we're adding so much more CO_2 to the situation.

GUNTER: The whole balance is very delicate and has now been upset to some extent by humanity introducing additional sources. But the greenhouse effect existed before there was any human existence. If we didn't have the natural greenhouse effect, the temperature on earth would be 0°F. It would be below freezing all the time, and we couldn't exist here. So we are not against the greenhouse effect. We're against the enhanced greenhouse effect, the industrial pollution, excessive auto emissions, and so on.

YAR: There's a flip side to that coin. It looks like we're nearing the end of our interglacial age, and it is possible that the expected transition to an ice age has been delayed by the extra greenhouse gases we're putting into the atmosphere. If what we've seen in ice cores and other kinds of records of the past holds true, we should be at the end of a ten-thousand-year warm period, and it should be getting colder. It would be ironic if what we're doing to the environment is actually staving off an ice age.

Should we keep doing what we're doing and expect the end effect to be beneficial? This is a major question.

GUNTER: Which would you prefer? An ice age is pretty unpleasant—ice sheets covering Europe and North America—not so great. Or would you prefer heat deaths and starvation, droughts and other catastrophes associated with warming? And if Wallace Broecker's theory about the Great Ocean Conveyer Belt is correct, excessive warming might bring on an ice age in any case.

Isn't there something in the middle? Surely staving off the ice age doesn't require this much CO_2*? Couldn't we just put less into the atmosphere?*

YAR: There's been nothing comparable anywhere anytime to the volume of CO_2 we're putting into the atmosphere now. That's the real concern.

Something I read about ice core samples said the information from them is so exact that it shows a decrease in CO_2 *in the*

1930s because of the Depression. There was less industrial activity. And then there was a big increase during World War II. I was amazed to learn that the information from ice core samples shows a decrease of CO_2 in the 1970s, and this is probably because of the Clean Air Act of 1974 enacted in the United States!

GUNTER: That would coincide with a slight cooling in the 1970s. There is a pretty good correlation between CO_2 in the atmosphere and warming, although there are fluctuations. In the big picture, there is no doubt that there has been a 30 percent increase of CO_2 in the atmosphere since the beginning of the Industrial Revolution about a hundred and fifty years ago and, at the present rate, CO_2 in the atmosphere will double in seventy to eighty years' time. Doubling could bring a one- to three-foot rise in sea level.

That would submerge most of Florida! But I gained hope when I learned that data from ice cores actually shows a decrease in CO_2 because of the Clean Air Act. Think what we could do! I had been putting global warming out of my mind, not wanting to hear about it because I didn't think there was a way to get a handle on it. But we did pass the Clean Air Act, and it did make a difference. And that act didn't even directly address the global warming issue.

YAR: We were also driving at a fifty-five MPH speed limit then.

Could we do that again? Pass another law? There is hope, isn't there?

GUNTER: There are a lot of things we could do. How about some fuel efficiency in SUVs? SUVs have escaped the fuel efficiency rules for autos because they are classified as light trucks. They don't need to be as fuel inefficient as they are.

Maybe we could have a Commission on Global Warming to regulate emissions, like the Securities and Exchange Commission regulates Wall Street, or even like the Federal Reserve Board regulates the monetary supply. We could have someone like Alan Greenspan in charge.

GUNTER: It's not a far-fetched idea. We make predictions of great importance to the nation in matters of commerce and monetary policy based on pretty poor economic models. Climate models are based on precise physics, and are more accurate than any economic model you can think of. We make decisions based on economic models every day, and yet we're not willing to make any decisions based on climate models.

We might be starting to think about it. In 2003, Senators John McCain and Joseph Lieberman sponsored a bill called the Climate Stewardship Act that for the first time ever would have put federal restrictions on emissions of greenhouse gases. An article in the Economist *magazine said there was a possibility that it could actually pass, even though President Bush was against it, because many people in business are convinced that CO_2 rules are going to come and they want them to be written by a business-friendly administration. It didn't pass, but it got forty-three votes, more than many people thought it would.*

GUNTER: Even though it didn't pass, it had the advantage that it increased awareness. And McCain and Lieberman say they will try again.

YAR: That was an emissions trading law, wasn't it? They were essentially saying, "Let's keep CO_2 emissions from going above a certain level." As an example, one thousand units of emissions might be allowed for a particular industry. Your business might have five hundred, and another business might have five hundred, and if the other business wants to pollute more and you are cleaning things up, you can sell it some of your units.

GUNTER: We do emissions trading in my family too. I drive the SUV and my wife walks.

You have an SUV*?*

GUNTER: A small one, a Toyota. In Alaska, in winter, you need something a little more powerful. I'm going to make up for it because I've just ordered a Toyota Prius, an electric-gasoline hybrid. It charges the electric cells when it's running on gas, and can switch from one fuel to the other. Toyota is doing well with that car—you have to get on a waiting list to get one. And, through its Lexus division, Toyota is planning to offer the first hybrid SUV in 2004.

YAR: I have a Toyota SUV, too, a T100, which is called the Tundra, a four-wheel-drive.

Because you go out in the Arizona desert all the time.

YAR: Exactly.

If the McCain-Lieberman bill had passed, emissions from major industries would have been set to decline to their 2000 levels by 2010, and farther by 2016. The Economist *article said it was too bad that Bush wouldn't support the bill.*

GUNTER: That's a British magazine, isn't it? There's more awareness in Europe. They are already doing emissions trading there, in accord with the Kyoto Protocol, which the European Union has adopted even though the United States has not. But even in the United States, I think the general population is behind environmental protection. We care about the environment and we don't want to continue to mess things up for the future. We are willing to make some sacrifices—not too many, maybe, but some. This kind of thinking eventually will percolate upward into the political system. It has already arrived in a few big companies. Alcoa Aluminum has decreased its greenhouse gas emissions and enhanced its business productivity at the same time. It is something that can be done. Even some of the oil companies are onboard.

Oil companies?

GUNTER: At the moment, unfortunately, they are European only —BP [British Petroleum] and Shell. Certainly not Exxon. BP calls itself Beyond Petroleum now. It is one of the biggest investors in solar cell technology. The people in charge know that eventually we're going to run out of fossil fuels.

YAR: All the oil companies must be fully aware of it.

But the American ones, such as Exxon, want to get every last drop of oil out of the ground, and they want government subsidies to help them. What will they do when it runs out? File for bankruptcy, like Enron, after making big payouts to their executives?

YAR: About drilling in ANWAR—the Alaska National Wildlife Refuge. If we legislated to improve mileage on SUVs by two miles per gallon, in one year we would save more fuel than is available in ANWAR.

GUNTER: Would Congress have the guts to do it?

I don't know about legislating SUV *efficiency, but I don't think Congress will allow the* ANWAR *drilling. People don't want that.*

GUNTER: Only in Alaska do people want it. It's money directly in their pockets. In general, I don't buy the economic arguments against doing something about global greenhouse warming. Some companies would have to rethink what they are doing, but others are already making money on environmentally friendly things: hybrid cars, windmills in Holland, various products made out of recycled materials. I think we could meet the Kyoto Protocol targets in the United States with no overall impact on the economy whatsoever if we had the will to do it. And the opposite route will be very expensive in the long run. The insurance industry is very concerned, as you can guess. They are facing huge losses as weather-related catastrophes continue. And at municipal levels people are beginning to take global warming seriously, particularly in coastal cities.

Are weather-related catastrophes part of the global warming pattern? It's not just warmer, warmer, warmer? Droughts and storms, tremendous shifts in heat and cold?

GUNTER: We don't know for sure, but that seems to be the case: hurricanes, tornadoes, extreme events overall. Our models are not very good at predicting them.

YAR: Some of the global warming models show predictions of swings in temperature and also storms. You're looking at accelerated heat transfer. That's what storms are, heat transfer. There's a bigger difference between the high temperatures at the equator and the polar temperatures, so the storms are more violent.

Yar, what is it exactly that you do when you go out into the desert in your SUV*?*

YAR: In general, I look at population dynamics of animals in the desert. It's an extreme environment. I do a lot of work with rodent populations, and I study bats, too—we have twenty-eight species in Arizona. At the time that I got interested in weather, I had ten years of data, but now it's gone to twenty-four years of continuous capture, mark, and release. I have documented extreme fluctuations in populations of pack rats, pocket mice, and other species. There will be a tremendous increase one year, and then in the next year or two the numbers will drop again.

GUNTER: Is the change cyclic?

YAR: No, it's not cyclic. I had to try to explain it, and I began to look at rainfall patterns. It's El Niño derived.

GUNTER: That's interesting.

YAR: El Niño, in our area, produces rainfall that counteracts the desert dryness. This produces desert blooms, and the rodent population takes advantage of the increase in biomass and increases dramatically. That affects the predators, and so on.

GUNTER: What are the predators there?

YAR: Snakes. Animals like coyotes and foxes, raptors such as owls and hawks. All of them feed on the rodent base and it feeds on the plants and seeds. So there is a food pyramid that is brought about by El Niño.

Would you tell me in a couple of sentences what El Niño is?

What causes it?

YAR: I don't think we really know what causes it. Some have a theory but I don't agree with it. Essentially El Niño is a warming of surface waters in the eastern part of the Pacific Ocean. There are rich fisheries there because of cold-water upwelling. El Niño reverses the cold-water upwelling, and warm waters pile up along the South American coast, up to Central America, even clear up to Baja and Southern California. This reversal affects atmospheric circulation, the jet stream in particular. In the northern hemisphere, the jet stream moves farther south over North America. This affects the position of high- and low-pressure areas, thus influencing where it rains and where it doesn't rain.

The jet stream circles the globe in the atmosphere at high altitude, very far north, doesn't it? Any change in its pattern causes storms.

YAR: Flooding conditions in some places and droughts elsewhere.

And it's not the same every year?

YAR: No. That's the thing. On the average, El Niño occurs every four and a half to five years, but that's an average. Some El Niños have come back to back. There was one span of over ten years between El Niños, 1930 to 1941.

That roughly coincides with the Great Depression. There was less industrial activity.

YAR: It would be interesting to try to find out if there is a relationship, but I don't think you can draw any conclusions at this point.

GUNTER: What causes El Niño is unclear. But it has consequences for weather and climate around the entire world, including as far as Alaska. It simply changes the whole atmospheric circulation pattern.

Why is it called El Niño?

YAR: El Niño is the Christ Child. It occurs around Christmastime. The fishermen of Peru and northern Chile would notice that sometimes around Christmas their catch would go to hell, and they called it El Niño.

Yar, didn't you tell me that there's a connection to global warming research in what you're doing? Something about pack-rat urine?

YAR: It's another tool used to look at past climate. Pack rats bring all kinds of material into their middens: pieces of cactus, tree bark, other things. They usually make their middens in rock crevices where they are protected from the weather, and they keep the same middens for generation after generation. In the midden, the rats have a bathroom where they pee, and the urine cements the vegetation, the dust, the pollen, and whatever else.

Like a little ice core!

YAR: A substance is produced that has been created in layers over thousands of years. It looks like amber. The climate people can date this and whatever's in the layers, they analyze. From bits of pollen, things like that, they can reconstruct the paleo-environment. The oldest turned out to go back forty-two thousand years.

GUNTER: Urine research.

YAR: They learned that our giant cactus, the saguaro, appeared in the Southwest only about six thousand years ago. That's recent. Prior to that there was piñon and juniper woodland in much of what is desert now.

GUNTER: Paleo-climatic research can use all kinds of stuff—tree rings and ice cores and pack rat urine and ocean sediments—it's pretty innovative.

And it all says the same thing?

GUNTER: They tend to agree well with each other. You cross correlate. You can deduce temperatures from pollen, for example. You might know that a particular species of plant lives only in a very narrow temperature range. So if you see its pollen, you know something about the temperature.

YAR: In these middens, you find scales of lizards, bones of this or that, and you know where those animals occurred and when. It corroborates other evidence.

Can you project that kind of thing into the future using computers?

GUNTER: Knowing as much as possible about the past helps you develop good climate models. You can also hind-cast. You can run your computer model backward. If you have some data from the past, and you've set up a model for the future, you can run the model to cover the time you know about in the past. How does it perform? Does it match the conditions you've discovered in the paleo-data? If it does, you have a little more confidence that what it projects for the future might be reliable. So the paleo-data are extremely important. The instrumental records don't go back that far. We are measuring climate by instruments now, but from the paleo-data you can extend records back hundreds of thousands of years.

What about carbon dating?

Gunter: You need a time line, and for that, if you can use carbon dating, it can give you the best indication. The time line can be difficult. If you compare ice core records with sediment records, for example, you have two wiggly curves. And you need to put them side by side and see if you can determine a common time line. In the recent past we've had very good indicators. The nuclear bomb tests of the 1950s give you a very nice line—it looks like a horizon—in the ice cores. Volcanic eruptions are also good; they deposit a layer of dust and their dates are known. The time line is critical. Once you have that, you can anchor everything else to it.

We have really come a long way.

YAR: Oh, yes.

GUNTER: Definitely.

Scientists often say, "Oh, we don't know very much." Of course, this is the scientist's state of mind, always to think that you don't know much.

YAR: You're always looking to answer questions.

GUNTER: And every answer you have raises two or three more questions.

YAR: And that's why you're still doing this kind of stuff.

And that's why the scientific argument is always vulnerable to the political argument. Politicians act as if they know everything. Political commentators do that especially, and people listen to them. People like confidence.

GUNTER: Confidence is one thing. Certainty is another. The politicians keep asking for 100 percent certainty. That is just not possible in science. They ought to forget about it.

Gunter, I'd like to find out more about your background. When I met you, you told me that you are "an ice and snow man."

GUNTER: My background is in the physical sciences, and my university degrees are from the University of Melbourne. I started my professional career as an engineer—my first degree was in aeronautical engineering. I was always interested in planes. For a couple of years in Australia I worked for the weapons industry, designing rockets. But I didn't care much for that. At that time I was a glider pilot. I really liked glider flying. Terrific. So that got me into the atmosphere and I studied meteorology. I went to Antarctica as a forecaster in meteorology. I knew absolutely nothing about forecasting in Antarctica. We had a couple of planes, and there was a tremendous blizzard and both aircraft were destroyed, so I had practically nothing to do. Next to our station was a Russian station, and the Russians flew in occasionally, and I would give them a forecast. But I had a lot of time on my hands, and I started a research project of my own. And that got me my master's degree, but I realized the project was pretty lousy. I needed to go back to Antarctica for my PhD, this time fully organized. I did that and got my PhD in meteorology and glaciology. My interest has always been in high latitude—polar—meteorology and climatology. All my early experience was with Australian expeditions. Later, I went back to Antarctica with

U.S. expeditions at the South Pole and on the high plateau of Antarctica—twelve thousand feet up, annual mean temperature of minus 75°F.

I didn't know anything could be that cold.

GUNTER: It was a pretty cold place. When the temperature went up to minus 4°F, we thought it was a pleasant day. Pancake flat, an ideal place for doing boundary-level meteorology. Really perfect. I worked for the U.S. expedition for several years, going there in summer only. Then I decided I needed to see the other polar region. I said to my spouse, "Let's go to Alaska for a couple of years." We've been there for thirty-five years now. In Alaska I've worked on glaciers and on the tundra. I've done some studies close to the North Pole on ice islands, sometimes spending the whole summer there. These were mostly sponsored by the U.S. Navy.

What were you looking for on the ice islands?

GUNTER: The navy was looking for Russian submarines, but I wasn't. I was concerned with the way pack ice behaves, the dynamics. How does it melt, how does it move, how much energy comes into it? Ice and snow. On the mainland, I did similar research on glaciers. How fast do glaciers melt? What does long-term climate change do to glaciers? I slowly made the transition into thinking about long-term climate change. I was always interested in climate in both polar regions, and then when the whole paradigm of global greenhouse effect came up ten to fifteen years ago, it was a very interesting question to me. What causes climate change? What does climate change really mean? It's not just an esoteric study. It has impact on humanity, on social and economic conditions. That's my present interest. At the moment, I'm running a very large international project under the Arctic Council, which is a council of the eight countries that have territory in the Arctic. We're doing a very thorough and comprehensive assessment. We're presently producing a fifteen-hundred-page book, which no one will read, of course. But it is spelling out in detail what climate change does to the ocean, the marine ecosystem, the terrestrial ecosystem, freshwater, and economic activities, as well as the social impact on native communities all around the Arctic: Siberia, Canada, Alaska.

Are a lot of people are working on this?

GUNTER: Yes. We have two hundred authors. So I have a superficial knowledge of a very large area.

You hope someone will read the report, someone in government maybe?

GUNTER: We have the usual executive summaries, but in order to make the whole project credible we want to fully document it. The book is fully referenced and has all the background information. People will use it to look things up.

YAR: It will be an important reference for people in the field. The general public, no, but scientists will use it to see their own work in a bigger context.

Do you hope the project will make a difference in getting lawmakers to act on global warming?

GUNTER: You always have to be an optimist. Perhaps reason will prevail. I am really convinced that there is enough evidence, certainly in Alaska and in the Arctic in general. It is much warmer, and already there have been economic impacts. There's the melting of the permafrost that we talked about, and a slow movement of forests northward, and an introduction of species—some of which are harmful—that haven't lived in high latitudes before. The coastal erosion is already bad enough that relocation of some native villages has been discussed at a cost of about a million dollars a person, 150 million for one village. And who is going to pay for this? All of us. These are current practical concerns, not even talking about future projected catastrophes. I think eventually there has to be a groundswell that will bring global greenhouse warming to the full attention of lawmakers.

CHAPTER FOUR

THE NORTH POLE

Journey: the North Pole

We reached the North Pole on July 24 and there was water there. It was not much water, just a small triangular lead with irregular cracks leading to it from our bow. Leads can open up anywhere, and this one was at the pole before we arrived. It kept us from putting down our gangway and walking out onto the ice just exactly there.

The passengers and ship's officers gathered on the bridge, where throughout the journey we had gone whenever we wished to scan the ice in company with others. A prominent feature of the bridge was a drafting table spread with a nautical chart of the area surrounding the pole; our course was plotted on it by hand. Above the drafting table were two modest-looking Global Positioning System devices which received signals constantly broadcast by a network of twenty-four satellites in space. Both display screens showed essentially the same information: the latitude and longitude of our ship. The top line indicated latitude, the one below it longitude. We would know we had reached the North Pole when the top line showed 90° north. We gathered in a knot around the devices and I watched the numerals reach N89°57′. The ship stuttered and jerked; passengers stood with their cameras pointed at the display. The numbers barely budged for several minutes while the ship maneuvered. Many of us moved to look out the windows. Finally, the ship's horn sounded, and the stewards served champagne.

We toasted the captain, the ship, and one another. We took each other's pictures, swapping cameras, though there was no distinctive backdrop. Then, the ship crept forward for fifteen or twenty minutes and found an unbroken spot in the ice. The gangway went down. Some crew members got off first, dragging a heavy circle of rope they laid out at the ship's side. They tried to place a marker saying "North Pole 90N", but the ice was so hard they couldn't sink the support. People held it upright to have their photos taken. Throughout the day that we spent at the North Pole, the marker was always in someone's hand, a photo being taken while a little group huddled together and watched.

Otherwise, people scattered, stepping across the ice unsteadily by themselves or with a few others. In some spots the surface crust gave way with a crunch and a layer of water appeared around our feet, even though we stood firmly on ice that was five or six feet thick. In other spots it was very slippery. I was one of many whose legs unexpectedly gave way. I was dazed. Perhaps it was the fall. Perhaps it was the strange uncertainty underfoot combined with the glittering light.

Before we had left on our trip, we were sent a packet of information that included an article describing a Soviet scientific expedition that landed three planes and twenty-four Russians at the North Pole on April 23, 1948. Almost everyone who nowadays discounts Robert E. Peary's 1909 claim to have been the first to stand at the pole gives the twenty-four Russians that distinction instead. They planted the Soviet flag, and soon a lead opened up and the flag drifted off, much to their consternation. The next day, the flag returned, but they were nine miles from the pole. Another day passed, and their instruments showed they were at 90° north again, but one of their planes was drifting away. In such a state of affairs, how can anyone know who was exactly there?

In 1989, an organization called the Navigation Foundation in Rockville, Maryland, analyzed Peary's 1909 photographs to try to determine if they were taken at the pole. The foundation studied shadows in the photographs to calculate the sun's elevation at the spot where they were taken, and it concluded from that analysis that Peary, his assistant Matthew Henson, and four Eskimo companions had been within five miles of the pole. Was that close enough? Most people would say so. But the photo analysis may not be reliable. If the real figure is sixty to a hundred miles, as several experts have suggested, most people would judge the claim unfavorably. Peary used a sextant to take latitude readings, and it is possible that he faked them. No one checked at the time. He did not measure longitude, a serious omission that has fueled the argument against his claim.

The concepts of latitude and longitude are elements of a system of geometric coordinates developed over centuries, so distances on our spherical earth can be translated onto flat maps that can accurately show travelers on land and sea where they are. Latitude is based on distance from the equator, and longitude is based on distance from the prime meridian, a line from the North Pole to the South Pole that runs through Greenwich, England.

Imaginary lines of latitude girdle the globe horizontally from the equator to each of the two poles. The equator is at 0° latitude. Because a straight line drawn from either pole to the center of the earth is at a right angle to a straight line from earth's center to the equator, the poles are at 90° north or south. The latitude of any place on the arc of the earth's surface is its position between 0° and 90° north or south.

Early explorers measured their latitudes with a sextant, an instrument with a movable scale that covers one-sixth of a circle. It has an attached mirror that allows the person using it to see the sun and the horizon at the same time. On the sextant's scale, the explorer would read the angle between the noontime sun and the horizon. Then he would consult navigation tables to adjust for the sun's apparent movement as the earth's axis tilts.

Longitude lines run from one pole to the other, and as they approach a pole the lines converge into a point impossible to register. When the *Yamal* reached the North Pole, our GPS display registered longitude 69°54′ east (and was constantly changing) even as the latitude line read 90° north.

The concept of longitude is the foundation of many of our timekeeping conventions, and some of the people in our group walked around in a circle when we were on the ice, theoretically passing through all the time zones of the earth. Longitude lines are also called meridians, a word derived from the Latin *meri* "middle," and *diem* "day." *Meridian* once meant "noon." (The abbreviations *a.m.* and *p.m.* stand for ante and post meridian.) However, only one meridian at a time is the "noon meridian." It is the one that at that moment is directly facing the sun; it registers noon all along its length. The earth takes twenty-four hours to rotate 360°, so each 15° of longitude equals an hour. Moving 15° west of the noon meridian would take you to an hour past noon, or 1 p.m. If you were 15° east of the noon meridian, it would be 11 a.m.

To take longitude readings, early explorers observed the angle of the sun at noon to obtain their exact local time and compared that time to clocks they carried that showed Greenwich Mean Time, the time at 0° longitude, the prime meridian. It is located in England because it was the British (in 1675) who stabilized the longitude concept. Early explorers, like Nansen and Peary, could accurately calculate longitude if their clocks were accurate. But, calculations of longitude were often inaccurate because of the difficulty of keeping clocks running. Peary, it seems, decided that since longitude lines converge at the pole, taking longitude readings was not worth the time and effort required.

The primitive methods of calculating position that I have described seem esoteric now, when ships like the *Yamal* and automobiles with occupants lost on country roads use GPS devices to display their individual latitudes and longitudes at any given moment. When the *Yamal* reached the pole, some of the passengers were on the deck checking their own personal devices.

Before I left home, to celebrate my decision to go to the North Pole, I bought an elegant-looking compass. I thought it would point unerringly to our destination as the trip progressed, but I was wrong. We went to the Geographic North Pole, true north, a fixed place. The Magnetic North Pole, the North Pole where compass needles point, is something else. It is located in a different (relatively nearby) place that is not fixed. As of June

2002, it is at latitude 78°30′ north, 111°48′ west in the ocean near Ellef Ringnes Island, one of the Sverdrup Islands, frozen bits of land that are fragmented across the top of Canada. The liquid iron at the center of the earth conducts electric currents that enter the earth at the Magnetic South Pole and exit at the Magnetic North Pole as lines of magnetic force. The existence of the Magnetic North Pole was postulated in 1546 by Gerardus Mercator, but it was not reached until 1831 when Captain James Ross discovered it. It was then on the Boothia Peninsula, lower in latitude than Ellef Ringnes Island but in the same vicinity.

That such a thing as a wandering Magnetic North Pole could exist seems not to have occurred to early explorers, though they did notice that as they traveled north their compasses shifted away from the North Pole, the spot they had mathematically determined to be true north. Some compass manufacturers would offset north on their dials in order to compensate for the variations, and it was commonplace for a ship to carry two compasses that would have different readings.

After the Magnetic North Pole was discovered, another century passed, and then, in 1956, the Geomagnetic North Pole was proven to exist as a result of activities of several scientists in preparation for the International Geophysical Year in 1957. This pole is at the north end of the axis of the magnetosphere, the spot where the electron flux from the sun is concentrated. It is the focus for the Northern Lights, or Aurora Borealis, and is in a fixed location over northwest Greenland.

Now, I must load one more block on an already teetering tower of geographic concepts and point out the existence of the Northern Pole of Inaccessibility. This one is fixed, but—like the Geographic North Pole—it is fixed in a field of drifting and cracking ice. It is the spot in the Arctic Ocean most distant from land, about seven hundred miles from any coast. The first person to go there was a Russian, Ivan Cherevichny, in 1941, and he went by air.

There has been only one tourist trip by icebreaker (it was the

Yamal) to the Northern Pole of Inaccessibility, and no expeditions have been organized to travel there over the ice by dogsled, skis, or other means. People have attempted trips to the Geographic North Pole by snowmobile, motorcycle, and motorized sledge, as well as by more traditional means, and many of these trips are listed in the backs of adventure books about Arctic travel. The comparative lack of interest in trips to the Northern Pole of Inaccessibility seems to show that overcoming inaccessibility alone is not what makes adventure travelers tick. No matter how many North Poles there are, only one exists in the popular imagination and that was where we were.

Not that we were adventure travelers. Some of us—aware of the sacrifices and privations of those who came before us—were embarrassed at how easily we achieved the goal. Probably the desire to experience some difficulty and to overcome some vulnerability influenced the twenty people, a quarter of our number, who—one by one—jumped into the freezing water at the North Pole and were pulled out by means of a harness. Even for those of us who didn't "swim," our emotions on being at that place were complex.

For me, all the North Poles were close enough in my mind to roll their attributes into one: the magnet where all magnets point; a place so inaccessible that only about fourteen thousand people have ever been there; a place where each year there is only one long day and one long night; one of the two places on which the axis of the earth turns; a place where the only creatures to survive year-round are microscopic organisms, algae, and tiny shrimp clinging underneath the ice.

In the sky above are the mysterious Northern Lights. The North Star marks this spot on earth by always staying above it. And finally (there's no escaping this), the North Pole is the home of Santa Claus, the Frankenstein Monster, and the Thing, a demonic mutant of science fiction. These creatures of human imagination are at the extremes of comfort and of fear.

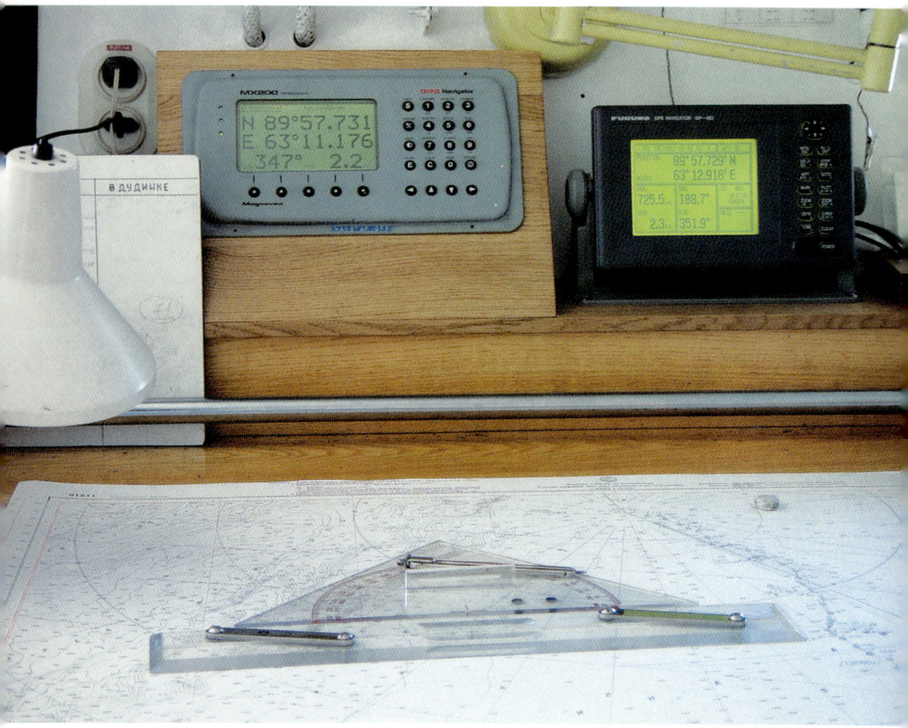
MX200
GPS Navigator
N 89°57.731
E 63°11.176
347° 2.2
В ДУДИНКЕ
89°57.729' N
63°12.918' E
725.5
188.7°
2.3
351.9°

The Journal of Fridtjof Nansen
April 2 to May 30, 1895

Tuesday, April 2

In spite of my being up by seven o'clock on Monday evening to do the cooking, it was nearly two this morning before we got clear of our camping-ground. The load on Johansen's sledge had to be re-lashed, as the contents of one grip had been eaten up, and we had to put a sack of bread in its place. Another grip had to be sewed together, as it was dripping pemmican. Then the sledge from which the bread-sack had been taken had to be lashed secure again, and while we had the ropes undone it was just as well to get out a supply of potatoes. During this operation we discovered that there was a hole in the fish-flour sack, which we tied up, but no sooner had we done so than we found another large one which required sewing. When we came to pack the potato-sack, this too had a hole in it, which we tied up, and so on.

The south wind had become what on board the *Fram* we should have called a "mill breeze" (i.e., 19 to 23 feet per second) and, with this at our back, we started off in driving snow. Everything went splendidly at first, but then came one pressure ridge after another, and each one was worse than the last. We had a long halt for dinner at eight or nine in the morning, after having chosen ourselves a sheltered place in the lee of a ridge. We spread out the sleeping bag, crept down into it with our food, and so tired was I that I went to sleep with it in my hand.

The ridges and leads which had frozen together again, with rubble on either side, became worse and worse. Making one's way through these new ridges is desperate work. One cannot use snowshoes, as there is too little snow between the piled-up blocks of ice, and one must wade along without them. It is also impossible to see anything in this thick weather—everything is white—irregularities, holes, and the spaces between the blocks are covered with a thin deceptive layer of snow, which lets one go crashing through it into cracks and pitfalls, so that one is lucky to get off without a broken leg. It is necessary to go long distances on ahead in order to find a way; sometimes one must search in one direction, sometimes in another, and then back again to fetch the sledges, with the result that the same ground is gone over many times.

Yesterday, when we stopped, I really was done. The worst of it all, though, was that when we finally came to a standstill we had been on the move so long that it was too late to wind up our watches. Johansen's had stopped altogether; mine was ticking, and happily still going when I wound it up, so I hope that it is all right.

Wednesday, April 3

Got under way yesterday about three in the afternoon. The snow was in first-rate condition after the southeast wind, which continued blowing till late in the day. The ice was tolerably passable and everything looked more promising; the weather was fine, and we made good progress. But after several level tracts with old humpy ice came some very uneven ones, intersected by leads and pressure ridges, as usual. Matters did not grow any better as time went on, and at midnight or soon after we were stopped by some bad ice and a newly frozen lead which would not bear.

As we should have had to make a long detour, we encamped, and Russen was killed. This was the second dog to go. The meat was divided into twenty-six portions, but eight dogs refused it, and had to be given pemmican. The ice ahead does not look inviting. These ridges are enough to make one despair, and there seems to be no prospect of things bettering.

I turned out at midday and took a meridian observation, which makes us in 85°59′N. It is astonishing that we have not got farther; we seem to toil all we can, but without much progress.

Beginning to doubt seriously of the advisability of continuing northward much longer.

It is three times as far to Franz Josef Land as the distance we have now come. How may the ice be in that direction? We can hardly count on its being better than here, or our progress quicker. Then, too, the shape and extent of Franz Josef Land are unknown, and may cause us considerable delay, and perhaps we shall not be able to find any game.

I have long seen that it is impossible to reach the pole itself or its immediate vicinity over such ice as this and with these dogs. If only we had more of them! We must turn, sooner or later. But as it is only a question of time, could we not turn it to better account in Franz Josef Land than by traveling over this drift ice, which we have now had a good opportunity of learning to know? In all probability it will be the same right to the pole. We cannot hope to reach any considerable distance higher before time compels us to turn.

Saturday, April 6

Two a.m., minus 11.4°F. The ice grew worse and worse. Yesterday it brought me to the verge of despair, and when we stopped this morning I had almost decided to turn back. I will go on one day longer, however, to see if the ice is really as bad farther northward as it appears to be from the ridge, thirty feet in height, where we are encamped. We hardly made four miles yesterday. Leads, ridges, and endless rough ice, it looks like an endless moraine of ice blocks; and this continual lifting of the sledges over every irregularity is enough to tire out giants.

Monday, April 8

The ice grew worse and worse, and we found no way. Ridge after ridge, and nothing but rubble to travel over. We made a start at two o'clock or so this morning, and kept at it as long as we could, lifting the sledges all the time; but it grew too bad at last. I went on a good way ahead on snowshoes, but saw no reasonable prospect of advance, and from the highest hummocks only the same kind of ice was to be seen. It was a veritable chaos of ice-blocks, stretching as far as the horizon.

There is not much sense in keeping on longer; we are sacrificing valuable time and doing little. If there be much more such ice between here and Franz Josef Land, we shall, indeed, want all the time we have. I therefore determined to stop, and shape our course for Cape Fligely [on Franz Josef Land].

On this northernmost camping-ground we indulged in a banquet, consisting of lobscouse [a mixture of pemmican and seasoned dried potatoes], bread and butter, dry chocolate, stewed red whortleberries, and our hot whey drink, and then, with a delightful and unfamiliar feeling of repletion, crept into the dear bag, our best friend. I took a meridian observation yesterday, by which I see that we should be in latitude 86°10′N, or thereabouts. This morning, I took an observation for longitude. At 8:30 a.m., minus 25.6°F.

Tuesday, April 9

Yesterday's was our first march homeward. We expected the same impracticable ice, but, to our amazement, had not gone far before we came on tolerable good ground, which improved steadily, and with only a few stoppages we kept at it till this morning. We came upon ridges, to be sure, but they always allowed themselves to be negotiated pretty easily, and we did well. Started yesterday about two in the afternoon, and kept going until one this morning.

Thursday, April 11

Better and better. Found nothing but beautiful level tracts of ice yesterday, with a few ridges, which were easy to get over, and some leads with young ice on them which gave us rather more trouble. They ran, however, about in our direction (our course is now the magnetic south 22°) and we could go alongside them.

At last, however, we had to make a crossing, and accomplished it successfully, although the ice bent under us and our sledges more than was desirable. Later in the afternoon we came across a channel, which we proposed to cross in the same way. We reached the other side with the first sledge safely enough, but not so with the other. Hardly had the leaders of the team got out to the dangerous place where the ice was thinnest, and where some water had come up onto it, when they stopped and warily dipped their paws in the water.

Then through went one of them, splashing and struggling to get out. The ice began to sink under the weight of the other dogs and the sledge, and the water came flowing up. I dragged the dogs and sledge back as quickly as possible, and succeeded in driving them all onto the firm ice again in safety. We tried once again at another place, I running over first on snowshoes and calling to the dogs, and Johansen pushing behind, but the result was no better than the first time, as Suggen fell in and we had to go back. Only after a long detour, and very much fagged, did we finally succeed in getting the last two sledges over.

Saturday, April 13

We have traversed nothing but good ice for three days. If this goes on, the return journey will be quicker than I thought. I do not understand this sudden change in the nature of the ice. Can it be that we are traveling in the same direction with the trend of the ridges and irregularities, so that now we go along between them instead of having to make our way over them? The leads we have come across seem all to point to this; they follow our course pretty closely. We had the misfortune yesterday to let our watches run down; the time between our getting into the bag on the previous night and encamping yesterday was too long. Of course we wound them up again, but the only thing I can now do to find Greenwich Mean Time is take a time-observation and an observation for latitude, and then estimate the approximate distance from our turning-point on April 8th, when I took the last observation for longitude. By this means the error will hardly be great.

I conclude that we have not gone less than fourteen miles a day on an average the last three days, and have consequently advanced 40 or more miles in a direction south 22°W.

April 14. Easter Day

We were unfortunate with leads yesterday, and they forced us considerably out of our course. We were stopped at last by a particularly awkward one, and after I had gone alongside it to find a crossing for some distance without success, I thought we had better, in the circumstances, pitch our tent and have a festive Easter-eve. In addition, I wished to reckon out our latitude, longitude, our observation for time, and our variation; it was a question of getting the right time again as quickly as possible.

The tent up, and Johansen attending to the dogs, I crept into the bag; but lying thawing in this frozen receptacle, with frozen clothes and shoes, and simultaneously working out an observation and looking up logarithms, with tender, frostbitten fingers, is not pleasurable, even if the temperature is only minus 22°F. It is slow work, and Easter day has had to be devoted to the rest of the calculation, so that we shall not get off before this evening.

I have calculated our previous latitudes and longitudes over again to see if I can discover any mistake in them. I find that we have come farther south than 86°N, but, according to our reckoning, assuming that we covered fifty miles during the three days, we should have come down to 85°. I cannot explain this in any other manner than that we have been drifting rapidly northward, which is very good for the *Fram* but less so for us. I assume that we are now in longitude 86°E, and have reckoned the present reading of our watches accordingly.

Tuesday, April 16

As we were about to start off at one o'clock yesterday morning, Baro sneaked away before we could harness him. He had seen a couple of the other dogs being put to, and knew what was coming. As I did not wish to lose this dog—he was the best I had in my team—this caused some delay. I called and called, and went peering round the hummocks in search of him, but saw nothing, only the ice-pack, ridge upon ridge disappearing towards the horizon, and the midnight sun shining over all. The world of ice was dreaming in the bright, cool morning light. We had to leave without the dog but, to my great delight, I soon caught sight of him far behind us in our wake. I thought I had seen his good face for the last time. He was evidently ashamed of himself, and came and stood quite still, looking up at me imploringly when I took him and harnessed him. I had meant to whip the dog, but his eyes disarmed me.

Friday, April 19

We now have provender for the dogs for two or three days more, but I think of saving it a little longer and having the worst dogs eaten first. Yesterday Perpetuum was killed. This killing of the animals, especially the actual slaughtering, is a horrible affair. We have hitherto stuck them with a knife, but it was not very satisfactory. Yesterday, however, we determined to try a new method—strangulation. According to our usual custom, we led the dog away behind a hummock, so that the others should not know what was going on. Then we put a rope round the animal's neck, and each pulled with all his might, but without effect, and at last we could do no more. Our hands were losing all sense of feeling in the cold, and there was nothing for it but to use the knife. Oh, it was horrible! Naturally, to shoot them would be the most convenient and merciful way, but we are loath to expend our precious ammunition on them. The time may come when we shall need it sorely.

Sunday, April 21

At four o'clock yesterday we got under way. During the night we stopped to have something to eat. These halts for dinner, when we take our food and crawl well down to the bottom of the bag, where it is warm and comfortable, are unusually cozy. After a good nap we set off again, but were soon stopped by the ugliest lead we have yet come across. I set off along it to find a passage, but only found myself going through bad rubble.

The lead was everywhere equally broad and uncompromising, equally full of aggregated blocks and brash, testifying clearly to the manner in which, during a long period, the ice here has been in motion and been crushed and disintegrated by continual pressure. This was apparent, too, in numerous new ridges of rubble and hummocky ice, and the cracks running in all directions.

I finally found a crossing, but when, after a long circuit, I had conveyed the caravan there it had changed in the interval, and I did not think it advisable to make the attempt. Though I went "farther than far" as we say, I only found the same abominable lead, full of lumps of ice grinning at one, and pressure ridges on each side. Things were becoming worse and worse.

Nearly the most annoying thing about it was that on the other side of the lead I could see fine flat ice stretching southward—and now to be obliged to camp here and wait! I had already possessed my soul with patience when, on coming back to our original stopping-place, I found a tolerably good crossing place close by it. We got to the other side, with the ice grinding under our feet the while, and by that time it was six o'clock in the morning.

We kept at it a little while longer over beautiful flat ice, but the dogs were tired, and it was nearly forty-eight hours since they had been fed. As we were hastening along we suddenly came across an immense piece of timber sticking up obliquely from the surface of the ice. It was Siberian larch, as far as I could make out, and probably raised in this manner through pressure long ago. Many a good meal we could have cooked with it had we been able to drag it with us, but it was too heavy. We marked it "F.N., H.J. 85°30′N." and went on our way.

Monday, April 22

If we have made good progress the previous days, yesterday simply outdid itself. I think I may reckon our day's march at twenty-five miles, but, for the sake of certainty, lump the two last days together and put them down at forty miles. The dogs, though, are beginning to get tired; it is approaching the time for us to camp. They are impatient for food and, grown more and more greedy for fresh dog's flesh, throw themselves on it like wolves as soon as a smoking piece, with hair and all on, is thrown to them. Kvik and Barnet only still keep back as long as the flesh is warm, but let it become frozen and they eat it voraciously. Twelve midnight, minus 27.8°F.

Friday, April 26

I was not a little surprised yesterday morning when I suddenly saw the track of an animal in the snow. It was that of a fox, came about WSW true, and went in an easterly direction. The trail was quite fresh. What in the world was that fox doing up here? There were also unequivocal signs that it had not been entirely without food. Were we in the vicinity of land? Involuntarily I looked round for it, but the weather was thick all day yesterday, and we might have been near it without seeing it. It is just as probable, however, that this fox was following up some bear. In any case, a warm-blooded animal in the 85th parallel!

It would seem as if we were getting nearer inhabited regions again. I have just pricked out our course on the chart according to our bearings, calculating that we have gone sixty-nine miles in the four days since our last observation, and I do not think this can be excessive.

Sunday, April 28

We made good way yesterday, presumably twenty miles. We began our march about half-past three in the afternoon the day before yesterday, and kept at it till yesterday morning. Land is drawing nigh, and the exciting time beginning, when we may expect to see something on the horizon. Oh, how I am longing for land, for something under one's feet that is not ice and snow; not to speak of something to rest one's eyes on. Another fox track yesterday; it went in about the same direction as the previous ones.

Later in the day Gulen gave in; it seemed to be a case of complete exhaustion. He could hardly stand on his legs, reeled over, and when we placed him on one of the loads he lay quite still without moving. We had already decided to kill him that day. Poor beast; faithfully he worked for us, good-tempered and willing to the end, and then, for thanks when he could do no more, to be killed for provender. He was born on the *Fram* on December 13, 1893, and, true child of the polar night, never saw aught but ice and snow.

Saturday, May 4

During the night the ice began to be bad in earnest, lead after lead, the one worse than the other, and they were only overcome by deviations and intricate by-ways. It was terrible work and when the wind increased to a good mill-breeze, matters became desperate. This is indeed toil without ceasing; what would I not give to have land, to have a certain way before me, to be able to reckon on a certain day's march, and be free from this never-ending anxiety and uncertainty about the leads. Nobody can tell how much trouble they may yet cause us, and what adversities we may have to go through before we reach land; and meanwhile the dogs are diminishing steadily. They haul all they can, poor things, but what good does it do? I am so tired that I stagger on my snowshoes and when I fall down only wish to lie there to save myself the trouble of getting up again. But everything changes, and we shall get to land in time.

At five this morning we came to a broad lead, and as it was almost impossible to get the dogs on any farther, we camped. Once well down in the bag with a pot of savory-smelling lobscouse in front of one, a feeling of well-being is the result, which neither leads nor anything else can disturb.

Thursday, May 9

Plus 9°F. Yesterday was a fairly good day. The ice was certainly first-rate, rather rubbly, and the going heavy, but all the same we are making steady way forward. There were long, flat stretches every now and then. The weather had become quite fine when we got under way about three o'clock this morning. The sun was shining through light cumulus clouds. It was hard work, however, making head against the ice, and soon the fog came down with the wind.

Tuesday, May 14

Plus 6.8°F. Yesterday was a cozy day of rest. Just as we were about to get under way after breakfast it clouded over, and a dense snowstorm set in, so that to start out in such weather, in the uneven ice we have now before us, would not have been worthwhile. I therefore made up my mind to halt for the time being and get some trifles done, and in particular the shifting of the load from the birch sledge onto the two others, and so at last get rid of this third sledge, for which we can no longer spare any dogs. This took some time; and as it was absolutely necessary to do it, we lost nothing by stopping for a day.

We had now so much wood from the sledge, together with broken snowshoe staves and the results of other casualties, that I thought we should be able to use it as fuel for some time to come, and so save the petroleum. We accordingly made a fire of it to cook the supper with, contrived a cooking-pot out of the empty petroleum tin, and hung it over in the approved fashion. At the first start-off we lighted the fire just outside the tent door, but soon gave that up as, for the first thing, we nearly burned up the tent and, secondly, the smoke came in till we could hardly see out of our eyes. But it warmed well and looked wonderfully cheerful.

Then we moved it farther off, where it could neither burn up the tent nor smoke us out; but therewith all the joy of it was departed. When we had about burned up the whole sledge and succeeded in getting a pot of boiling water, with the further result of having nearly melted through the floe on which we were living, I gave up the idea of cooking with sledges and went back to our trusty friend the Primus—and a sociable and entertaining friend, too, which one can have by one's side as one lies in the bag. We have as much petroleum, I should imagine, as we shall require for the journey before us, and why bother about anything else?

Sunday, May 19

The surprise which the 17th brought us was nothing less than that we found the leads about here full of narwhals. When we had just got under way, and were about to cross over the lead we had been stopped by the previous day, I became aware of a breathing noise, just like the blowing of whales. I thought at first it must be from the dogs, but then I heard for certain that the sound came from the lead. I listened. Johansen had heard the noise the whole morning, he said, but thought it was only ice jamming in the distance. No, that sound I knew well enough, I thought, and looked over toward an opening in the ice whence I thought it proceeded.

Suddenly I saw a movement which could hardly be falling ice, and—quite right—up came the head of a whale; then came the body. It executed the well-known curve, and disappeared. Then up came another, accompanied by the same sound. There was a whole school of them. I shouted that they were whales and, running to the sledge, had my gun out in a second. Then came the adjusting of a harpoon, and after a little work this was accomplished, and I was ready to start in pursuit.

Meanwhile, the animals had disappeared from the opening in the ice where I had first seen them, though I heard their breathing from some openings farther east. I followed the lead in that direction, but did not come within range, although I got rather near them once or twice. They came up in comparatively small openings in the ice, which were to be found along the whole length of the lead. There was every prospect of being able to get a shot at them if we stopped for a day to watch the holes; but we had no time to spare, and could not have taken much with us had we got one as the sledges were heavy enough already.

We soon found a passage over, and continued our journey with the flags hoisted on the sledges in honor of the day. As we were going so slowly now that it was hardly possible for things to be worse, I determined at our dinner-hour that I really would take off the under-runners from my sledge. The change was unmistakable; it was not like the same sledge. Henceforth we got on well, and after a while the under-runners from Johansen's sledge were also removed. As we furthermore came on some good ice later in the day, our progress was quite unexpectedly good, and when we stopped at half-past eleven yesterday morning, I should think we had gone ten miles during our day's march. This brings us down to latitude 83°20′ or so. At last we have come down to latitudes that have been reached by human beings before us, and it cannot possibly be far to land.

Sunday, May 26

When the ice is as uneven as it is now, the difficulty of making headway is incredible. The snow is loose, and if one takes one's snowshoes off for a moment one sinks in above one's knees. It is impossible to fasten them on securely, as every minute one must help the dogs with the sledges. Added to this, if the weather be thick, as yesterday, one is apt to run into the largest ridges or snowdrifts without seeing them; everything is equally white under its covering of new snow, and the light comes from all directions, so that it throws no shadows. Then one plunges in headlong, and with difficulty can get up and onto one's snowshoes again. This takes place continually, and the longer it lasts the worse it gets. At last one literally staggers on one's snowshoes from fatigue, just as if one were drunk. But we are gaining ground, and that is the chief thing, be one's shins ever so bruised and tender.

I have today reckoned out the observations made yesterday, and find, to our joy, that the longitude is 61°27′E, so that we have not drifted westward, but have come about south, according to our course. My constant fear of drifting past land is thus unfounded, and we should be able to reckon on reaching it before very long.

The ice we have before us looks practicable, but, to judge by the sky, we have a number of waterways a little farther on; we must manage somehow to fight our way across them.

Monday, May 27

Ever since yesterday morning we have seen the looming of water on the sky; it is the same looming that we saw on the previous day, and I set our course direct for the place where, to judge by it, there should be the greatest accumulation of ice, and where, consequently, a crossing should be easiest. During the course of the afternoon we came on one lead after the other, just as the water-sky had denoted, and towards evening the dark heavens before us augured open water of a worse kind. The reflection was particularly dark and threatening, both in the west and in the east. By seven o'clock I could see a broad lead before us, stretching away west and east as far as the eye could reach from the highest hummock. As the dogs were tired, our day's march had been a good one, and we had a splendid camping-place ready to hand, we decided to pitch the tent.

Yesterday evening Kvik was slaughtered. Poor thing, she was quite worn out, and did little or nothing in the hauling line. I was sorry to part with her, but what was to be done? Even if we should get fresh meat, it would have taken some time to feed her up again, and then, perhaps, we should have had no use for her, and should only have had to kill her, after all. But a fine big animal she was, and provided food for three days for our remaining eight dogs.

Thursday, May 30

At five o'clock yesterday morning we set forth with the buoyancy born of the belief that now at last the whole network of leads was behind us; but we had not gone far before the reflection of new channels appeared in front. I climbed up onto a hummock as quickly as possible, but the sight which met my eyes was anything but enlivening—lead after lead, crossing and re-crossing, in front of us and on each side, as far as the eye could reach. It looked as if it mattered little what direction we chose: it would be of no avail in getting out of the maze. I made a long excursion on ahead to see if there might not be a way of slipping through and over on the consecutive flat sheets as we had done before;

but the ice appeared to be broken up, and so it probably is all the way to land.

It was no longer with the compact, massive polar ice that we had to deal, but with thin, broken-up pack ice, at the mercy of every wind of heaven, and we had to reconcile ourselves to the idea of scrambling from floe to floe as best we might. What would I not have given at this moment for it to be March, with all its cold and sufferings, instead of the end of May, and the thermometer almost above 32°F? It was just this end of May I had feared all along, the time at which I considered it of the greatest importance to have gained land.

Unhappily, my fears proved to be well founded. I almost began to wish that it was a month or more later; the ice would then perhaps be slacker here, with more open pools and leads, so that in a measure one could make one's way in a kayak. Well, who could tell? This miserable thin young ice appeared to be utterly treacherous, and there was a water-sky in every direction, but mostly far, far ahead. If only we were there!

While we were making our way during the morning between some leads, I suddenly saw a black object come rushing through the air; it was a black guillemot (*Uria grille*), and it circled round us several times. Not long afterwards I heard a curious noise in a southwesterly direction—something like the sound made by a goat's horn when blown on; I heard it many times, and Johansen also remarked it, but I could not make out what it was. An animal, at all events, it must be, as human beings are hardly likely to be near us here. [It was a seal.]

A little while later a fulmar came sailing towards us, and flew round and round just over our heads. I got out my gun, but before I had a cartridge in it, the bird had gone again. It is beginning to grow lively here; it is cheering to see so much life, and gives one the feeling that one is approaching land and kindlier regions.

In front of us on the horizon we have a water-sky, or at any rate a reflection which is so sharply defined and remains so immovable that it must be over either open water or dark land; our course just bears on it. It is a good way off, and the water it is over can hardly be of small extent. I cannot help thinking that it must be over land. May it be so!

Fred Sandback

John Elton

Ed Staak

A Conversation with Fred Sandback, John Elton, and Ed Staak

This conversation is among three people who went to the North Pole as ordinary people with a simple curiosity about it, as I did. Fred Sandback (who unfortunately died a few months after the conversation took place) was a sculptor whose work is collected by major museums around the world. He traveled to the North Pole by air with a small group in 1985. I met John Elton and Edward (Ed) Staak on the Yamal. *John Elton, at eighty-seven years old, was the oldest passenger on our trip. He is a retired owner of an import business, now run by his son, in New York City. Ed Staak is a television producer who is also a stay-at-home dad (his children are aged two and four). His wife works in the pharmaceutical industry. They live in Chicago. At the North Pole, each of these three men experienced something they regarded as life affecting.*

FRED: My beloved wife, Amy, had been aware for a long time of my fascination with the North Pole, and one day she came home from her club, the Explorers Club, and said, "You're going to the North Pole." I had to go. Amy sent me off in a devoted company, and she stayed home. She doesn't like the cold very much. We went in a Twin Otter ski plane in April, before the ice started to break up. At that time it was properly cold, fifty below, and the wind was whistling.

JOHN: That's a real North Pole experience! It wasn't very cold when we went in July. It got down to 26°F at the pole, but for most of the trip it was in the mid-30s.

FRED: As the temperature drops it is awkward to start up your engine again. You have to take the—what is it?—the carburetor out and take it inside the tent, and heat up the tent.

JOHN: Some of my friends said to me that my going there was the most stalwart thing they'd ever heard of, and I let them keep that impression. But all we did was eat and drink.

We didn't have any hardship. It was a tourist trip.

FRED: Ours was too. There was no serious threat.

JOHN: So you flew straight to the North Pole? From where?

FRED: We left from Resolute Bay, in the Northwest Territory, Canada, in a little plane from an outfitter there. The Otter only has only a 250-mile capacity so we landed on the way at a town on Ellesmere Island and then at a radar station. And then at a navy outpost out on the ice where they said they were looking for fish but obviously they were looking for Russians. They supplied us with fuel.

ED: Flying out there in a small plane must be risky. Things can go wrong.

FRED: The year before, on a charter flight like the one I was on, one of the planes went through the ice. They didn't tell us about that till after we'd left. Still, our trip was an ordinary piece of tourism. It wasn't so long ago that Cook and Peary were making that trip in a much more rigorous manner.

It was almost a hundred years ago—1908 and 09. Now, it seems that neither Cook nor Peary made it to the pole.

ED: How far away was Peary?

It depends on who's writing about him. Maybe five miles, maybe sixty, maybe more. One author says a hundred miles. We're in the age of deconstruction now, and Peary is being deconstructed. He's up for it because there were questions about his claim even at the time he made it. Cook claimed to have gotten there earlier, in 1908, but his claim is more often discredited now than Peary's. Peary was so virulent about Cook at the time that he raised doubts about his own claim, too. And his geographic determinations are suspect because he didn't take along a recognized expert to vouch for them—he expected everyone to take his word for it.

JOHN: I thought he had another expert navigator, beside himself, on the trip.

He did. Robert Bartlett. But he sent him back. Peary's travel method was to start out with several units each made up of one man and a dog team. Each unit would take a turn at breaking the trail, and then turn back. That way, Peary and his own dog team arrived near the pole quite fresh, having followed a beaten track to that point. Peary sent Bartlett back at the last minute. He actually wrote in his journal that he didn't want to share the fame with Bartlett. He took a black man and some Eskimos on the last leg, and figured no one would expect them to share his fame.

FRED: Bartlett was his pilot on the ship. As I recall, he was bitter about it.

He agreed to go on the trip because Peary promised he could go all the way to the pole. But even though he was bitter, he said afterward that he believed Peary had gotten there.

FRED: They took off from the top of Canada?

Yes. Most of the explorers traveled from that side, where your trip began. They didn't go the way we went, starting at Spitsbergen.

ED: The polar ice cap is connected to land on the Canadian side. There was quite a bit of water between Spitsbergen and the place where we started breaking up ice.

There's a bit of the Gulf Stream off Spitsbergen that keeps the ice away a good part of the year. But everyone who wanted to be the first to fly to the Pole seems to have started from Spitsbergen.

ED: If you're flying to the North Pole, and you travel too far, did you travel too far north?

Every direction is south!

ED: How did your plane manage to land on the right spot?

FRED: It was very tricky to land. The pilot circled and circled. He found what he wanted to find, which was a lead where the ice had parted and then frozen over again. But he had to get a sense of the age and thickness of the ice before he would risk using that great landing strip.

Is it possible that the great landing strip wasn't exactly at the pole?

FRED: There was a GPS sort of device in the cockpit and it looked good. But who knows? We were just children at play. I borrowed my friend's stick with the candy stripe on it, and I stuck it in the ice for the pictures.

ED: We weren't able to get on the ice exactly at 90° north. I wanted to see what it would be like to walk around the world several times in one day. That did not happen.

Nobody organized the walk through the time zones, since we were not at the correct spot. Some people walked around in circles anyway, figuring we were close enough.

ED: What time is it at the North Pole? Did you notice on the ship that the crew was operating in a different time zone from the passengers?

There were clocks set to different times, Norway and—

ED: Russia. The Russians on the ship were operating two hours ahead of everybody else. That goes to show you that if the sun doesn't set, it really doesn't matter what time you say it is. That was the only time I ever lived in a controlled small environment with people living in two different time zones. And I never felt that I got over my jet lag. I didn't realize it till I got back to Oslo and experienced night again, but I was in a mild suspended jet lag for the entire trip, because it was always light. I was traveling with my dad, and we went on to Finland, and then started to feel horrible jet lag. We both agreed that we got on that ship and ten days later, when we got off, we started to adjust to a different time zone. Did you notice that, John?

JOHN: I've just been to Europe. I came back a couple of weeks ago. I had terrible jet lag in both directions. For five or six days, I was completely unusable. Nothing like that happened to me on the North Pole trip.

FRED: For myself, and also for my fellow travelers, we found that because the sun was out twenty-four hours we just didn't sleep. We would only stop for catnaps, when we were exhausted. Because there was no sense of night and day, we abandoned that idea.

ED: How many people were in your group?

FRED: There were fourteen of us. We had an odd structure because it was really a fundraising trip for a Canadian photographer named Pat Morrow, who is also an explorer. His mission was to be the first person to climb the highest peak on each of the seven continents, and he had only one peak to go—Mt. Vinson in Antarctica. He was neck-in-neck with another explorer who had no trouble with financing. Pat did, because he is a humble photographer. So we went to a couple of places in Canada—Edmonton was one—to solicit corporate funding for his expedition. We had some luminaries with us: Neil Armstrong, the first man on the moon, and Sir Edmund Hillary and his son, Peter. Ed Hillary led many expeditions in Antarctica, and he was the first to climb Everest. That was in 1953, at the beginning of his career. The quips were that Ed had only been to the South Pole, and Neil had only seen the North Pole from way up high! We got to Grise Fjord on Ellesmere Island and Neil stepped out of the airplane—

JOHN: A step for mankind!

FRED: Yes. It is a town of one hundred people, mostly Inuit, and one of the little boys said, "Right foot or left foot?" Our group also included two young outdoorsmen who were learning about the tourist route from the organizer of the trip. They were practicing so they could take their own groups. And at the high point on the tourism scale was a woman, whom I dearly love, who wore her mink coat all the way through.

The person the trip was about, Pat Morrow, in a way was not so different from Peary. He was trying to be the first to do something, and he was trying to beat somebody else out.

FRED: Yes, he was. His project involved a great deal of risk. And he failed. A crosswind caused damage to his plane, and the mission had to be scrapped. In the meantime his competitor from Texas climbed the summit and wrote the book. When I talked with Pat on the phone I said, "Are you sad?" and he said, "Naw—I can't wait to come to New York and have a cappuccino with you." That's a good disposition.

What is it about being the first one?

ED: The first one's remembered. Number two, nobody remembers.

In one of his lectures on our trip, Bob Headland said that the reasons explorers explore are fame, knowledge, and wealth. He was quoting from a fourteenth-century text.

FRED: It's mainly fame, and that can bring wealth. Speaking of fame, a relative non-performer in our group was a stockbroker from Chicago named Steve Fossett. On July 4, 2002, he was the first person to fly solo around the world in a balloon. He was the sleepyhead in our group, as if waiting for something more challenging.

ED: When did you do your trip?

FRED: 1985.

ED: Oh. That was way before the Russian icebreakers started taking tourists.

FRED: It was before the fall of the Soviet Union, when we eyed the Russians with a different kind of scrutiny.

ED: What kind of statement does the *Yamal* make about Russia today? Russia sold a place in its space program to a civilian who paid to go up there. Maybe we were in the same continuum. I don't think you could rent many ships from the U.S. Navy. For the Russians, is it capitalism or is it a sign of desperation?

JOHN: It's capitalism. This is good business. They don't need the *Yamal* in summer, and they want tourism.

The Yamal *isn't controlled by the Russian military. It is leased by the government to the Murmansk Shipping Company. I think the crew members enjoy the tourist trips. Did you notice that a lot of them were out there with us taking pictures of the polar bear?*

ED: What did they think about all those flags we wanted to fly?

I was a little surprised that so many people brought flags. There were several university flags and, of course, the country flags. And even a corporate flag.

FRED: With us, too. Everyone brought their toys.

ED: People gave a lot of thought to what they wanted to take up there and have photographed. I heard that on a previous trip one man paid to bring his car. But there are a lot of people who don't realize how unusual a place it is. After I got home, someone asked me what airport is closest to the North Pole.

There was a story going around the ship told by a passenger who went to the hairdresser before she left and mentioned she was going to the North Pole. A woman popped her head out of the dryer and said, "Do you have relatives there?"

ED: In one of Bob Headland's lectures, he said that fewer than fourteen thousand people had ever been to the pole. Do you remember how many he said had flown in?

I have an update from him, figures as of August 31, 2003. The Scott Polar Research Institute, where Headland is the archivist, keeps records. This list counts everyone who has stood at the North Pole, but if someone—like Bob—has gone more than once, it only counts the first time. It shows that 1,746 people have flown to the pole in fixed-wing aircraft, and 198 have flown there by helicopter from the Russian islands of Severnaya Zemlya or the drift ice base called Borneo.

ED: How many by icebreaker?

Icebreakers have taken 4,500 people to the North Pole since 1977 when the Soviet military sent the first ship there. The first ship to take tourists was in 1991. For those who went by surface, beginning in 1968, Headland lists 12 who made what he calls a "complete traverse—coast to pole to coast." In addition, 60 people went from one coast to the pole and were airlifted out. And 320 traveled "short distances" to the pole. They were dropped by aircraft somewhere near it and picked up later. I suppose that includes parachutists. And there is still another category, those who drifted to the pole on ice islands. There are 36 of them, scientists or military people working on drift stations.

JOHN: The largest number went underneath the water.

That is 5,660 who arrived at the North Pole on submarines that surfaced there: 42 submarines from the United States, 20 from the Soviet Union or Russia, and 7 from Britain. The total number of people who have ever been to the North Pole is 13,516.

ED: Four of those people are in this room.

Why did you go to the North Pole, Ed?

ED: I enjoy traveling with my dad, and all in all I've visited ninety countries in my life. It has become more and more difficult to find countries that are safe to visit and destinations that are exciting and unusual.

Your dad told me that at the time you suggested the trip, he thought he should have his head examined for letting you talk him into it.

ED: Yes. Well, I was curious about any life-changing experience that would take place at 90° north versus any other part of the world. And there was a desire to be on top of the world. I thought there must be a certain feeling in that.

Did you end up having a life-changing experience?

ED: Yes, but we can get into it later. Sitting on top of the world didn't feel dramatically different from sitting anywhere else. However, I did feel that the light we were experiencing at that time from the sun had a different feeling. It had a surreal feel to it. There was a surreal glow that you can't experience anyplace else in the world. I don't know if anybody else thought that.

I did. "Surreal" is a good description. I noticed from my photographs later that the length of the shadows didn't change over the five or six hours we spent on the ice. The sun stays close to the horizon all the time, making long shadows. It was very bright, and the ice was in tiny crystals, so everything was glittering. John, what was your reason for going?

JOHN: In a sense, you do it because it is there. It was offered. A brochure came from the American Museum of Natural History. I had to convince myself—it had not exactly been my dream for decades. After booking, my initial thought was not to tell anyone until I got to the gate. But that idea was impractical and was discarded. Then I told everybody. "Why are you doing this?" someone said. "Are you out of your mind?" "What's there to see?" And the clincher, something about my age and a rocking chair. My daughter was so upset she wouldn't stop talking about it. Finally, my son said, "Leave it alone. He's going to do what he wants anyway."

I had similar troubles with my husband. He didn't want to go and, out of some kind of fear for my safety, didn't want me to go.

JOHN: You can't really envision it. All you've ever read about the North Pole are hardships. And before I left, I did wonder if I was doing the thing that I ought to be doing. Then, throughout the trip and afterward, I had just a little bit of a bad conscience about it, because we were having four meals a day and people were always doing things for us.

ED: The term *expedition* does not quite fit.

JOHN: But the more we got into the higher latitudes, something sort of gripped me and I would spend hours looking out my window at nothing. And then, well, you start thinking about this, that, and the other. I think it's a very deep experience: religious, spiritual, whatever you want to call it. We were surrounded by loneliness. All we saw were a few birds here and there. We never saw a ship. We never saw a plane. You don't think anything like that exists in this world anymore, especially when you live in a big city. And that got ahold of me. I haven't shaken it yet. And I don't think I want to necessarily. Afterward, you are a different person vis-à-vis the cosmos.

ED: Did you experience this when you were up there, or was it something you experienced afterward?

JOHN: While I was there. I would stand at my window or outside at the rail of the ship and just keep staring out at nothing in particular. I saw a bear, fine. We saw a bear up close. But nothing else. It was so immense. You were just, well, just one with immensity. I'm not a writer. But it was a feeling like that.

The bear was part of the feeling to me—that big white animal, alone in all that space.

FRED: It was different for me. Once I was down on the ice, the imagined great vastness into which I would lose myself was only about three hundred yards wide, because the pressure ridges all around us defined that kind of a dish. You couldn't see beyond a couple of hundred yards out. So you're standing in the middle of a dish and looking out and really it's very small.

ED: We had a much bigger horizon. The dish seemed to be upside down. You could see the curvature of the earth.

FRED: It was a funny kind of come-uppance for me. I was expecting to dissolve into—however you want to view it—the nothingness or everythingness of the landscape, and then to realize you were right back here [pats chest] after all. It was kind of amusing. It was a trick.

ED: Did you feel that there was any revolution, revelation, whatever, for your art from that time forward?

FRED: It's impossible to say. At first glance, I'd say no. I was very bound up in the experience of the moment. It was, indeed, very moving. I can't imagine how it related to art. I didn't come home and make a great sculpture because of the pole. But there is a dim sort of parallel between it and what I like, how my mind works. One of the marvelous things about it was that I was in a place with no language, relatively speaking. We were a little bit beyond nomenclature. I think in my desire, and my personality—and in my artwork too—I need to work in those places that are pre-linguistic. I'll leave it at that. I went with no particular expectations except my romance, my fascination, with the North Pole. Who knows exactly how that could be realized? But it was realized, in spades.

ED: One other time that I tried to have a religious, spiritual, what-have-you experience was at the Great Wall of China. When we were there, I said to my father that I just wanted to have time to myself. I was expecting a great bolt to come out of the sky, but nothing hit me. The same was true at the North Pole. I was expecting to have a discovery right then and I didn't. But the experience as a whole had an impact.

But, Ed, you did say you would tell us about a life-changing experience that you had. You didn't mean the experience as a whole, did you?

ED: My life-changing experience at the North Pole was when

I decided to take the challenge to go swimming.

Oh, yes. People did that!

FRED: Oh, kahuna!

ED: I have to say that after I did that and reflected on it, it was definitely one of the most impactful, as well as one of the most unusual, things I've ever done in my life. With all that ice made from saltwater—saltwater freezes at a lower temperature than fresh—it was definitely below freezing. A strap is put around you in case you start to drown. I was also foolish in that I dove in, so I went out and I had to come back. I admit that going into that incredibly cold water was a stupid thing to do. But it was the experience after getting out of the water that mattered to me. When I first got out, I could feel the ice on my body, on my hairs, my chest hairs. Then I dried off and I didn't get dressed. I just put on my boots without socks and put a coat over my shoulders and moved toward the boat. But within five minutes, my temperature all of a sudden felt very comfortable. I was happy. I was standing there at the North Pole sign, and I got my picture taken, and I didn't feel cold. I felt like I could just walk around in my bathing suit. I didn't feel cold, and I just found it amazing. And I thought, if you set your mind to do something, you can do it, and afterward you find out that it's not bad. What it taught me was that you can actually do anything in the world you want to do if you just set your mind to it. You decide to do it, and you can do it. It's such a simple thing.

CHAPTER FIVE

FRANZ JOSEF LAND

Journey: Franz Josef Land

As I looked down from the helicopter, a black cloud lifted like a curtain to show horizontal stripes: dark clouds, blue sky, white clouds, white land, and dark blue sea, one stripe below another. In the sea, ice in irregular dots formed vertical stripes, setting off the horizontal stripes above. I poked my camera out the open window and pressed my face close, keeping back just enough to be able to see against the wind. The sun moved in and out of clouds. A brown conical hill turned gold as the sun picked it out. "Bell Island," our guide shouted above the roar. It looked like a volcano, but in fact it was just a hill. The volcanic action on Franz Josef Land took place one hundred million years ago. At that time, basaltic lava from the interior of the earth poured from fissures and covered existing tablelike sedimentary rocks. Later, some of the tables upended but many of them stayed flat. There are one hundred to two hundred islands in the Franz Josef Land group, depending on how you count the ones called plugs that are tentatively connected to others.

As the helicopter moved on, I could see that Bell Island was a plug at the end of a row of low peaks connected by ice caps. Franz Josef Land and the neighboring island groups of Novaya Zemlya and Severnaya Zemlya have permanent ice caps, as do the small island of Jan Mayen and the archipelago of Svalbard, which includes the large island of Spitsbergen. A permanent ice sheet—a very large ice cap—covers enormous Greenland. The Arctic island ice caps and the Greenland ice sheet have been here for at least two million years, and with luck they will still be here when the next great ice age overtakes the earth.

Ice cap and *ice sheet* are other words for glacier. Glaciers form only on land and are made entirely of freshwater that has come from snow. It snows here regularly but the air is nevertheless relatively dry, and these glaciers are considered "starved." They grow slowly. Not much of the snow that falls here melts, since the air temperature is usually below freezing and there is very little ice-free land. About 85 percent of Franz Josef Land is glacier covered.

The glaciers are thickened by each new snowfall, and gradually the layers of snow compress into ice. As the ice forms, it creates an expanding mound in the glacier's center and pushes the edges outward; often the edges keep moving to form ice shelves over the frozen sea. When the sea ice melts, the shelves break and icebergs float away, but here the icebergs are small and generally flat topped. The great icebergs like the one that sank the *Titanic* come from the Greenland ice sheet.

From the air, I could see some small icebergs in the open sea beyond Bell Island, and in front of it a glacier edge curved gracefully forward. I later learned it was about fifty feet high. The glacier had released a full-scale chunk of itself into partly frozen water —eventually the chunk would break down and float away in pieces.

At the perimeter of Bell Island where water gave way to land, there was a lip of rocky soil—a spillway of ice had pushed the lip (a moraine) out into the sea ahead of it. The glacier behind it was immense. Unlike pack ice, it was almost uniformly smooth. The sun was very low in the sky. Franz Josef Land is only about six hundred miles from the North Pole.

Later, back in my cabin, I watched the ship's shadow bulk wide across the ice, and the islands become a dotted line at the horizon. We were moving on, and I became engrossed in a book. I turned a page, looked up, and out the window I saw houses! There had been nothing like this for the entire eight days that we had been on the *Yamal*, and the sight was jarring. The ship was moving fast in a calm area free of ice, and almost the moment I saw the houses, they were gone. I rushed to the bridge to find out who was living there.

No one was living there anymore, said our lecturer, Bob

Headland. This was Tichaya Station, the first weather and research station to be established in Franz Josef Land. The Russians set it up in 1929, greatly enlarged it in 1934, and abandoned it in 1959, the year the Krenkel Research Station on nearby Hayes Island became fully operational. The Krenkel station closed in 2003. It was the last Russian base in Franz Josef Land. As recently as 1990 there were five: an airbase, a "top secret" base, and three weather stations, including the "modern" Krenkel station.

Abandoned at Tichaya are twenty buildings, including an airplane hangar and a radio station. A seaplane equipped for cartographic surveys had been based there. The Russian scientists had also recorded changing ice thicknesses and ocean temperatures. In the Arctic, ocean temperatures are almost always warmer than those of the air, but in Franz Josef Land the ocean, underneath the ice, is especially cold, barely above freezing. Air temperatures rise above freezing only an average of forty days a year. Two dozen scientists, some with families, lived at Tichaya year-round when it was active. Between 1934 and 1936 three babies were born there. Those are the only births ever recorded in Franz Josef Land, since this strange place has never been colonized, and has never been home to an indigenous population.

Because there have never been natives in Franz Josef Land, its history has been created by explorers, whose attentions were not on this place but on the pole. In their diaries they recounted their bear and walrus kills and remarked on the savage beauty of the ice-covered islands. But they longed to be free of them and dreamed of the pole. Nansen, having given up on the pole, longed for Franz Josef Land. Either way, explorers stayed here a year or two at most unless, like Georgiy Sedov, the discoverer and surveyor of Tichaya Bay, they are buried here.

Sedov arrived in September 1913 in the *Sveta Foka*, a poorly equipped sealer, and named this bay Tichaya (Russian for "calm") because the ice barely moved. On the way to Franz Josef Land, Sedov's ship had been stuck in ice in Novaya Zemlya, a glacier-covered island group close to the Russian mainland, and he had undertaken a survey of the place while he waited for the ship to free itself. A year later, when the *Sveta Foka* reached Tichaya, its fuel and provisions (not up to standard to begin with) were already depleted. Sedov the explorer was at his core a surveyor. Born into an illiterate family, he had left home at the age of eighteen to study navigation and subsequently gained the rank of second lieutenant in the Imperial Russian Navy. This was a difficult position to reach without connections, but Sedov had to his credit unparalleled achievements. He had sledged across Siberia to complete a survey of the area, and then had traversed Siberia's coastline by ship, producing information about undersea hazards and characteristics of the seabed and the tides.

Sedov set out for the pole in 1912, about three years after Cook and Peary had staked competing claims for having discovered it. Aware of questions as to whether either had been successful, he argued that Russia should create a backup claim. The Russian government ignored him, but he managed to get meager financing mainly through subscriptions from artists and scientists.

Sedov left the *Sveta Foka* on February 15, 1913, with two crewmen, three sledges, and twenty-four dogs, intending to walk to the pole. He died before the party got clear of Franz Josef Land, and his companions buried him with the Russian flag he had hoped to fly at the pole. Near death themselves, they returned to their ship. The crew of the *Sveta Foka* stoked her engines with walrus blubber and also burned for fuel every part of her except the hull, masts, and upper deck. They eventually made it back to Russia; the world was by then involved in World War I. Sedov's journals were deposited in the archives of the Russian navy and were not opened until 1956. By that time, the twenty-four Russians—the ones now credited with being the first to stand at the pole—had been there by plane in 1948.

Sedov's attempt to reach the pole via Franz Josef Land was unusual. The best route for combined ship and sledge travel had been established more than half a century earlier. It was the one Peary used: up Smith Sound, which runs between Greenland and Ellesmere Island in Canada. Sedov, the patriotic Russian, went through Franz Josef Land because it was close to Russia. At the time, however, it did not belong to Russia, as it does now. Austrians had discovered and claimed Franz Josef Land forty years before Sedov's trip.

Austria in the nineteenth century was not the small land-locked country it is today. It was an empire that included Hungary and reached as far as Venice. In the Austro-Hungarian Empire's first Arctic expedition (1872-74), Emperor Franz Josef I was pursuing a quasi-scientific theory called the Open Polar Sea that he hoped would place his country as the first to reach the North Pole; Franz Josef Land was an undesired detour. The Open Polar Sea theory at the time was capturing the imaginations of the governments of several countries, including the United States and Great Britain, because it cast the pole as a possible route to Asia. In the dozen years following Sir John Franklin's disastrous 1845 effort to go through the Northwest Passage, forty expeditions had been sent to search for him, and the difficulty of that route had become clear. The Northwest Passage was traversed for the first time in 1905 by Roald Amundsen, but only now, nearly a millennium later with global warming in play, does it seem promising for heavy commercial use.

The American Elisha Kent Kane had seen what he thought was the edge of the Open Polar Sea in 1852 when he had been ship's doctor on an expedition searching for Franklin. A year later he commanded his own Franklin search that was a thinly disguised pretext for an attempt to reach the pole. The idea of the Open Polar Sea was put into Kane's head by Matthew Maurey, an American naval officer who was known for his charts of ocean currents and winds. He was a deskman not a sailor, however, and he had formed his knowledge of ice by observing that ponds frozen at the edges often have open centers. It was an absurd notion to apply to the Arctic, but it engaged many explorers (armchair and otherwise) and was later elaborated by a renowned German geographer, August Petermann.

Kane believed that if he could sledge small boats across the ice, he could reach an ice-free sea surrounding the pole and sail through it to Asia. Orders given by the U.S. Navy to the captain of the ship Kane traveled on in 1852 instructed that the explorers should contact "United States naval forces or officers of the government serving in the waters of the Pacific or in China." Neither that expedition nor Kane's later one (1853-55) reached either the pole or China, but Kane discovered the Greenland ice sheet, which he named the Humboldt Glacier after German Baron Alexander von Humboldt, a great naturalist of the time. Darwin's *Origin of the Species* was published in 1859, four years after Kane returned. Science as we know it was just beginning to take hold.

After Kane, two other Americans—Isaac Hayes who set off in 1860 in a ship called the *United States* and Charles Francis Hall who traveled in the *Polaris* in 1871-73—tried to reach the pole from the Canadian side via the imagined Open Polar Sea. They were frankly searching for glory for America, and the British Navy took up the challenge in 1875 and sent George Nares out by the same route in a cumbersome expedition with man-hauled sledges and canned food of the type experts think contributed to the death of the Franklin party. Many members of the Nares expedition contracted scurvy, and if their leader had not decided to come home a year early, his expedition probably would have shared the fate of Franklin's.

Nares gained a new Farthest North record of 83°20′. Much

later, in 1964, the governments of Canada and Greenland named the strait he discovered above Smith Sound for him. He had seen the frozen Arctic Ocean—he told everyone who would listen that there was no Open Polar Sea. But his views were discounted, and his expedition labeled "The Polar Failure" in the press. There was even an official commission set up to investigate, and it blamed him for the scurvy, charging that he did not require his men to drink the lime juice provided by the navy. Nares never accepted that censure. In fact, the lime juice had been canned at a high temperature and consequently contained no vitamin C. Although it was known at the time that lime juice prevented scurvy, vitamin C was not discovered until 1928. The failure of the British Navy and the public to give Nares the benefit of the doubt may have had something to do with the famous telegram he sent in advance of his return to London: "North Pole impracticable."

Franz Josef I, monarch of the Austro-Hungarian Empire, made his bid for the pole in 1872, after the American expeditions of Kane, Hayes, and Hall, and before Nares's British one. He placed two young explorers in charge of a state-of-the-art Arctic-exploration ship, the *Admiral Tegetthoff*, built in Germany. Karl Weyprecht, who had been born in Germany but was a lieutenant in the Austrian navy, was the ship's captain. Julius Payer, an Austrian alpine expert and experienced dog-sledger, was director of off-ship exploration. Both Weyprecht and Payer had been members of an 1869-70 German expedition in which two ships, the *Germania* and the *Hansa*, set out to explore a route to the pole at the east side of Greenland specified by the geographer August Petermann, who had expected it to lead to the Open Polar Sea. The *Germania* had returned home unsuccessful; the *Hansa* was crushed in the ice (its crew returned safely).

Petermann also determined the route taken by the Austrian

expedition in the *Admiral Tegetthoff*. He was a respected geographer with no Arctic experience who had amended the Open Polar Sea idea to include something he called "thermometric gateways." His theories prescribed explorations that would follow (supposedly to the pole) three Arctic tongues of the Gulf Stream: off the east coast of Greenland, off Spitsbergen, and at the Bering Strait. The *Admiral Tegetthoff*'s assignment was the Spitsbergen tongue. Petermann considered himself a "natural philosopher." He did not describe himself as a scientist; that word was just coming into use to differentiate those whose speculations were based on observation rather than on the pure reason considered sufficient by naturalists like Petermann. Petermann committed suicide in 1878 but, nevertheless, a year later a ship departed to explore the third of his "thermometric gateways," the one at the Bering Strait. That ship was the *Jeannette*, captained by the American George Washington De Long. It was crushed by ice in 1882 and its captain and twenty of its thirty-three crew members lost their lives. Artifacts from the *Jeannette*, including a pair of oilskin trousers, drifted across the polar sea and inspired Nansen's drift theory.

On July 14, 1872, the Austrian expedition headed by Weyprecht and Payer set out for the Spitsbergen tongue of the Gulf Stream, departing from the German port city of Bremerhaven where its ship had been built. Only five weeks later, on August 20, the *Admiral Tegetthoff* got stuck in ice. The drifting floe in which it was imprisoned carried its occupants past the Russian islands of Novaya Zemlya into an ice-filled open sea. "We were no longer discoverers, but passengers against our will on the ice," Payer wrote later. "From day to day we hoped for the hour of our deliverance. At first we expected it hourly, then from week to week, then at seasons of the year and changes of the weather, then in the chances of a new year. But that hour never came." The *Admiral Tegetthoff*, locked in ice, drifted more than five hundred miles. It never moved under its own power again.

It drifted through a four-month-long Arctic night, and over and over again the crew threw personal belongings, dogs, sledges, and provisions into their small boats at moments when the ship seemed about to break up under the pounding of the ice. But when the sun came back, the *Admiral Tegetthoff* was intact. The floe that held the ship was more than twenty-five feet thick, and the ice that surrounded it wasn't solid enough to walk on.

On August 30, 1873, many of the men, including Payer, were on deck when a cloud bank lifted to reveal the unmistakable dark shapes of rocks. Payer recorded the event in his journal: "At first we all stood transfixed, hardly believing what we saw. Then, carried away by the reality of our good fortune, we burst into shouts of joy: land, land at last!" They celebrated with grog, draped the *Admiral Tegetthoff* in bunting, and named their discovery Franz Josef Land after their emperor. "All cares, for the present at least, disappeared, and with them the passive monotony of our lives. There was not a day, there was hardly an hour, in which this mysterious land did not henceforth occupy our thoughts and attentions." But they could not reach the land; there was too much ice to launch a boat and too little to allow walking. It was a full month before Payer managed to set foot there, and then the mist was so thick he could not see anything. He returned to the ship unfulfilled. On November 1, with winter imminent, he tried again and this time succeeded. "Snow and rock and broken ice surrounded us on every side," he wrote. "A land more desolate could not have been found on earth than the island we walked on; all this we saw not. To us it was a paradise, and this paradise we called Wilczek Island [after a patron]. The vegetation was indescribably meager and miserable, consisting of a few lichens. The driftwood we expected to find was nowhere to be seen. We looked for traces of the reindeer and fox, but our search was utterly fruitless. The land appeared to be without a single living creature."

A second winter passed, and in March 1874 Payer began serious explorations. Weyprecht worried that the ship might free itself from the ice while Payer was gone, but Payer, with a small group, went anyhow. He took along his journals, since he and Weyprecht had agreed that if the ship became free, it would sail off. Provisions for the shore party would be left behind.

In his explorations, Payer and his party traveled 165 miles across Franz Josef Land, walking from island to island on the frozen sea. On April 12, they reached the land's northernmost tip, which Payer named Cape Fligeley, on an island he named Crown Prince Rudolf Land. In the distance he thought he saw two more islands, and he named them King Oscar Land and Petermann Land. He did not try to reach them. The ice was starting to break up, and he turned back to the ship, still stuck as he had left it.

In his journal, Payer wrote that as the men walked, they were accompanied by a strange tinkling sound. It was the crystals of their frozen breath dropping to the ground. The crystals surrounded each man, so that sometimes the members of the party were invisible to one another. The temperature was minus 59°F. It was a harrowing journey. At one point when the dogs, a sledge, and one man fell into a crevasse, Payer ran six miles back to his camp, throwing off articles of clothing as he ran. At the camp he collected some rope and another man, and ran back. The round trip took him five hours, and after that the two men managed to use the rope to bring up the fallen man, the dogs, and the sledge, one by one. The sledge had contained Payer's journals, along with food and equipment for the journey.

After Payer returned to the ship, he and Weyprecht decided to abandon it. Their provisions were low, and they couldn't imagine spending a third winter there. They had lost only one crew member, whom they had buried on Wilczek Island (a cross and a nameplate are still there). Twenty-two men set out on May 20, walking south, pushing and pulling three small boats filled with everything they thought they might need for a long journey. The ice they were traveling over was meanwhile drifting north, and it took them two months to go the first nine miles. "I am very much aware that we are probably lost if conditions do not change radically," Weyprecht wrote in his journal. Eventually, conditions did change. There was more and more open water, and they floated when they could. On August 24, 1874, a Russian fishing ship rescued the group—still numbering twenty-two.

In 1875, after his return to Austria, Karl Weyprecht proposed to a group of German scientists the idea of an International Polar Year in which nations would cooperate with one another in polar research, and in 1879 he put the same proposal to a meeting of the International Meteorological Congress. He died in 1881, but in the following year, 1882-83, twelve countries participated in the first International Polar Year. Fourteen stations were created and operated on islands or in countries near the North Pole to study the structure and motion of ice, auroral phenomena, geomagnetism, and other subjects of polar science. A Second International Polar Year occurred in 1932-33 with forty-four nations participating, and the International Geophysical Year in 1957-58, in which sixty-seven nations participated, was based on the earlier Polar Year examples. Weyprecht's legacy went beyond his discovery of Franz Josef Land.

Franz Josef Land remained unexplored until six years after its discovery when, in 1880, a young Englishman named Benjamin Leigh Smith arrived in the *Eira*, a steam yacht that he had had built especially for Arctic travel. He found the spot off Wilczek Island where Weyprecht and Payer had left the *Admiral Tegetthoff*, but there was no trace of her. He moved on about 130 miles and made a camp on Bell Island, then spent the summer mapping 110 miles of coastline at Franz Josef Land's western edge. He named the islands Hall, McClintock, Hooker, Newton, Bell, David, and Northbrook, and noted that on Northbrook Island, the southernmost of the group, there was a good harbor with an abundance of flowering plants. He named the spit of land Cape Flora and brought home samples of the vegetation.

The following summer, Leigh Smith returned with the *Eira*, and this time was not so lucky. The ship was nipped in the ice and sank off Cape Flora, and Leigh Smith and his men were stranded there over the winter of 1881-82. On June 22, 1882, a ship named the *Hope* left England to search for the *Eira*, and in two months it was back with Leigh Smith and his entire crew on board. One of the rescuers on the *Hope* was Henry Gore Booth, whose daughter, Constance (age fourteen at the time), in 1918 became the first woman elected to the British Parliament.

Benjamin Leigh Smith's father had provided independent wealth for his five children, including a daughter, Barbara. Barbara Leigh Smith (later, Barbara Bodichon) studied art at Bedford Square Ladies College in London. She succeeded as an artist—her paintings were complimented by the most respected critic of the time, John Ruskin. She also studied law and wrote influential pamphlets in favor of women's rights. She was the model for the title character in *Romola*, a novel by her friend George Eliot (Mary Ann Evans).

The Leigh Smiths and their friends inhabited a stratum of Victorian society that was creative and adventurous. Exploration for men and the suffragette movement for women were ways out of a constricting culture. Medical students often spent the last year of their studies as ships' doctors—Arthur Conan Doyle did this, and the references to the Arctic in his Sherlock Holmes novels came from his experiences there—and well-bred young men explored with their own ships or signed on with private expeditions. This same stratum of society also produced Mary

Shelley, known for her gothic novel, *Frankenstein*, the story of a man's creation of a monster that slips from his control and ultimately destroys him. The setting for the telling of this tale is a frozen wasteland near the North Pole.

When Benjamin Leigh Smith mapped islands in Franz Josef Land, he made no attempt to claim them for his country, although it might have been possible for him to do so. The Austrians had made a claim in the usual way—they built a cairn and left a note inside stating that they claimed the entire group of islands, however many they might be, for the Austro-Hungarian Empire. But no one from the empire returned. Franz Josef Land was a conduit, not a place where anyone wanted to be (except perhaps Leigh Smith and, later, another Englishman named Frederick Jackson). Nevertheless, it was exciting. Because of Payer's erroneous sighting of King Oscar Land and Petermann Land, Franz Josef Land briefly replaced Canada's Smith Sound as the most promising route to the pole. If King Oscar Land and Petermann Land had existed, they would have been closer than any other land to the North Pole. Payer's mistake, or mirage, conferred on Franz Josef Land an important episode in its history, an episode that includes its most memorable incident: the meeting of Fridtjof Nansen and Frederick Jackson on Cape Flora in the summer of 1896.

But I am getting ahead of my story. For the moment, I want to mention only that in 1894 Englishman Frederick Jackson set up a semipermanent camp at Cape Flora with the idea of using it as a base for mapping Franz Josef Land and, if it should prove possible, for reaching the pole. He was a cautious man. Before getting as far as Franz Josef Land he had spent a year on an island between Siberia and Novaya Zemlya studying the ways of native people who used reindeer and ponies for sledge hauling. He took ponies and dogs to Cape Flora and also materials to build a camp, including a large wooden building that he named Elmwood and furnished with chairs, tables, books, and even etchings on the walls. Jackson mapped Franz Josef Land north from Cape Flora and, as he wrote in his journal, "Our explorations entirely upset existing maps and our route to the North Pole as planned by land has been frustrated by the non-existence of it."

Despite Jackson's (and, later, Nansen's) doubts that King Oscar Land and Petermann Land existed, other expeditions tried to reach the pole by way of them. An American newspaperman, Walter Wellman, on his second of five unsuccessful attempts on the pole, went that way in 1898-99. He discovered and named Graham Bell Island after the inventor of the telephone, one of his patrons, and returned home after reaching Cape Fligeley at Franz Josef Land's northernmost tip. An Italian expedition led by the Duke of Abruzzi in 1899-1900 celebrated the arrival of the twentieth century with fireworks at Cape Fligeley, then sent Umberto Cagni with a small group of men (three of whom were lost) sledging toward the pole over the ice.

Cagni bettered Nansen's 1895 Farthest North record by twenty-two miles and then turned back, unable to find land beyond Cape Fligeley. "Should we give up all hope of reaching the North Pole?" wrote the Duke of Abruzzi in his diary. "It would be useless to repeat the attempt following the same plan. What I should recommend would be to the north of Kennedy Sound." This is the Smith Sound route, on the opposite side of the pole from Franz Josef Land. When Abruzzi recommended it in 1900, Robert E. Peary was already venturing it, making his first attempt (1898-1900) on the pole. He went by ship to Greenland, and then through Baffin Bay, then—with Greenland on one side and Canada on the other—he entered Smith Sound. Peary's attempts on the pole all took more or less the same route. From Smith Sound he would continue by ship—if ice conditions permitted—through Nares Strait, Kennedy Sound, and Robeson Channel before setting off on foot over the ice. On his third attempt, in 1909, Peary claimed success. But Otto Sverdrup, commander of Nansen's ship, the *Fram,* in its three-year drift, maintained that "the fast currents along that route carry the ice away and make it impossible to reach the pole." He recommended setting out for the pole on the northwest side of Ellesmere Island. This route was used by Peary's rival, Frederick Cook, who claimed in 1909 to have reached the pole in 1908.

Sverdrup, after returning the *Fram* to Norway in 1896, took it out again in 1898, this time to explore and map the small islands near Ellesmere Island that are now named for him. One evening in October of 1898 when Sverdrup was in a remote camp, he received an unexpected visit from Peary, who announced to him that Robeson Channel was closed by ice, and then abruptly left without accepting Sverdrup's invitation to warmth and refreshment. Peary lost eight of his toes on that expedition at least partly because of his imagined rivalry with Sverdrup, who had no plan to try for the pole.

Sverdrup mapped many of Canada's northern islands and he suggested that Norway claim them, especially the three largest ones, which he named Axel Heiberg, Ellef Ringnes (the nearest land to the current location of the magnetic North Pole), and Amund Ringnes, after the Norwegian patrons of his expedition. After Norway failed to press a claim, Sverdrup sent the Canadian government an invoice for approximately $67,000 for mapping and surveying services. The invoice was paid, and the Sverdrup Islands today are Canadian.

Sverdrup remained an Arctic explorer all his life and in 1914 went to Franz Josef Land to search unsuccessfully for the lost Russian expedition of Georgiy Sedov, an expedition that had seemed ridiculous to Russian authorities who believed the North Pole had already been discovered. Fifteen years later, the land where Sedov died became a Russian territory. This was accomplished by Otto Yulyevich Shmidt, who raised the flag of the Soviet Union there on August 29, 1929, in the presence of witnesses. Russia had issued a decree in 1926 that all land north of the Russian coastline to the North Pole was Russian territory, and Shmidt's gesture in 1929 was backed up by the establishment of the Tichaya Station the same year. Russia's claim to Franz Josef Land has not seriously been questioned since, although Norwegian hunters of walruses and polar bears continued to go there until protections were established. Now, hunting of the big land/marine mammals (with some exceptions, mainly for Eskimo or Inuit people) is illegal, and the laws are enforced.

In 1952 the Soviet Ministry of Fisheries began to regulate the number of walruses that could be taken in the Arctic areas under its control, and the Russians still police the area. Polar bears have been protected since 1973 by the International Agreement on Conservation of Polar Bears and their Habitat, signed by Russia, Norway, Canada, the United States, and the other nations where the bears live. And both walruses and polar bears are protected by CITES, the Convention on International Trade in Endangered Species that came into force in 1975. In the United States, the Fish and Wildlife Service enforces the Marine Mammal Protection Act of 1972. There are only about twenty thousand polar bears alive in the world today and about two hundred and twenty thousand walruses.

On Franz Josef Land, polar bears and walruses were certainly abundant at the time of its discovery. The Austrian Weyprecht-Payer expedition killed sixty-seven polar bears in the two years it spent there (1872-74), and Jackson killed seventy-three in three years (1894-97). Leigh Smith's group survived almost a year (1881) on Cape Flora by killing thirty-four bears, twenty-four walruses, and about twenty-five hundred birds.

Now, tourists like us count ourselves lucky to see a polar bear or a group of walruses on an Arctic trip. Birds, however, could almost be called abundant. We didn't see any in the vicinity of the North Pole, but as we approached Franz Josef Land they began to appear. We were glad to see them, one or two or more, flapping and skidding across the water—a sign of life. Then, the ship edged close to an enormous gold-topped, white-bottomed cliff with dark rocks making its leading edge look like a dinosaur tail, and all at once we saw hundreds of chattering birds. Some were in the air around us, but most of them were on the cliff, sitting close together in rows on stairlike ledges. When I show my friends photographs of these birds, they often say, "Penguins!" But penguins live near the South Pole. If they lived in Franz Josef Land, the polar bears would make short work of them, since penguins do not fly.

The black-and-white birds we saw on the cliff are thick-billed murres (also called Brünnich's guillemots), northern members of the family *alcidae.* The thick-billed murre is distinguished from an ordinary murre by a white stripe on its bill. It stands upright somewhat like a penguin but, unlike a penguin, it rarely walks. Its very short wings prevent it from soaring but it does fly. Mostly, it swims. It can dive more than three hundred feet. It chases small fish underwater, folding its short wings into a streamlined shape. The chicks jump off the precarious ledges where they are born only two or three weeks after hatching, before they have grown enough feathers to be able to fly. Accompanied by adult males, they swim more than a hundred miles south into the Barents Sea or other ice-free waters where they spend the winter. The adults molt on the journey (they cannot fly either in this period).

Thick-billed murres, like most of the other birds that breed in the Arctic, find food easily in summer, but no food is available when the pack ice is solid. The murres, in particular, must time their breeding carefully so that when their chicks jump from the cliffs they fall into water not onto ice. The awareness of ice overrides everything for every creature, bear, bird, or human that ventures into Franz Josef Land.

Weyprecht, Payer, Leigh Smith, Nansen, Jackson, Wellman, Cagni, Abruzzi, Sedov, Sverdrup, Shmidt, and the few tourists like us who have been here have all seen the same landscape, the islands like dark waves in the sea, shrouded by ice, set upon by mists and clouds. This is the way most of the world must have looked two million years ago when the glaciers in Franz Josef Land were formed.

The Journal of Fridtjof Nansen
June 1 to August 24, 1895

Saturday, June 1

So this is June. What has it in store for us? Will not this month, either, bring us the land we are longing for? Must hope and believe so, though the time is drawing out. Luck, for that matter, is a wonderful thing. I expected this morning as little of the day as was possible; the weather was thick and snowy, and we had a strong contrary wind. It was no better when we came on a lead directly after we started which appeared to be nearly impassable; everything was dark and dull. However, the day turned out to be better than we expected. By means of a detour to the northeast I found a passage across the lead and we got on to long flat plains that we went over until midday.

Curious how different things are. If we only reach land before our provisions give out we shall think ourselves out of danger, while to Payer land stood for certain starvation if he should have to remain there and not find *Tegetthoff* again. But he had not been roaming around in the drift ice between 83° and 86° for two months and a half without seeing a living creature. Just as we were going to break up camp yesterday morning, we suddenly heard the angry cry of an ivory gull; there, above us, beautiful and white, were two of them sailing right over our heads. I thought of shooting them, but it seemed, on the whole, hardly worthwhile to expend a cartridge apiece on such birds; they disappeared again too, directly. A little while afterwards we heard them again. As we were lying in the bag today, and waiting for breakfast, we suddenly heard a hoarse scream over the tent, something like the croaking of a crow. I should imagine it must have been a gull.

Is it not curious? The whole night long, whenever I was awake, the sun smiled in to us through our silken walls and it was so warm and light that I lay and dreamed dreams of summer far from leads and drudgery. How fair life seems at such moments and how bright the future! But no sooner do I turn out at half past nine then the sun veils his countenance and snow begins to fall. This happens nearly every day now. Is it because he will have us settle down here and wait for the summer and the slackening of the ice and open water, to spare us the toil of finding a way over this hopeless maze of leads? I am loath that this should come to pass. Even if we could manage, so far as provisions are concerned, by killing and eating the dogs and with a chance of game in prospect, our arrival in Spitsbergen would be late and we might have to pass the winter there, and then those at home would have another year to wait.

Sunday, June 2

The lead which stopped us yesterday did not close, but opened wider until there was a big sea to the west of us, and we were living on a floe in the midst of it without a passage across anywhere. So, at last, what we have so often been threatened with has come to pass: we must set to work and make our kayaks seaworthy. But first we moved the tent into a sheltered nook of the hummock where we are lying to, so that the wind does not reach us and we can imagine it is quite still outside instead of a regular mill-breeze blowing from the southwest. To rip off the cover of my kayak and get it into the tent to patch it was the work of a very short time, and then we spent a comfortable, quiet Sunday evening in the tent. The cooker was soon going, and we had some smoking-hot lobscouse for dinner, and I hardly think either of us regretted he was not on the move; it is undeniably good to make a halt sometimes.

Wednesday, June 5

Yesterday we shot our first game. It was an ivory gull (*Larus eberneus*), which went flying over the tent. There were other gulls here, yesterday, too, and we saw as many as four at once; but they kept at a distance. I went after them once and missed my mark. One cartridge was wasted; this must not be repeated. If we had taken the trouble we could easily have got more gulls; but they are too small game, and it is also too early to use up our ammunition. In the pool here I saw a seal, and Johansen saw one too. We have both seen and heard narwhals. There is life enough here, and if the kayaks were in order and we could row out on the water I have no doubt we could get something.

Yesterday we had to kill Klapperslangen. He gave twenty-five rations, which will last the six remaining dogs four days. They are beginning to be pretty well starved now. Lilleraven ate up the toe-strap (the reindeer skin which is placed under the foot to prevent the snow from balling), and a little of the wood of Johansen's snowshoes which the dog had pulled down onto the ice. The late Kvik ate up her sailcloth harness, and I am not so sure these others do not indulge in a fragment of canvas now and then.

Saturday, June 8

Finished and tried the kayaks yesterday at last, but only by dint of sticking to our work from the evening of the day before yesterday to the evening of yesterday. It is remarkable that we are able to continue working so long at a stretch. If we were at home we should be very tired and hungry, with so many working hours between meals, but here it does not seem more than it should be, although our appetites certainly are first-rate and our sleeping powers good. It does not seem as if we are growing weak or sickening from scurvy just yet. As a matter of fact, so far as I know, we are unusually strong and healthy just now and in full elasticity.

Sunday, June 9

We got away from our camping ground at last yesterday, and we were more than pleased. In spite of the weather, which was as bad as it could be, with a raging snowstorm from the east, we were both glad to begin our wanderings again. It took some time to fix grips under the kayaks, consisting of sack, sleeping bag, and blankets, and so load the sledges; but eventually we made a start. We got well off the floe we had lived on so long, and did not even have to use the kayaks which we had spent a week in patching for that purpose. The wind had carefully closed the leads. We found flat ice country, and made good way in spite of the most villainous going, with newly fallen snow, which stuck to one's snowshoes mercilessly, and in which the sledges stood as if fixed to the spot as soon as they stopped.

We came across the track of a bear again yesterday. How old it was could not easily be determined in this snow, which obliterates everything in a few minutes, but it was probably from yesterday, for Haren directly afterwards got scent of something and started off against the wind, so that Johansen thought the bear must be somewhere near. Well, well, old or new, a bear was there while we were a little farther north, stitching at the kayaks, and one day it will come our way, too, no doubt. The gull which Johansen shot brought up a large piece of blubber when it fell, and this tends to confirm us in the belief that bears are at hand, as the bird hardly could have done so had it not been in company.

Tuesday, June 11

No sign of land in any direction and no open water, and now we should be in the same latitude as Cape Fligely, or at most a couple of minutes farther north. We do not know where we are, and we do not know when this will end. Meanwhile our provisions are dwindling day by day and the number of our dogs is growing seriously less. Shall we reach land while we yet have food, or shall we, when all is said, ever reach it?

It is wonderful how little it takes to give one fresh courage.

Yesterday, I found dead in a lead a little polar cod (Gadus polaris), and my eyes, I am sure, must have shone with pleasure when I saw it. It was a real treasure-trove. Where there are fish in the water we can hardly starve, and before I crept into the tent this morning I set a line in the lead beside us. But what a number of these little fish it would require to feed us; many more in a day than we could catch in a week, or perhaps in a month! Yet one is hopeful, and lies counting the chances of there being larger fish in the water here, and of being able to fish to one's heart's content.

Friday, June 14

It is three months today since we left the *Fram*. A quarter of a year have we been wandering in this desert of ice, and here we are still. When we shall see the end of it I can no longer form any idea. I only hope whatever may be in store for us is not very far off, open water or land—Wilczek Land, Zichy Land, Spitsbergen, or some other country. These are moments full of anxiety, when from some hummock one looks doubtingly over the ice, one's thoughts continually reverting to the same question: have we provisions enough to wait for the time when the snow will have melted, and the ice will have become slacker and more intersected with leads so that we can row between the floes? Or is there any probability of our being able to obtain sufficient food, if that which we have should fall short? That it will take a long time before all this snow melts away, and advance becomes fairly practicable, is certain. At what time the ice may become slacker and progress by means of the leads possible, we cannot say. Up to this we have taken nothing, with the exception of two ivory gulls and a small fish. We did, indeed see another fish swimming near the surface of the water, but it was no larger than the other. Where we are just now there seems to be little prospect of capturing anything.

Saturday, June 15

The middle of June, and still no prospect of an end to this; things only became worse instead. So bad as yesterday, though, it had never been, and worse, happily it can hardly be. The sledges ran terribly heavy in the loose, wet, newly fallen snow, which was deep to boot; and sometimes when they stopped—and that was continually—they stuck as if glued to the spot. It was all we could do to move them when we pushed with all our might.

To keep on longer in such circumstances is only wearing out men and dogs to no purpose, and is also using up more provender than is necessary. We therefore renounced dinner, and halted at about ten yesterday evening, after having begun the march at half-past four in the afternoon. I had, however, stopped to take an observation on the way. It is not easy to get hold of the sun nowadays, and one must make the most of him when he is to be seen through the driving clouds; clear he will never be. Yesterday afternoon, after an unconscionable wait, and after having put up the instrument in vain a couple of times, I finally got a wretched single altitude.

Yesterday evening I reckoned out these observations and find that, contrary to our expectations, we have drifted strongly westward, having come from 61°16′E, which was our longitude on June 4, right to 57°40′E. But then we have also drifted a good way north again, up to 82°26′N, after being down in 82°17.8′ on the same date, and we have been pushing southward as hard as we could the whole time. However, we are glad to see that there is so much movement in the ice, for then there is hope of our drifting out eventually towards open water. That we can get there by our own efforts alone over this shocking ice I am beginning to doubt. This country and this going are too bad, and my hope now is in leads and slack ice. Happily, a northeast wind has spring up. Yesterday there was a fresh breeze from the north-northwest (magnetic), and the same again today. Only let it blow on; if it has set us northwest it can also set us southwest, and eventually out towards our goal—towards Franz Josef Land or Spitsbergen.

I doubt more than ever our being east of Cape Fligely after this observation, and I begin to believe more and more in the possibility that the first land we shall see—if we see any, and I hope we may—will be Spitsbergen. In that case we should not even get a glimpse of Franz Josef Land, the land of which I have dreamed golden dreams day and night. But still, if it is not to be, then well and good. Spitsbergen is good enough, and if we are as far west as we seem to be, I have greater hope than before of finding slacker ice and open water; and then for Spitsbergen! But there is still a serious question to be faced, and that is to procure ourselves enough food for the journey.

Sunday, June 16

Yesterday was as bad as it well could be—the surface enough to make one desperate and the ice rough. I very much doubted whether the wisest thing would not be to kill the dogs and keep them as food for ourselves, and try to make our way on as best we could without them. In that manner we should have provender for fifteen or perhaps twenty days longer, and should be able to make some progress at the same time. There does not seem much to be done in that line, however, and perhaps the right thing to do is to wait. But, on the other hand, perhaps it is not far to land or open water, or, at any rate, to slack ice, and then every mile we can make southward is of importance. I have therefore come to the conclusion that we must use the dogs to get on with as best we can—perhaps there will be a change before we expect it; if nothing else, then, perhaps, some better ice, like that we had before.

Meanwhile we were obliged to kill two dogs yesterday. Lilleraeven could hardly go when we started; his legs seemed to be quite paralyzed and he fell down and could not get up again. After I had dragged him and the sledge for a time and had tried in vain to make him go, I had to put him on the load, and when we came to some hummocks where there was shelter from the north wind, Johansen killed him while I went forward to find a way. Meanwhile, my other dog, Storraeven, was in almost as bad a plight. Haul he could not, and the difficulty was to make him go on so that he was not dragged by the sledge. He went a little way, stumbling and falling, and being helped up repeatedly, but soon he was just as bad as Lilleraeven had been, lagged behind, got caught in the traces under the sledge runners and was dragged with it. As I thought I had enough to do in hauling the sledge I let him go, in the hope that he would, at any rate, follow us. He did so for a little while, but then stopped behind and Johansen was compelled to fetch him and put him on his load, and when we camped he was killed too.

Kaifas is the only dog I have left to help me haul my sledge, and Johansen has Haren and Suggen. We have rations for them for ten days from the two slaughtered dogs, but how far we shall be able to get with them the gods alone know. Not very far, I am afraid. Meanwhile our hitherto somewhat primitive method of hauling had to be improved on. With two dog harnesses we accordingly made ourselves proper hauling gear, and therewith all idea of using snowshoes not securely fastened on had to be abandoned. One's feet twisted and slipped and slid off the snowshoes and deep down into the bottomless snow, which in addition turned to ice under our feet, and with our smooth soles was as slippery as eel skin to stand on. Then we fastened the snowshoes on, and where the ice was even it really was possible to drag the sledge with only one dog beside one.

To judge by the sky, there must be a number of leads in the south and southwest. Perhaps our trying mode of advance is leading us to something better. We began at about ten yesterday evening, and stopped at six this morning. We have not had dinner the last few days, in order to save a meal, as we do not think this ice and our progress generally are worth much food. With the same object, we this morning collected the blood of Storraeven and converted it into a sort of porridge instead of the fiskegratin [farina and dried fish]. It was good, even if it was only dog's blood, and at any rate we have a portion of fish flour to the good. Before we turned into the bag last night we inspected our cartridges, and found, to our joy, that we had 148 shotgun cartridges, 181 rifle cartridges, and in addition 14 spherical-shot cartridges. With so much ammunition, we should be able to increase our provisions for some time to come, if necessary. If nothing else should fall to our guns there would always be birds, and 148 birds will go a long way. This discovery has put me in good spirits, for, truth to tell, I did not think our prospects were inordinately bright. We shall now, perhaps, be able to manage for three months, and within that time something must happen.

Saturday, June 22

Half-past nine a.m. After a good breakfast of seal's flesh, seal liver, blubber, and soup, here I lie dreaming dreams of brightness; life is all sunshine again. Yesterday and the last few days were dull and gloomy; everything seemed hopeless, the ice impassable, no game to be found; and then comes the incident of a seal rising near our kayaks and rolling about round us. We have eaten our fill both at supper and breakfast, after being ravenous for many days. The future seems bright and certain now, no clouds of darkness to be seen any longer.

It was hardly with great expectations that we started off on Tuesday evening. A hard crust which had formed on the top of the soft snow did not improve matters; the sledges often cut through this, and were not to be moved before one lifted them forward again. We came to a long pool, which it was necessary to ferry over. The kayaks were soon launched and lying side by side on the water, well stiffened, with the snowshoes under the straps, a thoroughly steady fleet. Then the sledges, with their loads, were run out to them, one forward, one astern. We had been concerned about the dogs and how we should get them to go with us, but they followed the sledges out onto the kayaks and lay down as if they had done nothing else all their lives. Kaifas seated himself in the bow of my kayak, and the two others were astern.

A seal had come up near us while we were occupied with all this, but I thought to wait before shooting it till the kayaks were ready, and thus be certain of getting it before it sank. Of course, it did not show itself again. These seals seem to be enchanted, and as if they were only sent to delay us. Twice the day before I had seen them and watched for them to appear again in vain. I had even achieved missing one—the third time I have missed my mark. It looks bad for the ammunition if I am going on like this, but I have discovered that I aimed too high for these short ranges, and had shot over them.

So then we set off across the blue waves on our first long voyage. A highly remarkable convoy we must have been, laden as we were with sledges, sacks, guns, and dogs; a tribe of gypsies, Johansen said it was. If anyone had suddenly come upon us then, he would hardly have known what to make of the troupe, and certainly would not have taken us for polar explorers.

At last we reached the end of the pool. I jumped ashore on the edge of the ice to pull up the kayaks and suddenly heard a great splash beside us. It was a seal which had been lying there. Soon afterwards I heard a similar splash on the other side, and then for the third time a huge head appeared, blowing and swimming backward and forward, but, alas! Only to dive deep under the edge of the ice before we had time to get the guns out. It was a fine, large blue or bearded seal (*Phoca barbata*).

We were quite sure that it had disappeared for good, but no sooner had I got one of the sledges halfway up the side than the immense head camp up again close beside the kayak, blowing and repeating the same maneuvers as before. I looked round for my gun, but could not reach it where it was lying on the kayak. "Take the gun, Johansen, quick, and blaze away, but quick!" In a moment he had thrown the gun to his cheek and just as the seal was on the point of disappearing under the edge I heard the report. The animal made a little turn, and then lay floating, the blood flowing from its head. I dropped the sledge, seized the harpoon and, quick as lightning, threw it deep into the fat back of the seal, which lay quivering on the surface of the water. Then it began to move; there was still life in it; and, anxious lest the harpoon with its thin line should not hold if the huge animal began to quicken in earnest, I pulled my knife out of its sheath and stuck it into the seal's throat, whence a stream of blood came flowing out. The water was red with it for a long distance, and it made one quite sorry to see the wherewithal for a good meal being wasted. But there was nothing to be done; not on any account would I lose that animal, and for the sake of safety gave it another harpoon.

Meanwhile, the sledge, which had been half dragged up onto the ice, slid down again, and the kayaks, with Johansen and the dogs, came adrift. He tried to pull the sledge up onto the kayak, but without success, and so it remained with one end in the water and one on the canoe. It heeled the whole fleet over, and Johansen's kayak canted till water rose in it with alarming rapidity. The cooker, which was on the deck, fell off and drifted gaily away before the wind with all its valuable contents, borne high up in the water by the aluminum cap, which happily was watertight. The ski fell off and floated about, and the fleet sank deeper and deeper in. Meanwhile I stood holding our precious prize, not daring to let go. The whole thing was a scene of the most complete dissolution.

Johansen's kayak had by this time heeled over to such an extent that the water reached the open seam on the deck, and the craft filled immediately. I had no choice left but to let the seal go and drag up the kayak, heavy as it was and full of water, before it sank. This done, the seal's turn came next, and this was much worse. We had our work cut out to haul the immense animal hand over hand up onto the ice; but our rejoicings were loud when we at last succeeded, and we almost fell to dancing round it in the excess of our delight. A waterlogged kayak and soaked effects we thought nothing of at such a supreme moment. Here were food and fuel for a long time.

Then came the rescuing and drying of our things. First and foremost, of course, the ammunition; it was all our stock. But happily the cartridges were fairly watertight, and had not suffered much damage. Even the shot cartridges, the cases of which were of paper, had not lain long enough to become wholly permeated. Such, however, was not the case with a supply of powder; the small tin box in which we kept it was entirely full of water. The other things were not so important, though it was hardly a comforting discovery to find that the bread was soaked through with salt water.

We found a camping-ground not far off. The tent was soon pitched, our catch cut up and placed in safety, and, I may say, seldom has the drift ice housed beings so well satisfied as the two who sat this morning in the bag and feasted on seal's flesh, blubber, and soup as long as they had any room to stow it in.

It is my opinion that for the time being we can do nothing better than remain where we are, live on our catch without encroaching on the sledge provisions, and thus await the time when the ice shall slacken more or the condition of the snow improve. Meanwhile we will rig up wooden grips on our sledges, and try to make the kayaks watertight. Furthermore, we will lighten our equipment as much as we possibly can. If we were to go on we should only be obliged to leave a great deal of our meat and blubber behind us, and this, in these circumstances, I think, would be madness.

Sunday, June 23

So this is St. John's Eve, and Sunday too. How merry and happy all the schoolboys are today; the folk at home are starting out in crowds for the beautiful Norwegian woods and valleys. And here we are still in the drift ice cooking and frying with blubber, eating it and seal's flesh until the train oil drips off us and, above all, not knowing when there will be an end to it all. Perhaps we still have a winter before us. I could hardly have conceived that we should be here now!

It is a pleasing change, however, to be able to launch out into excesses and eat as much and as often as we like. The food is agreeable to the taste and we like it better and better. My own opinion is that blubber is excellent both raw and fried, and it can well take the place of butter. The meat, in our eyes, is as good as meat can be. We had it yesterday for breakfast in the shape of meat and soup served with raw blubber. For dinner I fried a highly successful steak not to be surpassed by the Grand Hotel, though a good seidel of bock beer would have been a welcome addition. For supper I made blood pancakes fried in blubber instead of butter, and they were a success inasmuch as Johansen pronounced them first class, to say nothing of my own sentiments.

This frying, however, inside the tent over a train oil lamp is a doubtful pleasure. If the lamp itself does not smoke the blubber does, causing the unfortunate cook the most excruciating pain in the eyes; he can hardly keep them open and they water copiously. But the consequences can be even worse. The train oil lamp which I had contrived out of a sheet of German silver became overheated one day, under the hot frying pan, and the whole thing caught fire, both the lumps of blubber and the train oil. The flame shot up into the air, while I tried by every means in my power to put it out, but it only grew worse. The best thing would have been to convey the whole lamp outside, but there was no time for it. The tent began to fill with suffocating smoke, and as a last resort I unfortunately seized a handful of snow and threw it onto the burning train oil. It sputtered and crackled, boiling oil flew in all directions, and from the lamp itself rose a sea of flames which filled the whole tent and burned everything it came near. Half suffocated, we both threw ourselves against the closed door bursting off the buttons, and dashed headlong into the open air. With this explosion the lamp went out, but when we came to examine the tent we found an enormous hole burned in the silk wall above the place where the frying pan had stood. One of our sledge sails had to pay the penalty for that hole.

We crept back into the tent again, congratulating ourselves, however, on having got off so easily, and after a good deal of trouble rekindled a fire so that I could fry the last pancake. We then ate it with sugar, in the best of spirits, and pronounced it the most delicious fare we had ever tasted.

Wednesday, June 26

June 24 was celebrated with great festivities. In the first place, it was that day two years since we started from home; secondly, it was a hundred days since we left the *Fram* (not really, it was two days more), and thirdly, it was Midsummer Day. It was, of course, a holiday, and we passed it in dreaming of good times to come, in studying our charts, our future prospects, and in reading anything readable that was to be found, i.e., the almanac and navigation tables.

At midday I got up and went out to take a meridian altitude.

The weather was brilliant, and it was so long since we had had anything of the kind that I could hardly remember it. I sat up on the hummock waiting for the sun to come to the meridian; basking in its rays and looking out over the stretches of ice where the snow glittered and sparkled on all sides and at the pool in front of me lying shining and still as a mountain lake, and reflecting its icy banks in the clear water. Not a breath of wind stirred—so still, so still; and the sun baked, and I dreamed myself at home.

Wednesday, July 3

Why write again? What have I to commit to these pages? Nothing but the same overpowering longing to be home and away from this monotony. One day just like the other, with the exception, perhaps, that before it was warm and quiet, while the last two days there has been a south wind blowing, and we are drifting northwards.

Saturday, July 6

Rain. At last, after a fortnight, we seem to have got the weather we have been waiting for. It has rained the whole night and forenoon, and is still at it, real good rain. So now, perhaps, this everlasting snow will take itself off; it is as soft and loose as scum. If only this rain would go on for seven days! But before we have time to look round there will be a cold wind with snow, a crust will form and again we must wait. I am too used to disappointment to believe in anything. This is a school of patience; but nevertheless the rain has put us in good spirits.

The days drag wearily on. We work in an intermittent way at the kayak grips of wood for our sledges, and at caulking and painting our kayaks to make them watertight. The painting, however, causes me a good deal of trouble. I burned bones here for many days till the whole place smelled like the bone-dust works at Lysaker; then came the toilsome process of pounding and grating them to make them perfectly fine and even. The bone dust was thereupon mixed with train oil, and at last I got as far as a trial, but the paint proved to be perfectly useless. So now I must mix it with soot, as I had first intended, and add more oil. I am now occupied in smoking the place out in my attempts to make soot, but all my exertions, when it comes to collecting the soot, only result in a little pinch although the smoke towered in the air and they might have seen it in Spitsbergen. There is a great deal to do battle with when one has not a shop next door. What would I not give for a little bucket of oil paint, only common lamp black! Well, well, we shall find a way out of the difficulty eventually; but meanwhile we are looking like sweeps.

On Wednesday evening Haren was killed. Poor beast, he was not good for much latterly, but he had been a first-rate dog and it was hard, I fancy, for Johansen to part with him. He looked sorrowfully at the animal before it went to the happy hunting grounds, or wherever it may be that draught dogs go; perhaps to places where there are plains of level ice and no ridges and leads. There are only two dogs left now—Suggen and Kaifas—and we must keep them alive as long as we can, and have use for them.

The day before yesterday, in the evening, we suddenly discovered a black hillock to the east. We examined it through the glass and it looked absolutely like a black rock emerging from the snows. It also somewhat exceeded the neighboring hummocks in height. I scrutinized it carefully from the highest ridge hereabouts, but could not make it out. I thought it too big to be only a piled-up hummock mixed with black ice or earthy matter, and I have never seen anything of the kind before. That it is an island seems highly improbable for although we are certainly drifting, it remains in the same position in relation to us. We saw it yesterday, and we see it still today in the same quarter. I think the most reasonable supposition is that it is an iceberg.

Wednesday, July 10

It is a curious thing that now, when I really have something of a little more interest than usual to relate, I have less inclination to write than ever. Everything seems to become more and more indifferent. One longs only for one single thing, and still the ice is lying out there covered with impassable snow.

But what was it I had to say? Oh, yes, that we made ourselves such a good bed yesterday with bearskins under the bag, that we slept the clock round without knowing it, and I thought it was six in the morning when I turned out. When I came out of the tent I thought there was something remarkable about the position of the sun, and pondered over it for a little while, until I came to the conclusion that it was six in the evening, and that we had slumbered for twenty-two hours.

This beneficent rain continued the whole day on Saturday, doing away with a fair amount of snow, and we rejoice to hear it. To celebrate the good weather we determined to have chocolate for supper; otherwise we live entirely on our catch. We had the chocolate accordingly, and served with raw blubber it tasted quite excellent. It was the cause of a great disappointment, however, for after having looked forward immoderately to this, now so rare, treat, I managed clumsily to upset my whole cup, so that all the precious contents ran out over the ice.

While I was lying waiting for a second cup—it was boiling over the train oil lamp—Kaifas began to bark outside. Not doubting but that he had seen an animal, I jumped up to hurry off to the lookout hummock to scan the ice. Not a little surprised was I when I poked my head out of the tent door to see a bear come jogging up to the dogs and begin sniffing at Kaifas. I sprang to the gun, which stood ready in the snow beside the tent, and pulled off the case, the bear meanwhile standing astonished and glaring at me. I sent it a ball through the shoulder and chest, certain that it would drop on the spot. It half staggered over, and then turned round and made off, and before I could extract a new cartridge from my pocket, which was full of everything else, was away among the hummocks.

I could not get a shot at it where it was, and set off in pursuit. I had not gone many steps before we saw (Johansen had followed me) two more heads appearing a little way farther on. They belonged to two cubs, which were standing on their hind legs and looking at their mother, who came reeling towards them with a trail of blood behind her. Then off they went, all three, over a lead, and a wild chase began over plains and ridges and leads and every kind of obstacle, but it made no difference to their pace. A wonderful thing, this love of sport; it is like setting fire to a fuse. Where at other times it would be laborious work to get on at all, where one sinks to the knees in the snow, and where one would hesitate before choosing a way over a lead, let only the spark be kindled and one clears every obstacle without thinking about it.

The bear was severely wounded, and dragged her left foreleg; she did not go fast but always so fast that I had my work cut out to keep near her. The cubs ran round her in their solicitude, and generally a little way in front, as if to get her to come with them; they little knew what was the matter with her. Suddenly they all three looked back at me, as I was crashing after them as fast as I could. I had been within range many times, but the bear had had her hindquarters towards me, and when I fired I meant to be sure of making an end of her, as I only had three cartridges with me, one for each of them.

At last, on the top of a huge hummock, I got a sight of her broadside on, and there, too, she dropped. The cubs hurried anxiously up to her when she fell—it made one sorry to see them—they sniffed at and pushed her, and ran round and round, at a loss what to do in their despair. Meanwhile I had put another cartridge in the rifle, and picked off one of the cubs as it was standing on a projection. It fell over the declivity with a growl, and down onto its mother. Still more frightened than before, the other cub hastened to its succor but, poor thing, what could it do? While its brother rolled over, growling, it stood there looking sorrowfully sometimes at it, sometimes at the mother, who lay dying in a pool of blood. When I approached, it turned its head away indifferently; what did it care about me now? All its kindred, everything it held dear, lay there mutilated and destroyed. It no longer knew where to go, and did not move from the spot. I went right up to it and, with a spherical ball through the breast, it fell dead beside its mother.

Johansen soon came up. A lead had detained him, so that he had lost ground. We opened the animals, took out the entrails, and then went back to the tent to fetch the sledges and dogs and proper flaying knives. Our second cup of chocolate in the tent tasted very good after this interruption. When we had skinned and cut up the two bears we left them in a heap, covered over with the skins to protect the meat from the gulls; the third one we took back with us. The next day we fetched the others, and now have more meat food than we shall be able to consume, I hope.

It is a good thing, though, that we can give the dogs as much raw meat as they will eat; they certainly require it. Suggen, poor thing, is in a very bad way, and it is a question whether we can get any more work out of him. When we took him with us after the bears the first day, he could not walk, and we had to place him on the sledge; but then he howled so terrifically, as much as to say it was beneath his dignity to be transported in this way, that Johansen had to take him down again. The dogs seem to be attacked with a paralysis of the legs: they fall down, and have the greatest difficulty in rising. It has been the same with all of them, from Gulen downwards. Kaifas, however, is as fresh and well as ever.

It is remarkable how large these cubs were. I could hardly

imagine that they were born this year, and should without hesitation have put them down as a year old if the she-bear had not been in milk. It is hardly to be supposed that the cubs would suck for a year and a half.

Wednesday, July 17

At last the time is drawing near when we can be off again and start homeward in earnest. The snow has decreased sufficiently to make advance fairly easy. We are doing our utmost to get ready. The grips on the sledges are nicely arranged and provided with cushions of bearskin on Johansen's and of cloth on mine. This is in order to give the kayaks a firm and soft bed and prevent chafing. The kayaks are painted with soot and train oil, and have been caulked with my pastels (for drawing) crushed and mixed with train oil.

Meanwhile, we have lain here—Longing Camp, as we call it—and let the time slip by. We have eaten bear meat morning, noon, and night and, far from being tired of it, have made the discovery that the breast of the cubs is quite a delicacy. It is remarkable that this exclusive meat and fat diet has not caused us the slightest discomfort in any way, and we have no craving for farinaceous food, although we might, perhaps, regard a large cake as the acme of happiness. Every now and then we cheer ourselves up with lime juice grog, a blood-pancake, or some stewed whortleberries, and let our imaginations run riot over all the amenities of civilization, which we mean to enjoy to the full when we get home! Perhaps it will be many a long day before we get there; perhaps there will be many a hard trial to overcome. But, no; I will believe the best. There are still two months of summer left, and in them something can be done.

Tuesday, July 23

Yesterday forenoon we at last got clear of Longing Camp, and now—I am thankful to say—we are again on the move. We have worked day and night to get off. We were determined to start on our last journey home in good repair, and so we did. Everything goes like wild fire. The chances of progress are better than we expected, although the ice is anything but even. The sledges are lighter to draw now that everything that can be dispensed with is left behind, and the snow, too, has decreased considerably. On the last part of the journey yesterday we could even go without snowshoes, and progress among the ridges and irregularities is quicker without them. Johansen performed a feat by crossing a lead alone in his kayak, with Suggen lying on the foredeck while he himself knelt on the afterdeck and balanced the craft as he paddled. I began to try the same with mine, but found it too cranky to risk the attempt and preferred to tow it over, with Kaifas on the deck, while I went carefully alongside and jumped over on some pieces of ice.

We have now the advantage of finding drinking water everywhere. We are also eating our old provender again. But curiously enough, neither Johansen nor I think the farinaceous food as good as one might suppose after a month of meat diet. It is good to be under way again, and not the least pleasant part about it is our lighter sledges.

We certainly left a good deal behind at Longing Camp. In addition to a respectable mound of meat and blubber, we left three fine bearskins. Our friend the bag, too, is lying on top of the bears, a quantity of wood consisting of the boards from under the sledges, the snowshoes and other things, more than half of Blessing's fine medicaments—plaster of Paris bandages, soft steam-sterilized gauze bandages, hygroscopic cotton wadding—to say nothing of a good aluminum glass horizon, rope, our combined frying-pan and melter, half an aluminum cap belonging to the cooker, sheets of German silver, a train oil lamp of the same, bags, tools, sailcloth, Finn shoes, our wolf skin fingerless gloves, also woolen ones, a geological hammer, half a shirt, socks, and other sundries, all strewn about in chaotic confusion. Instead of all these we have an augmentation in the form of a sack of dried seal's and bear's flesh and the other half of the aluminum cap full of blubber. We are now thoroughly divested of all superfluous articles, and there is hardly so much as a bit of wood to be had if one should want a stick to slip through the end of the hauling rope.

Wednesday, July 24

At last the marvel has come to pass—land, land, and after we had almost given up our belief in it! After nearly two years, we again see something rising above that never-ending white line on the horizon yonder—a white line which for countless ages has stretched over this lonely sea, and which for millenniums to come shall stretch in the same way. We are leaving it, and leaving no trace behind us; for the track of our little caravan across the endless plains has long ago disappeared. A new life is beginning for us; for the ice it is ever the same.

It has long haunted our dreams, this land, and now it comes like a vision, like fairyland. Drift-white, it arches above the horizon like distant clouds, which one is afraid will disappear every minute. The most wonderful thing is that we have seen this land all the time without knowing it. I examined it several times with the telescope from Longing Camp in the belief that it might be snowfields, but always came to the conclusion that it was only clouds, as I could never discover any dark point. Then, too, it seemed to change form, which, I suppose, must be attributed to the mist that always lay over it. But it always came back again at the same place with its remarkable regular curves. I now remember that dark crag we saw east of us at the camp, which I took to be an iceberg. It must certainly have been a little islet of some kind.

The ice was worse and more broken than ever yesterday. It was, indeed, a labor to force one's way over pressure ridges like veritable mountains, with valleys and clefts in between, but on we went in good spirits and made some progress. At leads where a crossing was difficult to find we did not hesitate to launch kayaks, and were soon over in this manner. Sometimes after a very bad bit we would come across some flat ice for a short distance and over this we would go like wildfire, splashing through ponds and puddles.

While I was on ahead at one time yesterday morning, Johansen went up onto a hummock to look at the ice, and remarked a curious black stripe over the horizon; but he supposed it to be only a cloud, he said, and I thought no more about the matter. When, sometime later, I also ascended a hummock to look at the ice, I became aware of the same black stripe; it ran obliquely from the horizon up into what I supposed to be a white bank of clouds. The longer I looked at this bank and stripe the more unusual I thought them until I was constrained to fetch the glass. No sooner had I fixed it on the black part than it struck me at once that this must be land, and not far off. There was a large snowfield out of which black rocks projected. It was not long before Johansen had the glass to his eye, and convinced himself that we really had land before us. We both of us naturally became highly elated. I then saw a similar white arching outline a little farther east, but it was for the most part covered with white mist from which it could hardly be distinguished and moreover was continually changing form. However, it soon came out entirely, and was considerably larger and higher than the former, but there was not a black speck to be seen on it. So this was what land looked like now that we had come to it! I had imagined it in many forms, with high peaks and glittering glaciers, but never like this. There was nothing kindly about this, but it was indeed no less welcome, and on the whole we could not expect it to be otherwise than snow covered with all the snow which falls here.

So then we pitched the tent and had a feast suited to the occasion: lobscouse made of potatoes (for the last time but one, we had saved them long for this occasion), pemmican, dried bear's and seal's flesh and bear tongues chopped up together. After this was a second course consisting of breadcrumbs fried in bear's grease, and a piece of chocolate to wind up.

Tuesday, July 30

We make incredibly slow progress, but we are pushing our way nearer land all the same. Every kind of hindrance seems to beset us: now I am suffering so much from my back (lumbago?) that yesterday it was only by exerting all my strength of will that I could drag myself along. In difficult places Johansen had to help me with my sledge. It began yesterday, and at the end of our march he had to go first and find the way. Yesterday I was much worse, and how I am today I do not know before I begin to walk. But I ought to be thankful that I can drag myself along at all, though it is with endless pain. We had to halt and camp on account of rain yesterday morning at three, after only having gone nine hours. The rain succeeded in making us wet before we had found a suitable place for the tent. Here we have been a whole day while it has been pouring down, and we have hardly become drier. There are puddles under us and the bag is soaked on the underside. The wind has gone round to the west just now, and it has stopped raining, so we made some porridge for breakfast and think of going on again; but if it should begin to rain again we must stop, as it will not do to get wet through when we have no change of clothes. It is anything but pleasant as it is to lie with wet legs and feet that are like icicles, and not to have a dry thread to put on. Full-grown Ross's gulls were seen singly four times today, and when Johansen was out to fetch water this morning he saw two.

Wednesday, July 31

The ice is as disintegrated and impracticable as can well be conceived. The continual friction and packing of the floes against each other grinds up the ice so that the water is full of brash and small pieces. To ferry over this in the kayaks is impossible, and the search is long before we eventually find a hazardous crossing. Sometimes we have to form one by pushing small floes together, or must ferry the sledges over on a little floe. We spend much time and labor on each single lead, and progress becomes slow in this way. My back is still painful. Johansen had to go ahead yesterday, also, and evening and morning he is obliged to take off my boots and socks, for I am unable to do it myself. He is touchingly unselfish and takes care of me as if I were a child; everything he thinks can ease me he does quietly, without my knowing it. Poor fellow, he has to work doubly hard now, and does not know how this will end. I feel very much better today, however, and it is to be hoped shall soon be all right.

Thursday, August 1

Ice with more obstacles than here—is it to be found anywhere, I wonder? But we are working slowly on, and that being the case we ought, perhaps, to be satisfied. One thing, however, I am rejoicing over: my back is almost well, so that I shall not delay our progress any more. I have some idea now what it would be like if one of us became seriously ill. Our fate would then be sealed, I think.

Saturday, August 3

Inconceivable toil. We never could go on with it were it not for the fact that we must. We have made wretchedly little progress even if we have made any at all. We have had no food for the dogs the last few days except the ivory gulls and fulmars we have been able to shoot, and that has been a couple a day. Yesterday the dogs only had a little bit of blubber each.

Sunday, August 4

These leads are desperate work and tax one's strength. We often have to go several hundred yards on mere brash or from block to block, dragging the sledges after us, and in constant fear of their capsizing into the water. Johansen was very nearly in yesterday, but as always hitherto, he managed to save himself. The dogs fall in and get a bath continually.

Monday, August 5

We have never had worse ice than yesterday, but we managed to force our way on a little, nevertheless, and two happy incidents marked the day: the first was that Johansen was not eaten up by a bear; and the second, that we saw open water under the glacier edge ashore.

We set off about seven o'clock yesterday morning and got onto ice as bad as it could be. It was as if some giant had hurled down enormous blocks pell-mell, and had strewn wet snow in between them with water underneath; and into this we sank above our knees. There were also numbers of deep pools in between the blocks. It was like toiling over hill and dale, up and down over block after block, ridge after ridge, with deep clefts in between. To put a coping-stone to our misery, there was such a mist that we could not see a hundred yards in front of us. After an exhausting march we at last reached a lead where we had to ferry over in the kayaks. After having cleared the side of the lead from young ice and brash, I drew my sledge to the edge of the ice, and was holding it to prevent it slipping in when I heard a scuffle behind me, and Johansen, who had just turned round to pull his sledge flush with mine cried, "Take the gun!" I turned round and saw an enormous bear throwing itself on him, and Johansen on his back. I tried to seize my gun, which was in its case on the foredeck, but at the same moment the kayak slipped into the water. My first thought was to throw myself into the water over the kayak and fire from there, but I recognized how risky it would be. I began to pull the kayak, with its heavy cargo, onto the high edge of the ice again as quickly as I could, and was on my knees pulling and tugging to get at my gun. I had no time to look round to see what was going on behind me. I heard Johansen quietly say, "You must look sharp if you want to be in time."

Look sharp? I should think so! At last I got hold of the butt-end, dragged the gun out, turned round in a sitting posture, and cocked the shot barrel. The bear was standing not two yards off, ready to make an end of my dog, Kaifas. There was no time to lose in cocking the other barrel, so I gave it a charge of shot behind the ear, and it fell down dead between us.

The bear must have followed our track like a cat and, covered by the ice-blocks, have slunk up while we were clearing the ice from the lead and had our backs to it. We could see by the trail how it had crept over a small ridge just behind us under cover of a mound by Johansen's kayak. While Johansen, without suspecting anything or looking round, went back and stooped down to pick up the hauling rope, he suddenly caught sight of an animal crouched up at the end of the kayak, but thought it was Suggen. And before he had time to realize that it was so big he received a cuff on the ear which made him see fireworks, and then over he went on his back. He tried to defend himself as best he could with his fists. With one hand he seized the throat of the animal, and held fast, clenching it with all his might. It was just as the bear was about to bite Johansen in the head that he uttered the memorable words, "Look sharp!" The bear kept glancing at me continually, speculating, no doubt, as to what I was going to do. But then it caught sight of the dog and turned towards it. Johansen let go as quick as thought, and wriggled himself away, while the bear gave Suggen a cuff which made him howl lustily, just as he does when we thrash him. Then Kaifas got a slap on the nose. Meanwhile, Johansen had struggled to his legs, and when I fired had got his gun, which was sticking out of the kayak hole. The only harm done was that the bear had scraped some grime off Johansen's right cheek so that he has a white stripe on it, and had given him a slight wound in one hand. Kaifas had also got a scratch on his nose.

Hardly had the bear fallen before we saw two more peeping over a hummock a little way off—cubs who, naturally, wanted to see the result of the maternal chase. They were two large cubs. I thought it was not worthwhile to sacrifice a cartridge on them, but Johansen expressed his opinion that the young bear's flesh was much more delicate in flavor than old. He would only shoot one, he said, and started off. However, the cubs took to their heels, although they came back a little while later and we could hear them at a long distance growling after their mother.

Johansen sent one of them a ball, but the range was too long and he only wounded it. With some terrific growls it started off again, and Johansen after it; but he gave up the chase soon as he saw it promised to be a long one. While we were cutting up the she-bear the cubs came back on the other side of the lead, and the whole time we were there we had them walking round us. When we had fed the dogs well and had eaten some of the raw meat ourselves, and had furthermore stowed away in the kayaks the meat we had cut off the legs, we at last ferried over the lead and went on our way.

The ice was not good and, to make bad worse, we immediately came on some terrible leads, full of nothing but tightly packed lumps of ice. In some places there were whole seas of it, and it was enough to make one despair. Among all this loose ice we came on an unusually thick old floe, with high mounds on it and pools in between. It was from one of these mounds that I observed through the glass the open water at the foot of the glacier, and now we cannot have far to go. But the ice looks very bad on ahead, and each piece when it is like this may take a long time to travel over.

As we went along we heard the wounded bear cub lowing ceaselessly behind us; it filled the whole of this silent world of ice with its bitter plaint over the cruelty of man. It was miserable to hear it; and if we had had time, we should undoubtedly have gone back and sacrificed a cartridge on it. We saw the cubs go off to the place where the dead mother was lying, and thought to ourselves that we had got rid of them, but heard them again soon afterwards, and even when we had camped they were not far off.

Wednesday, August 7

At last we are under land! At last the drift ice lies behind us, and before us is open water, open, it is to be hoped, to the end. Yesterday was the day. When we came out of the tent the evening of the day before yesterday we both thought we must be nearer the edge of the glacier than ever, and with fresh courage and in the faint hope of reaching land that day, we started on our journey. Yet we dared not think our life on the drift ice was so nearly at an end. After wandering about on it for five months and suffering so many disappointments, we were only too well prepared for a new defeat. We thought, however, that the ice looked promising farther on.

We eagerly harnessed ourselves to the sledges again, and put on a spurt and away we went through snow and water, over mounds and ridges. We went as hard as we could, and what did we care if we sank into water till far above our fur leggings, so that both they and our shoes filled and gurgled like a pump? What did it matter to us now so long as we got on?

We soon reached plains, and over them we went quicker and quicker. We waded through ponds where the spray flew up on all sides. Nearer and nearer we came, and by the dark water-sky before us, which continually rose higher, we could see how we were drawing near to open water. We did not even notice bears now. There seemed to be plenty about, tracks, both old and new, crossing and re-crossing; one had even inspected the tent while we were asleep, and by the fresh trail we could see how it had come downwind in lee of us. We had no use for a bear now: we had food enough. We were soon able to see the open water under the wall of the glacier, and our steps lengthened even more. As I was striding along, I thought of the march of the Ten Thousand through Asia, when Xenophon's soldiers, after a year's war against superior forces, at last saw the sea from a mountain and cried, "Thalatta! Thalatta!" This sea was just as welcome to us after our months in the endless white drift ice.

At last, at last, I stood by the edge of the ice. Before me lay the dark surface of the sea, with floating white floes. Far away the glacier wall rose abruptly from the water; over the whole lay a somber, foggy light. Joy welled up in our hearts at this sight, and we could not give it expression in words. Behind us lay all our troubles, before us the waterway home. I waved my hat to Johansen, who was a little way behind, and he waved his in answer and shouted, "Hurrah!" Such an event had to be celebrated in some way, and we did it by having a piece of chocolate each.

While we were standing there looking at the water the large head of a seal came up, and then disappeared silently; but soon more appeared. It is very reassuring to know that we can procure food at any minute we like.

Now came the rigging of the kayaks for the voyage. Of course, the better way would have been to paddle singly, but with the long sledges on the deck this was not easy and leave them behind I dared not. We might have good use for them yet.

For the time being, therefore, there was nothing else to be done but to lash the two kayaks together side by side in our usual manner, stiffen them out with snowshoes under the straps, and place the sledges athwart them, one before and one behind.

It was sad to think we could not take our two last dogs with us, but we should probably have no further use for them and it would not have done to take them with us on the decks of our kayaks. We were sorry to part with them. We had become very fond of these two survivors. Faithful and enduring, they had followed us the whole journey through; and now that better times had come they must say farewell to life. Destroy them in the same way as the others we could not. We sacrificed a cartridge on each of them. I shot Johansen's and he shot mine.

So then we were ready to set off. It was a real pleasure to let the kayaks dance over the water and hear the little waves plashing against the sides. For two years we had not seen such a surface of water before us. We had not gone far before we found that the wind was so good that we ought to make use of it, and so we rigged up a sail on our fleet. We glided easily before the wind in towards the land we had so longed for all these many months. What a change after having forced our way inch by inch and foot by foot on ice. The mist had hidden the land from us for a while, but now it parted and we saw the glacier rising straight in front of us. At the same moment the sun burst forth, and a more beautiful morning I can hardly remember.

We were soon underneath the glacier, and had to lower our sail and paddle westwards along the wall of ice, which was from fifty to sixty feet in height, and on which a landing was impossible. It seemed as if there must be little movement in this glacier; the water had eaten its way deep underneath it at the foot, and there was no noise of falling fragments or the cracking of crevasses to be heard as there generally is with large glaciers. It was also quite even on the top, and no crevasses were to be seen. Up the entire height of the wall there was stratification, which was unusually marked.

We soon discovered that a tidal current was running westwards along the wall of the glacier with great rapidity, and took advantage of it to make good progress. To find a camping-ground, however, was not easy, and at last we were reduced to taking up our abode on a drifting floe. It was glorious, though, to go to rest in the certainty that we should not wake to drudgery in the drift ice.

Wednesday, August 14

In the evening we at last reached the islands we had been steering for over the last few days, and for the first time in two years had bare land underfoot. The delight of the feeling of being able to jump from block to block of granite is indescribable, and the delight was not lessened when in a little sheltered corner among the stones we found moss and flowers, beautiful poppies (*Papaver nudicaule*, *Saxifrago nivalis*, and a *Stellaria*). It goes without saying that the Norwegian flag had to wave over this our first bare land, and a banquet was prepared. Our petroleum, meanwhile, had given out several days previously, and we had to contrive another lamp in which train oil could be used. The smoking hot lobscouse, made of pemmican and the last of our potatoes, was delicious and we sat inside the tent and kicked the bare grit under us to our hearts' content.

Where we are is becoming more and more incomprehensible. There appears to be a broad sound west of us, but what is it? The island we are now on, and where we have slept splendidly (this is written on the morning of August 16th) on dry land with no melting of the ice in puddles underneath us, is a long moraine-like ridge running about north and south (magnetic), and consists almost exclusively of small and large—generally very large—blocks of stone with, I should say, occasional stationary crags. We must have come to a new land in the western part of Franz Josef Land, and so far west that we had seen nothing of the countries discovered by Payer. But so far west that we had not even seen anything of Oscar Land, which ought to be situated in 82°N and 52°E? This is indeed incomprehensible. But is there any other explanation?

Wednesday, August 24

It was at midnight between the 17th and 18th that we set off from our last camping ground in splendid weather. Though it was cloudy and the sun invisible, there was along the horizon in the north the most glorious ruddy glow with golden sun-tipped clouds, and the sea lay shining and dreamy in the distance: a marvelous night. On the surface of the sea, smooth as a mirror, without a block of ice as far as the eye could reach, glided the kayaks, the water purling off the paddles at every silent stroke. It was like being in a gondola on the *Canale Grande*. But there was something almost uncanny about all this stillness, and the barometer had gone down rapidly. Meanwhile, we sped toward a headland in the southwest, which I thought was about twelve miles off. After some hours we saw ice ahead, but both of us thought it was only a loose chain of pieces drifting with the current, and we paddled confidently on. But as we gradually drew nearer we saw that the ice was fairly compact, and extended a greater and greater distance, though from the low kayaks it was not easy to see the exact extent of the pack.

We accordingly disembarked and climbed up on a hummock to find out our best route. The sight that met us was anything but encouraging. Off the headland we were steering for were a number of islets and rocks, extending some distance out to sea. It was they that were locking the ice, which lay in every direction between them and outside them. Near us it was slack, but farther off it looked much worse, so that further advance by sea was altogether out of the question. Our only expedient was to take to the edge of the shore-ice, and hope for the chance that a lead might run along it some way farther on. On the way in we passed a seal lying on a floe, and as our larder was beginning to grow empty, I tried to get a shot at it, but it dived into the water before we came within range.

As we were paddling along through some small bits of ice, my kayak suddenly received a violent shock from underneath. I looked round in amazement as I had not noticed any large pieces of ice hereabouts. There was nothing of the kind to be seen, and worse enemies were about. No sooner had I glanced down than I saw a huge walrus cleaving through the water astern, and it suddenly came up, raised itself, and stood on end just in front of Johansen who was following in my wake. Afraid lest the animal should have its tusks through the deck of his craft the next minute, he backed as hard as he could and felt for his gun, which he had down in the kayak. I was not long, either, in pulling my gun out of its cover. The animal crashed snorting into the water again, however, dived under Johansen's kayak, and came up just behind him. Johansen, thinking he had had enough of such a neighbor, scrambled onto the floe nearest him. After having waited a while with my gun ready for the walrus to come up close to me, I followed his example. I very nearly came in for the cold bath which the walrus had omitted to give me, for the edge of the ice gave way just as I set my foot on it and the kayak drifted off with me standing upright in it, and trying to balance it as best I could in order not to capsize.

If the walrus had reappeared at that moment, I should certainly have received it in its own element. Finally, I succeeded in getting up onto the ice, and for a long time afterwards the walrus swam round and round our floe, where we made the best of the situation by having dinner. Sometimes it was near Johansen's kayak, sometimes near mine. We could see how it darted about in the water under the kayaks, and it had evidently the greatest desire to attack us again. We thought of giving it a ball to get rid of it, but had no great wish to part with a cartridge, and besides it only showed us its nose and forehead, which are not exactly the most vital spots to aim at when one's object is to kill with one shot. It was a great ox-walrus. There is something remarkably fantastic and prehistoric about these monsters. I could not help thinking of a merman, or something of the kind, as it lay there just under the surface of the water blowing and snorting for quite a long while and glaring at us with its round glassy eyes. After having continued in this way for some time, it disappeared just as trackless as it had come; and as we had finished our dinner we were able to go on our way again, glad not to have been upset, or destroyed by its tusks. The most curious thing about it was that it came so entirely without warning, suddenly rising up from the deep. Johansen had heard a great splash behind him some time before, which he took to be a seal, but perhaps it may have been the walrus.

The lead along the shore-ice gave us little satisfaction, as it was completely covered with young ice and we could make no way. In addition to this, a wind from the S.S.W. sprang up, which drove the ice onto us, so there was nothing for it but to put in to the edge of the ice and wait until it should slacken again. We spread out the bag, folded the tent over us, and prepared for rest in the hope of soon being able to go on. But this was not to be. The wind freshened, the ice packed tighter and tighter, and there was soon no open water to be seen in any direction. Even the open sea, whence we had come, had disappeared. All our hopes of getting home this year sank at one blow.

After a while we realized that there was nothing to be done but to drag our loads further in onto the shore ice and camp. To try to haul farther over this pack, which was worse than any ice we had come across since we began our voyage, we thought was useless. We should get very little distance in the day, and it might cost us dear with the kayaks on the sledges, among all these ridges and hummocks. And so we lay there day and night waiting for the wind to go down or to change. But it blew from the same quarter the whole time, and matters were not improved by a heavy fall of snow that made the ice absolutely impracticable.

Our situation was not an attractive one: in front of us, massive broken sea-ice, close by land, and the gods alone know if it will open again this year; a good way behind us, land that looked anything but inviting to spend the winter on; around us, impassable ice, and our provender very much on the decline. The south coast of the country and Eira Harbor now appeared to our imagination a veritable land of Canaan, and we thought that if only we were there all our troubles should be over. We hoped to be able to find Leigh Smith's hut there, or at any rate some remains of it, so that we should have something to live in, and we also hoped that in that spot where there no doubt was much open water it would be easy to find game. We regretted not having shot some seals while they were numerous. On the night we left our last camping place there were plenty of them about. As Johansen was standing on the edge of the ice doing something to his kayak, a seal came up just in front of him. He thought it was of a kind he had not seen before, and shouted to me. But at the same moment up came one black head after another quiet and silent, from ten to twenty in number, all gazing at him with their great eyes. He was quite nonplussed, thought there was something uncanny about it, and then they disappeared just as noiselessly as they had come. I consoled him by telling him they really were of a kind we had not seen before on our journey; they were young harp, or saddleback seals (*Phoca groenlandica*). We saw several schools of them again later in the day.

Meanwhile we killed time as best we could, chiefly by sleeping. On the early morning of the 21st, just as I lay thinking what would become of us if the ice should not slacken and we had no opportunity of adding to our larder—the chances I thought did not seem very promising—I heard something pawing and moving outside. It might as usual be the packing of the ice, but still I thought it was more like something on four legs. I jumped up, saying to Johansen that it must be a bear, and then I suddenly heard it sniffing by the tent wall. I peeped out through some holes in one side and saw nothing. Then I went across to a big hole on the other side of the tent and saw an enormous bear just outside. It caught sight of me, too, at the same moment and slunk away, but then stopped again and looked at the tent. I snatched my gun down from the tent pole, stuck it through the hole and sent the bear a ball in the middle of the chest. It fell forward, but raised itself again and struggled off, so I had to give it the contents of the other barrel in the side. It still staggered on, but fell down between some hummocks a little way off. An unusually large he-bear, and for the time all our troubles for food were ended. The wind, however, continued steadily from the same quarter. As there was not much shelter where we were encamped and, furthermore, as we were uncomfortably near the ridge where the ice was continually packing, we removed and took up our abode farther in on the shore ice, where we are still lying. Last night there was a bear about again, but not so near the tent.

Today, at last, the change we have longed and waited for so long has come. Last night the southwest wind quieted down; the barometer, which I have been tapping daily in vain, has at last begun to rise a little, and the wind has gone round to the opposite quarter. The question now is whether it will be able to drive the ice out again.

Al Duba

Jack Brink

A Conversation with Al Duba and Jack Brink

This conversation took place in a staff conference room at the American Museum of Natural History in New York. Alfred (Al) Duba is a geophysicist who works in the Department of Earth and Planetary Sciences there. He is scientific advisor to the Education Department's Earth Bulletins *and also works on the* Earth Wall *in the museum that shows changing geophysical events. The Discovery Tours of the* AMNH *sponsored the trip to the North Pole on which I traveled, and Al Duba was a lecturer on that trip. J. W. (Jack) Brink is Curator of Archaeology at the Provincial Museum of Alberta, in Edmonton, Alberta, Canada. He is an active research scientist who studies native cultures in the Arctic and in the Great Plains of Canada. Our conversation began with the geology of Franz Josef Land, detoured into a short discussion about global warming, and continued with a discussion of the first occupants of the Arctic. We also talked about Robert E. Peary's relationship with the Polar Eskimos, and whether or not Peary made it to the pole.*

AL: There's a lot of sedimentary rock in Franz Josef Land, underneath hundred-million-year-old volcanic rock that came from rift volcanism. The sedimentary rock is about three hundred million years old. It was formed near the equator and reached the Arctic by continental drift. Plant and animal remains produced coal, and some oil and gas, as the sediments were heated and compressed.

Do you think there is oil in Franz Josef Land today?

AL: Oh, yes. Listen, there is going to be a tremendous battle in this century for oil and mineral rights in the Arctic as the ice melts. I have a book here, for example, that is part of a series: "Geology of North America and the Arctic Region." Here's a list of the companies that supported publication: Amoco, Arco, Chevron, Exxon, Getty, Gulf, and so on. They funded the science. The Geological Society of America got all these big rollers on board. I use this series. It's a great series. Good science. What we do at the museum is to try to present a balanced story on the science. We also try to let people know what the issues are. Hydrocarbons are important not only for energy but because clothing, plastics, lots of things are made from them. This table is full of hydrocarbons that aren't running your car. We don't have a full appreciation of how shortsighted we are being as a species.

JACK: A friend of mine says that one hundred years from now people will look back and say, "I can't believe they burned it all." We make so many things out of oil that we need for daily use, and yet its primary purpose has been as fuel. Its most important purpose in years to come will not be as fuel. It will be manufacturing. There are other possibilities for fuel.

AL: There's a theory that compares the earth to Venus—we're sister planets, very similar. But no one can live on Venus because there's so much CO_2 there. There is equilibrium on earth. But when we mess with that we can have trouble. When we get extra CO_2 in the atmosphere, it gets too hot and that can melt glaciers, and the melting may cause it to get too cold. Of course, if the glaciers come back in a big way they'll wipe out Canada first.

JACK: We'll be the test case.

You have a lot of glaciers.

JACK: We do. And they're melting.

They're all receding?

JACK: Not all of them. Some are actually accumulating. But natural phenomena are never going to happen in unison everywhere. The deglaciation at the end of the ice age was not a uniform melting of ice, and now also the melting of glaciers is not completely uniform. But the majority are melting. And significantly. The rate of melting is increasing dramatically. But as Al knows, when you look way back in history, we've had advances and we've had retreats. What's new is global warming, pollutants, and so forth. This has never happened before.

AL: Exactly. Unless the dinosaurs drove cars.

What about Wallace Broecker's theory of the Great Ocean Conveyer Belt? Was that what you were referring to when you said if it gets too hot, glaciers can melt, and then it will get too cold? Broecker's proposition is that a new ice age could result from global warming because the melting of Arctic glaciers, or what he calls freshening events, will interfere with ocean currents in which the ratio of salt water to fresh is critical.

AL: I recently heard one of Broecker's students talking about this. Four different guys are arguing four different things, and he says, "All I've done in my research now is to show how all of them could be right."

Broecker is very complicated.

AL: Any natural system is very complicated. Take the weather. There are so many systems we can measure and see, and we still can't do good predictions. There are too many things that affect it. We talk about this Conveyer Belt—the oscillation between the densities of salt water and freshwater—but in addition you've got heat transfer from hot regions to cold ones.

In the sky, you mean?

AL: Yes, in the sky. You've got the atmosphere, the ocean, and the land. And, in addition, the continents keep moving. Even if it's only centimeters a year, it changes everything. In 2003, a really big El Niño caused a lot of problems, fires in Australia, droughts in Africa, and a NASA weatherman who specializes in El Niño got headlines by saying our weather in New York was caused by a "quirky" El Niño. New England and New York had a very warm wet winter, yet there were also some of the coldest temperatures on record. But this was basically because of the North Atlantic Oscillation, the circulation in the atmosphere between the European coast and North America. Things aren't simple. You can't say it's just this or that. It's impossible to think of all the interactions. So forget it.

We can't forget it.

AL: President Bush can argue forever that CO_2 doesn't make a difference, and he can find people to agree with him. But CO_2 is dangerous stuff the way we're treating it.

JACK: No one doubts, even President Bush doesn't doubt, that global warming is going on. But people like Bush don't want to say that industry has a big part in it. They want to say it's the natural cycling of the earth's changes in temperature—we've seen this before and we're going to see it again. Scientists can be lined up to support that because there are natural cycles of the earth when it is colder and warmer. The real question is if there is a smoking gun this time, different from the natural oscillations. A lot of scientists believe there is.

It's also that Bush and the ones who agree with him think the consequences of global warming are going to be gradual and we'll be able to adjust to them. But everything I've read suggests that they are not going to be gradual.

JACK: That's certainly the Canadian experience. The melting of our glaciers has been abrupt.

AL: It's going to be abrupt for the polar bears when they can't get out on the ice to get their seals.

The polar bears are doomed, I'm afraid.

JACK: There is a gradual progression in everything about the earth, whatever causes a change, until the change reaches a point. Then it becomes vastly accelerated. You can see this in extinctions. An animal species declines and declines and then all of a sudden it just stops existing. If the same thing happens with the melting of glaciers, they will keep receding and receding, and then all of a sudden there will be a big consequence. You get to the point where you can't sustain gradual decline and it becomes catastrophic.

AL: You get to the point where you can't renew.

If emissions keep on growing as they are now, in about seventy years the CO_2 *in the atmosphere will double.* CO_2 *doubling is used as a benchmark by some scientists for the point of no return. Of course, Bush will be dead in seventy years and so will we, but it does seem irresponsible not to worry what the world will be like then.*

AL: It's all a matter of power and politics. I quit my job at the Lawrence Livermore National Laboratory because of that sort of thing. I quit in 2000 because of the Wen Ho Lee affair at Los Alamos—remember, he was accused of a security breach. That resulted in the placing of too many restrictions on how science was to be conducted at both Los Alamos and Livermore. Losing free exchange of nonclassified ideas with colleagues from over twenty-five countries was just more than I could accept.

Now, we should get to the topic we are supposed to be discussing: Franz Josef Land. Jack, you asked me why I wanted you—an archaeologist and anthropologist—to talk about a place that has never had an indigenous population. And I admit it is a stretch. But my thinking is that Franz Josef Land is symbolic of all cold and desolate places. I'm sure there were others, Greenland especially, that were settled. Why not Franz Josef Land?

JACK: It's an interesting question, and I'm not sure what the answer is. It may be as simple as the fact that nobody ever found it. It's surrounded by pack ice in the north and virtually inaccessible from there.

Nansen reached it from the north, and his journal shows how difficult the approach would have been from that direction.

JACK: The occupation of the northern hemisphere was from Siberia through Alaska, and then to the Canadian Arctic and Greenland. It is understandable. People could travel almost that entire arc by land, and where they couldn't, they could walk a short distance across ice or use boats. Only a few miles separate Ellesmere Island from Greenland, which was settled just as early as the Canadian Arctic was. The radiocarbon dates coming out of northern Greenland are as old or older than anything coming out of Canada. And northern Greenland seems to be the first part of Greenland that was inhabited. Its first population was there about forty-five hundred years ago, and didn't live there very long—only about two hundred to three hundred years. This is an area that's still poorly understood archaeologically because of its remoteness.

AL: They got there forty-five hundred years ago and lasted only about two hundred years! Where was that in Greenland, exactly?

JACK: The top of northern Greenland. The entire Arctic region was populated by a single wave of people at a single point in time bearing ostensibly the same culture. And it seems to have happened within the blink of an eye, on a geologic timescale.

AL: They were even farther north than Peary's Polar Eskimos.

Were they ancestors of the Polar Eskimos, the ones who helped Peary in his attempts to reach the North Pole?

JACK: No, the earliest inhabitants died out in Greenland. The ancestors of the Inuit people came later, in another wave. The Polar Eskimos are Inuit. The Polar Eskimos were completely isolated. The Humboldt Glacier in the north and northwest was essentially a barrier and they did not go beyond that, and Melville Bay below them was a barrier and they did not go beyond that. They thought they were the only people on earth.

Peary picked them up with his ship from several villages, and sometimes one would want to get off at a different village than he started from. But all the villages were in the same general area.

JACK: Peary went there seven or eight times in total, and many times he overwintered at Etah, their main village. It is near Cape

York, the area where the Thule Airbase is now. The Polar Eskimos were first noted by William Baffin in 1616.

AL: Baffin, before Ross?

JACK: Yes, Baffin in 1616. Then there was no word for about two hundred years and then Captain James Ross met them in 1818. Ross noted the Cape York meteorites as well. He did not see them, but he reported their existence and the fact that native people used them for a source of metal.

AL: It's interesting that these people who were so isolated were using material from outer space. The Cape York meteorites came from a single piece of iron-nickel alloy that was the core of an asteroid that broke up sometime after forming four and a half billion years ago. As it entered the earth's atmosphere, the iron broke into several pieces before it fell to earth about ten thousand years ago. Pieces of it have been collected from Greenland and Canada. We have the three pieces downstairs that Peary brought back. The biggest one weighs thirty-four tons and is the biggest meteorite on display in the world. After Peary got it to New York on his ship, it took fourteen teams of horses to drag it to the museum. There are two or three more big pieces in Greenland, and one is on display in a museum in Denmark. Jack, when can you first document the use of Cape York meteoric iron by any Eskimo culture?

JACK: The oldest dates we have run around twelve hundred years ago. The very first people who inhabited Greenland weren't using the Cape York meteorites. There's no evidence of that. But evidence shows up later. One of the phenomenal things about Arctic occupation is that there were two separate movements of people with separate cultural groups. The early wave is generally referred to as Paleo-Eskimos. The Paleo-Eskimos were the first inhabitants of the Arctic region, and when they spread across the Arctic from west to east—that is, from Alaska to Greenland—they did so in an amazingly short period of time. One theory about why they spread so quickly across the vast Arctic is called the Muskox Way. It goes like this: When muskoxen are threatened they run together to a hilltop, put the young behind them or in the middle of a circle, and turn and face their horns outward toward their predators. This works against wolves —the muskoxen defend themselves as a group. But against people it doesn't work, because the people stand there with bows and arrows and shoot them all. The theory is that muskoxen were a prime food of the Paleo-Eskimos, partly because they were so easy to kill, and that people moved so quickly across the Arctic because they rapidly wiped out their main food source in each place they inhabited. So the Muskox Way is an attempt to explain how people got all the way from Alaska to Greenland in what appears to be perhaps just one or two hundred years. When you think of Eskimo people you probably think of whaling, which was a later development that comes with the second population wave.

AL: When they ran out of the easy food source, they had to go after the hard one.

JACK: Yes, but these were different people. The second wave of population was a totally different kind of culture, the ancestors of what we now call the Inuit people.

What's the difference between Eskimos and Inuit?

JACK: *Eskimo* is the term still used in Alaska for the Arctic and Sub-Arctic adapted people. *Inuit* is the term used by Canadian

Arctic native people. They are the same people, with the same language, and much the same culture; they decided to call themselves by different names. About one thousand years ago, a warming period opened up water throughout the lower part of the Arctic, which includes most of Alaska and the southwestern part of Arctic Canada, and allowed whales to go in there. The people followed them. They were ancestors of the Inuit, and are called the Thule culture.

I thought Thule was a place in Greenland.

JACK: It is. They were first named in Greenland. Archaeologists were doing work there, finding evidence of the culture. Then they found more evidence as they went across the Canadian Arctic and said, "They are all the same people." It was a replacement culture; it had a different language, different culture base, totally different tools. The Paleo-Eskimos had finely chipped stone tools and used bows and arrows. The Thule culture didn't use bows and arrows and hardly chipped stone at all. They had harpoon points and things like that, not uncommonly with metal tips on them.

They got the metal from Cape York?

JACK: Not in the western Arctic. Cape York metal has never been found there. The metal found in the western Arctic is Asiatic metal, coming from the great civilizations of Asia and traded through Siberia. Remember, it's easy to carry. These people are trading little slivers. All an Inuit person needs is a piece of metal the size of your thumb to make a very sharp barb that goes in the end of a harpoon. And these slivers were extremely valuable to them.

AL: You were talking about the Muskox Way. *Way* is an interesting term. It usually means "way of life" and this is a way of life defined by animal availability. It's just humans chasing muskoxen. The thing about all these animals is that we human beings kill them off and then we go after something else.

The muskox is almost extinct now.

AL: So then we go after the whales, and before we made some recent laws, some species of whales were very near extinction too—but that wasn't because of the Inuit. The reason the Inuit are tied to the Canadian Arctic and Alaska is because there's a big mass of land that animals can roam over, back and forth. The problem with Franz Josef Land is that it's a group of small islands without a large animal population for humans to live on.

Nansen and Johansen found seals and walruses and polar bears, and most of the expeditions that went there stayed healthy eating the meat along with the provisions they brought with them. But they were very small numbers of people.

AL: There aren't even whales up there because they can't get through the ice.

Nansen saw some whales. But it's not a major whaling area.

AL: Overall there is not much to sustain mammals like us. You can't live off those teeny mushrooms I took pictures of before I lost my camera. So I would say that the reason Franz Josef Land has no human population is because it has no animal population to speak of.

JACK: I agree. I don't know a lot about Franz Josef Land but I don't think it has nearly enough resources to sustain life. If it had ever been settled we might have found evidence of someone getting there and trying to live off the resources, but to my knowledge there's never been a find there of any archaeological site.

In some ways it's not very different from Northern Greenland, though, where the Polar Eskimos live. There aren't many animals roaming around on the big glacier in the center, and the area that is not frozen in summer is pretty small, certainly by comparison to Canada and Alaska.

JACK: That's true, but I just don't think anybody ever got to Franz Josef Land. You can see Greenland from Ellesmere Island, and Franz Josef Land is not visible from any other place.

It's hardly visible even when you're in it. There's so much mist and so many glaciers to blend with the pack ice. What about the Vikings in Greenland? If the Inuit second wave got there around 1500, that was just about when the Vikings were leaving, wasn't it?

JACK: They had already left. I went to a lecture two nights ago by a friend of mine, Charlie Schweger, who's working in Greenland, researching the abandonment of the early Norse villages. He's proposed an interesting new theory. The Norse farms had "inner lands" on the flatlands of the valley. These had the best soil and were the prime growing lands, fertile bottomlands that were scarce. They were fenced with stone to keep out livestock. Charlie Schweger's evidence suggests the inner lands were being repeatedly flooded about the time the Norse abandoned Greenland, and he thinks it was mainly the disappearance of the essential inner lands that drove them away. Without those lands for farming, they simply had no way to make a living.

But that was the time of the Little Ice Age when temperatures were getting colder. I thought the glaciers were expanding.

JACK: They were. But water-flow patterns changed. One theory is that rivers froze solid, then thawed more slowly in the spring; new melt water from the glaciers came down the frozen channels and, having no valley to occupy, overflowed onto the fields. With bigger glaciers, there was more ice to melt. There was still seasonal melting.

It's all so contradictory!

AL: Not contradictory, complicated.

JACK: My expertise isn't really Inuit material.

What is your expertise?

JACK: My major area is western North America, the high plains and central parklands. But I had an opportunity a few years ago to go to the Arctic and do some research and I fell in love with the place. I studied it almost as a hobby—I have published some papers on the north, but not much in comparison. If I can get off the track a little, what really got me interested in going north is that I was working with buffalo jumps.

AL: Buffalo jumps?

JACK: I spent ten years of my life at Head-Smashed-In Buffalo Jump. Buffalo jumps are where the Plains Indians would cause these animals to jump to their deaths over cliffs. What I was interested in wasn't the end of that story, where all the bones and arrowheads are. I looked back into the rolling prairies, beautiful landscapes of waving fields of grass, and saw lines of rocks that would go for miles, small piles, little cairns, and I realized they were the key to how the buffalo jumps worked. I started studying what we call in anthropology "communal hunting techniques." Large groups of people came together for the purpose of killing large numbers of animals in a cooperative unit that would not have formed otherwise. These are groups that don't live together, but come together for this special purpose. When I realized that the caribou hunters of the high Arctic and the central Arctic are among the best examples of that anywhere, I went north with some friends—I begged my way into their research group—and started studying caribou drives. And I found that the stone arrangements, the lay of the land, the use of wind and smell and sound were almost identical to the way the Plains Indians used those things. The caribou and bison are both large herd animals that run together in tight units when they panic. It was fascinating because of the similarity. The Inuit culture is also fascinating in itself. These people inhabit the most difficult, demanding place on earth.

AL: I'm not an anthropologist, but I just love your language. I just wrote these down: "buffalo jump," "caribou drive," "Muskox Way." You could write poetry with those phrases. But I want to make one point. We as human beings have been doing this to animals forever, killing and being wasteful. We're probably a little more wasteful now, but you send a hundred buffalo over a cliff and there's no way you can eat them all. The same with the caribou and the muskoxen.

JACK: You're right. Some native movements today seek to portray themselves as the original ecologists, the original environmentalists. There is a lot of truth to that, and I would support them in many aspects of it. But deep down their ancestors ultimately were human beings, which means that sometimes they killed way more food than was needed. But they did so for reasons that are different from our own cultural experience. We think of it as waste, but they might have viewed it in a different way. The result was waste, but that's not necessarily how they saw it. I know I've gotten an adrenaline rush when I've finally caught fish after years of getting skunked. Suddenly I'm holding an Arctic char and I look around me and I've got twenty of them and I think, "What the hell am I doing?"

AL: That's happened to me, too. But you said the Inuit had a different take on it?

JACK: The adrenaline rush was probably part of it, but for the Inuit there were other factors, too. I can give you two examples. In the case of a buffalo jump, they killed large numbers of animals. We don't know the exact number, but it was almost certainly in the hundreds. And as far as we know, they killed them all. They didn't say, "We've got enough. Let these stragglers go." But they saw the animal world as a very different world than we perceive it today. They thought animals had the ability to realize they had been put through this trap, to know that the hunters who had lined the cairns and waved and shouted and shot arrows at them were driving them toward the cliff. And once they understood it, if any escaped, the future hunts would fail because the animals would go back to the herd and inform the other animals about it. The case of the muskoxen is a little different. When the animals turned and faced their predators the Inuit could have picked off four or five and said, "That's all we can eat, so why not stop?" But they didn't do that. They killed them all, but not because they were a bunch of savages. They did it because they saw a family unit there. If you attack another Eskimo village you don't leave some alive, children, for example, because that's cruel. They would never survive. They killed all the muskoxen because that was the humane thing to do.

There was a type of Victorian explorer-hunter who went to Franz Josef Land to map the islands and shoot polar bears. Frederick Jackson stayed there three years and shot about two bears a month. He called himself a sportsman.

JACK: Read the journals of Audubon sometime. He was slaughtering everything that moves.

AL: What about Teddy Roosevelt?

JACK: The Indians and Eskimos were wasteful at times, but if the Europeans had never shown up with their technology, the native people could have gone on running buffalo jumps and all their other kinds of kills for thousands of years and never put a dent in the animal population.

I'm looking forward to going downstairs in the museum to see the Cape York meteorites that we talked about earlier. But first, could we talk a little bit about Robert Peary and how he used the Polar Eskimos to help him?

AL: I always thought Peary was a huckster.

JACK: On Peary's second attempt to cross the Greenland ice cap —his first attempt was a failure but the second time he was successful—he went diagonally across the northeast corner to an area now called Pearyland. It was about an eleven-hundred-mile trek. It was pretty substantial and there's no doubt he accomplished it. But when he looked at Pearyland he reported a channel of water in front of it, separating it from the mainland. There is no channel of water. Five years later he got back to the same place and his journal makes no mention that earlier he had seen this channel of water. He couldn't stand being wrong, even though it would have been in his interest to say, "What I thought was there wasn't there." But, nevertheless, I don't think that implicates him in lying. I've been in the Arctic and I know about the mirage confusion. We see what's called iceblink, essentially a mirage, all the time. People are simply fooled. Do you want me to go on about Peary?

Yes.

AL: I'd like to hear it.

JACK: Peary was a man who was obsessed with fame and fortune. He could not accept defeat. He could never come back and say, "I simply failed, but I'll try again," as many explorers did. For example, in the very first expedition he tried, crossing Greenland, he got less than one hundred miles and turned back after twenty-eight days. That would normally be called a failure, but it turned out that he had gone farther in that direction than anyone else had done except two Laplanders—we call them Saami now. So, Peary didn't say he failed. He said he had gone farther than any white man.

He was a big "white man" fan. He was always saying that.

JACK: It was the same thing with the Eskimos and Matthew Henson. They just didn't count in his mind.

In that society, they really didn't count. But Peary was pretty extreme. When he first saw the large meteorite, he wrote in his diary that it was "rudely awakened" by having the eyes of a white man on it for the first time.

AL: He was definitely a racist. It was surprising that Henson, who was black, spent most of his life exploring with Peary.

JACK: And in a very subservient relationship. Once Peary had lost all but two of his toes, he had to get hauled a lot.

He was carried most of the way on that last trip to the pole, on the sledges driven by the Eskimos and by Henson. But apparently he didn't plan for his need to be carried. He loaded all the sledges equally and then tried to get on top of various loads. Henson said later that whoever was carrying him resented it because he slowed them up so much. He and the Eskimos tried to outrun him so he wouldn't choose them. Peary just couldn't admit to any weakness.

JACK: In his book, you don't see anything about being carried. He decided to bring back the meteorites after another failed trip, because he needed a trophy.

AL: He spent three summers getting those meteorites.

He got money for them, didn't he?

AL: In the end, he did. Morris Jesup, a railroad magnate and one of the founders of the American Museum of Natural History, had pulled a lot of political strings to keep Peary in the job of explorer while the navy was paying his salary, and Peary collected all these wonderful articles for the museum. Peary wasn't making much money. His wife and children had a hard time making ends meet in New York while he was out playing hotshot explorer. Mrs. Peary wrote a heartbreaking letter to Jesup to get money for the meteorites, and the museum paid her forty thousand dollars for them. Peary, as far as I am concerned, was not a very loving or caring husband or father. He was even exploiting his daughter when she was ten. Look at this book, written by "the Snow Baby and her Mother" [picks up an antique Victorian-style book].

This is a nice-looking book. I wouldn't think it would be exploitation if it is a true story. I think it would be good for a child to write a book. It could be creative, not exploitative.

AL: Here's a story about an Arctic bunny rabbit that died. It's just awful.

Well, she was up there—she was born up there and lived there for a couple of seasons with her mother. That's pretty remarkable in itself. I wonder why Peary gave his daughter an Eskimo middle name if he was such a racist about the Eskimos. Marie Ahnighito Peary was her name.

AL: Ahnighito is the name of the largest of the three meteorites. A book about the museum, published by the museum, says that the meteorite got that name because little Marie, at the age of three, broke a bottle of champagne over it to christen it when they had gotten it onto the ship, and she mumbled that word as gibberish. The book says that Peary gave the name to her and to the meteorite at that time.

JACK: I can give you two ideas about that name. Kathan asked me if I could find out where it came from. The question is, did the meteorite already have the name from the native people and then Peary transferred it to Marie as her middle name? I think so. I sent an e-mail to a friend who asked this question of an Inuit linguistic expert, and he wrote back saying the translation of the word in Inuit is "which has few flat surfaces."

AL: That fits! The Ahnighito, the big one, the one the Eskimos called the Tent, is almost uniformly rough—there is a texture on it. It was not mined or chipped by the Eskimos. They got their iron from the little ones, the ones they called the Woman and the Dog, and they are smoother.

JACK: The Inuit word is *Annikittuq*, which can be transliterated into *Ahnighito*.

AL: This is a reasonable thing.

JACK: There is another story I found. I've no idea of the truth of this one since I got it from a website.

AL: I'll believe a website sooner than the museum's book at this point. What's the other story?

JACK: It was the name of the Eskimo woman who made Marie's first outfit of fur. She made these little baby clothes of fur, and her name was Ahnighito. Mrs. Peary gave the child that middle name in honor of the woman.

AL: That has some currency too.

JACK: It's not necessarily incompatible with the other idea because names can be spread around in different ways. People could have had that name, which was a descriptive title. It's possible that both are true.

AL: I didn't like the gibberish idea when I read it because I couldn't imagine coming up with gibberish that sounds like that.

No three-year-old would do that, especially since it is an Inuit word. I still have a nagging question. If Peary was so stiff and so conscious of being a "white man," it doesn't seem in character that he would give his daughter an Eskimo name? Why would he do that, given that he had a tremendous chip on his shoulder?

AL: He was able to do his work only because he used the natives. The Inuit were the salvation of Peary.

He definitely felt superior to them, but he also respected them. He learned their ways of traveling, wore their clothes, and sometimes ate their food. He took his wife up there at first, but later lived with an Eskimo woman. His son, Kali, was eighty years old in 2001 and still living near Etah.

AL: Didn't Henson also have an Eskimo son?

Yes. His name is Anaukaq, son of Mahri-Pahluk, "Matthew the Kind One."

JACK: Peary's mentality was different from the British. The British knew they were superior in every way. They would sail in there and see a primitive Stone Age race that was smelly and dirty and shuffling across the ice in skins. The Eskimos looked like animals, and they probably smelled like animals. It's all clear in this picture [pulls out a copy of a nineteenth-century engraving of explorers in uniforms and Eskimos in furs].

The British are dressed up in cocked hats and high-heeled boots!

JACK: All those people on the Franklin expedition died because they brought their culture with them. They couldn't say, "We're going to a place where another culture prevails. Let's find out what that is." They said, "We're British!" When the remains of the Franklin expedition were found, it was amazing what was in the small boats that they were dragging across the ice: monogrammed silverware, towels, brushes, and combs—

Scented soap!

JACK: Yes, scented soap, books—there were five Bibles and a novel. This is stuff they were dragging from their ship, which had already been frozen in the ice for two years! A British person has to be civilized to the end.

AL: And the end did come! Knut Rasmussen, who explored Greenland a little later than Peary, makes this point eloquently in his book. He says the explorers who were most successful were the ones who adopted the ways of the human beings who lived up there. He's absolutely right!

JACK: He is. When Peary was pushing for the pole, for example, he would send advance crews out to make snow houses for him. When Nares was pushing for the pole, his men dragged seventy-foot-long British-made sleds with tents on them. They would set the tents up and put fourteen men in each one, like sardines. Do you know the amount of body perspiration and breath that fourteen men would generate to condense on the tent wall while they slept? In the Arctic, it freezes. And then you have to pack the tent up in the morning. The tents had gained three times their weight by the time the expedition ended. They were loading sheets of ice on the sleds every day and hauling them. If you have a snow house, you don't have that problem.

And Nares knew what happened to Franklin by the time he went.

JACK: He was critical of the British approach in his report later. He said, "We learned nothing."

But no one listened to him because he said the North Pole was "impracticable" and came back early. He didn't want to die.

JACK: I'd like to make one more point about Peary's involvement with the Inuit. Peary wasn't the first to learn from them, but he did it more systematically. He traveled to their villages well in advance of his trip and started people preparing things for him. He stayed there for months and they sewed clothing and made sleds and snowshoes and got together things he would need. And then he began to recruit people and dogs. He went around to many different communities, not just Etah, and he took the best—the best dogs and the best dog drivers. The best hunters. This had a profound effect on the villages left behind.

AL: Some of those people didn't come back. They lost important contributors.

JACK: Yes. And even if they came back, they weren't there while the trip was going on. Peary also bought up things the Inuit used in their daily lives and sent them to the museum. So he depleted the society. Meanwhile, he was buying all this with things like metal needles, knives, and ax heads that were highly desired. But using them changed the Eskimo culture. It was definitely a two-way street.

AL: After Peary took the Eskimos' meteorites, he gave them almost nothing—a few cans of produce and some knives. It's amazing.

JACK: They didn't want to lead him to the meteorites because they were still using them as a metal source, even though by then a fair amount of metal was making its way in from whalers, who traded it for furs. And the Inuit discovered some Norse sites and took metal from those. But they wanted to keep the meteorites.

AL: Peary—and this is part of why I think he's a huckster—staged the way the Eskimos used the meteorites, how they mined them for iron. He got a painter to paint a group of Inuit that he hired to act out the mining of the Dog for iron. The painting was probably based on photographs. It shows a family: the son is working on the meteorite while the father is flattening a piece of iron and putting it into a whalebone, and the mother is busy cooking a blubber lunch. And meanwhile another group comes in with a seal! And after the pictures were made, Peary collected all the clothing for a display that never was put on anywhere. It's all documented in a rare book we have in our library at the AMNH.

He was a showman. He would go around the United States and give lectures in his furs to raise money for the next expedition. It's what fund-raisers today call the "dog and pony show."

AL: This went beyond fund-raising. This guy was obsessive about getting to his goal, and when he couldn't quite make it, he made it up.

Maybe he wasn't a likeable character. But that doesn't mean he didn't make his goal.

JACK: Let's talk for a minute about whether he got to the pole. I'm basing my doubts on what his claims are for the amount of area he traveled and the amount of time it took him to do it and the conditions we know existed at that time. You remember the fellow named Bartlett? He was the captain of the ship, extremely experienced.

Bob Bartlett, yes. Peary sent him back.

JACK: Bartlett had taken Peary north the previous trip and he turned out to be the most competent captain Peary had ever seen. He knew ice better than anyone. So Peary desperately wanted him for this trip, because he knew it was his last. He had only one more in him. Bartlett said, "I'll go on one condition. I want to go all the way to the pole with you." And Peary agreed. Then, when they got within 150 miles of the pole—and at that point almost everybody else had been sent back—he tells Bartlett to go back, leaving just Henson and the Eskimos. Bartlett says, "Wait a minute, we had an agreement." And Peary says, "Sorry, the deal's off." The excuse he used was a racial slur. He said Henson was not fit to lead the last group back. But Peary wrote this later, "The reason I sent him back was I felt it was my due, because of my long effort, to be the only white man to be the first to see the North Pole."

Over and over in Peary's history he seems to have let his prejudices get in the way of his success. But Peary wasn't that unusual for that time. I recently read a review of a book about a trial that took place in the South at the same time that Peary was making his explorations. Two black women were accused of killing a white person, and a white lawyer got them off. After the trial, the lawyer said that although they were innocent, they should be sent back to Africa along with all the other black people in the country. And he said it publicly. You can't even imagine something like that happening today.

JACK: No, Peary wasn't unique at all.

Donald MacMillan, another person on Peary's last North Pole expedition, wrote that Peary told him, "Henson must not turn back. I can't manage without him." What he should have done was to keep both Henson and Bartlett for the final push.

AL: He sent Bartlett back because he didn't want a guy there who could argue with him.

JACK: That's the secret reason. He wanted to get rid of an expert navigator who could show him up if he didn't make it.

It was his big mistake. The expert navigator could have proved that he made it if he really did.

JACK: The crippling part of his argument is that on April 1, 1909, he dismissed Bartlett, kept Henson and a few Eskimos, and then on April 6, in theory, reached the pole, but there's no entry in the journal for those days, especially April 6 and April 7. A separate loose-leaf sheet of paper was inserted that says, "The Pole at Last!" Why would you not write that in your journal? He doesn't write, "I am at the Pole," or put in any of his calculations. The calculations are on separate sheets too.

There is a possible explanation. It could be that Peary was really exhausted. He had tried to walk, but his feet were hurting because of his lack of toes, and the other men didn't like carrying him on their sledges. Maybe he couldn't write in his journal because he was delirious. Henson doesn't say this. It's my guess. Henson does say that he and the Eskimos knew they had reached the Pole on April 6, but Peary didn't realize it.

JACK: I thought Peary was the only one who knew how to read the instruments.

Henson says he and the Eskimos knew they were at the pole by the position of the sun and by judging how far they had traveled each of the five days. They were experienced in navigating this way. When Henson told Peary he thought they were at the pole, Peary went ahead for a short distance and took readings. Then he came back to the camp and took readings, and put the flag up there. It bothers me, in thinking about the later controversy, that if Peary was lying, Henson was lying too. If you read what Henson wrote later or anything other explorers wrote about Henson, you know he wasn't likely to have supported Peary in a lie. And, by the way, both Bartlett and MacMillan said that they believed Peary had made it to the pole.

AL: I read that Peary ignored Henson after that, and for the rest of his life was unfriendly to him. Henson attributed it to having been there when Peary first saw the pole. He said Peary had planned to go the last short distance alone.

JACK: The explanation I read for Peary's not speaking to Henson on the way back was that he knew he was concocting a lie that he was going to sell to the rest of the world and he just wasn't going to bring it up. You'd think a man who'd devoted his whole career to getting to the pole would get on that ship saying, "We made it! We made it!" But he shut himself up in his room and said hardly anything to anyone—not just Henson.

That's suspicious. But Peary was a complicated person psychologically.

JACK: The most damning evidence against him is still that the claims for the distances he covered seem totally unbelievable by any standard.

AL: Yes, that's the most damning.

I'm not capable of understanding that very well.

JACK: On April 1, when he turned Bartlett back, everyone agrees, he was 150 miles from the pole. He then claims to be at the pole on the April 6. That's only five days to go 150 miles. And then he gets back on the tenth, so in ten days he's gone roundtrip 300 miles. And then he goes on to rejoin the ship, and when he gets there Bartlett has been back only five days.

I'm waiting to see what Bob Headland thinks about this point. In his position as archivist at the Scott Polar Research Institute, I'm sure he's read all the material. I did look it up on the web, and I found a website telling about two people who recreated Peary's trip with dogsleds. They did it in very nearly the same time—four days longer, but they didn't have extra people breaking the trail in the early part of the trip as Peary did.

JACK: That's not what I read. Two people tried to do it, and they took seventy days longer than Peary. Maybe this is not the same group of people. One was German and one Russian.

The ones I read about were American. They had tried before and failed to get close in the amount of time. But this time they were lucky. Their explanation is that the Arctic is very mysterious.

JACK: And that's absolutely true.

CHAPTER SIX

CAPE NORWAY

Journey: Cape Norway

From the air the island looked barren, like the other islands of Franz Josef Land that we had seen. But when I stepped out of the helicopter, the rocky surface was not hard but yielding. Underfoot was the springiness of recently unfrozen land with permafrost beneath it, and interspersed among the rocks was the softness of moss and flowers; it was an enchanted place. "If only Nansen could have seen it in July," I thought, imagining his despair as he and Johansen beached their kayaks here on August 26, 1895, knowing they must remain through a winter of complete darkness and intolerable cold. The growing season in Franz Josef Land, especially on this island near the northern perimeter, is at most a month and a half. By the time Nansen got here, the thin layer of soil above the permafrost had already begun to freeze, and although there was moss (he used it to fill gaps between the stones of his hut), and there were flowers (he saw poppies under the snow), he could not have known the beauty that we saw. Frederick Jackson had visited this island and mapped it from his base on Cape Flora about two months before Nansen's arrival. He would have seen, as we did, the zenith of its bloom.

How strange it must have been for Nansen to be told by Jackson, nearly ten months later, that he had been on that island the previous spring just before Nansen and Johansen had arrived, and had been near it again just before they left. Both times he had had with him a small tin box of letters for Nansen. "I had no real expectation of seeing him," Jackson wrote in his journal, "but should have felt very annoyed had I met him sledging and had not his letters; consequently I always carried them with me."

After Nansen's August 24 entry in his journal, written just before reaching this place, there is a gap. The next entry is November 27, and soon after that, on December 6, he wrote: "I must at last try to patch the hole in my diary. There has been so much to see about that I have got no writing done; that excuse, however, is no longer available, as we sleep nearly the whole twenty-four hours." Nevertheless, he did not fill the hole. "The brain worked dully," he explained in his later book, "and I never felt inclined to write anything. Perhaps, too, this was owing to the impossibility of keeping what you wrote upon clean. If only you took hold of a piece of paper your fingers left a dark-brown, greasy mark, and if a corner of your clothes brushed across it, a dark streak appeared. Now, in writing this book it is all I can do to find out what was once written on these dirty, dark-brown pages." Nansen and Johansen stayed on the island for nearly nine months.

In his recollected summary of that time, Nansen describes his arrival with Johansen on Cape Norway after drifting out to sea in their kayaks. They had sailed before a storm and—fearful of again being stranded on drift ice—laboriously made their way back to land. A bear greeted them as they landed on the beach; they killed it and the meat was the beginning of their winter store.

Their great find was a pine log, and they made a ridgepole of it. Before the ground became solidly frozen, they dug out a site for a hut and a short passageway for an entry into it. They erected stone walls to surround a space ten feet long and six feet wide, with a stone bench inside for sleeping and a cooking hearth at one end. The chimney was made of ice. "It was not quite permanent, however," Nansen remembered. "The hole in it constantly widened with use, and it was not altogether guiltless of dripping down onto the hearth, but there was an abundance of this building material." The hut was high enough that they could stand up inside. "Fancy having a place sheltered from the wind where you could stretch your limbs a little! We had not had that since last March on board the *Fram*."

They used walrus hides for roofing material. Walruses were plentiful on the drift ice near the island, but to kill them meant hunting from kayaks, a perilous circumstance. And when they made a kill, there was still the job of getting the huge animal to shore and skinning it before it froze. All the stored skins froze, of course, and when the men were ready to make their roof, they had to drag them back into the sea. "Our hides were now so far softened in the sea that we could stretch them over the roof," Nansen wrote. "They were so long that they reached from one side of the hut right over the ridge-piece down to the other side, and we stretched them by hanging large stones at both ends, attached by strips of hide, thus weighing them down over the edges of the wall, and we then piled stones upon them. By the aid of stones, moss, strips of hide, and snow to cover everything we made the edges of the walls to some extent close-fitting." In Nansen's book, the hut is shown in a photograph he took. Without the caption, you wouldn't know this is a picture of a hut. You see only a ridge in the snow with an upended sledge in the foreground. In the background there is a hill with a distinctive notch in it. As I studied the photo, I realized with a little start that the notched hill appears in a photograph I took as the *Yamal* approached Cape Norway.

One hundred and seven years after Nansen and Johansen had built their hut, we stood looking at it: tumbled rocks in a slash in the earth, the bleached pine log, about a foot in diameter, stretched across the spot. In front were a few large bones, no doubt from a bear that Nansen and Johansen had eaten. Surrounding us were tiny flowers. The air was mild, certainly above freezing; water moved from the glacier above us through moss-lined channels at our feet. The climate here is very dry, and the growing season is short and cold. There is very little soil and not much sun. Nevertheless, there was life everywhere, beautiful life, pulsing and delicate.Red and green mosses were lush and abundant but, except where the water was running, the grass was short and dry. Dead plants or dead leaves of plants decompose here very slowly, if at all, and their presence helps hold heat and water and protects nearby plants from the wind. But in lands where plants don't decompose, the soil's nutrients are meager, and in Franz Josef Land the plant communities grow in patches interspersed with bare rocky soil. There were many flowers; they seemed to be varied, but the variety was provided mainly by four kinds of saxifrage, all in bloom.

Poppies were everywhere, and they created the special beauty of the place. Poppies continually move to face the sun, and their petals form parabolic receivers to trap warmth. In more sunny areas of the Arctic, they are mainly bright yellow, since yellow absorbs more sunshine than white. But it takes chemical energy to create the pigment, and here energy is conserved. The poppies we saw were the palest shade of yellow, almost white, and small, but they were definitely poppies, their round hairy buds unmistakable. The growing season here is not long enough for a poppy to both develop buds and open them, so the blooms we were seeing came from buds produced the previous year.

All the plants were low to the ground and small, but we learned that they were actually much larger than we thought. About 95 percent of their living material is underground in the form of roots and rhizomes that spread laterally through the soil above the permafrost. When plants or parts of plants die, they remain in the ground as peat, and since it is too cold for decomposition to take place with any efficiency, the carbon that the living plants withdrew from the atmosphere remains locked in the peat. This is why the Arctic is called a carbon sink.

If, however, a lot of Arctic peat should warm and decompose, it would release carbon dioxide and methane into the air in a quantity that the slow-growing Arctic plants could not begin to absorb. Methane is given off by the bacteria and fungi that cause decomposition. It is a greenhouse gas even more powerful than the CO_2 we are sending into the atmosphere by driving our cars.

Cars were far from our minds as we stood in Cape Norway's delicate and rugged landscape, however. Near the edge of the ice, vegetation ended abruptly in a beach of coarse sand gouged with deep rounded holes where ice boulders had recently lodged, then melted. We tested the sea ice with our feet—it was solid, and full of great blocks and mounds and towering structures. It had been much smoother when we had walked on it at the pole, and though we had seen rough ice from the *Yamal*, we had been twenty feet above it then. At Cape Norway I understood what Nansen had traveled over, dragging sledges and kayaks. "Ice with more obstacles than here—is it to be found anywhere, I wonder?" he wrote as he neared this place. "Inconceivable toil."

The Journal of Fridtjof Nansen
November 27, 1895 to June 15, 1896

Wednesday, November 27

9.4 below zero F. It is windy weather, the snow whirling about your ears, directly you put your head out of the passage. Everything is grey; the black stones can be made out in the snow a little way up the beach, and above you can just divine the presence of the dark cliff. But wherever else the gaze is turned, out to sea, or up the fjord, there is the same leaden darkness. One is shut out from the wide world, shut into oneself.

The wind comes in sharp gusts, driving the snow before it; but up under the crest of the mountain it whistles and roars in the crevices and holes of the basaltic walls—the same never-ending song that it has sung through the thousands of years that are past, and will go on singing through thousands of years to come. And the snow whirls along in its age-old dance; it spreads itself in all the crevices and hollows, but it does not succeed in covering up the stones on the beach. Black as ever, they project into the night. On the open space in front of the hut, two figures are running up and down like shadows in the winter darkness to keep themselves warm, and so they will run up and down on the path they have trampled out, day after day, till the spring comes.

Monday, December 2

Morning. Today I can hear it blowing again outside, and we shall have an unpleasant walk. It is bitterly cold now in our worn, greasy clothes. It is not so bad when there is no wind, but even if there is only a little it goes right through one. But what does it matter? Will not the spring one day come here too?

Evening. That fox is playing us a great many tricks; whatever he can move he goes off with. He has once gnawed off the band with which the door-skin is fastened, and every now and then we hear him at it again, and have to go out and knock on the roof of the passage. Today he went off with one of our sails, in which our saltwater ice was lying. We were not a little alarmed when we went to fetch ice, and found sail and all gone. We had no doubt as to who had been there, but we could not under any circumstances afford to lose our precious sail on which we depend for our voyage to Spitsbergen in the spring, and we tramped about in the dark, up the beach, over the level, and nothing was to be seen of it. At last we had almost given it up when Johansen, in going onto the ice to get more saltwater ice, found it at the edge of the shore. Our joy was great; but it was wonderful that the fox had been able to drag that great sail, full of ice too, so far. Down there, however, it had come unfolded, and then he could do nothing with it. But what does he want with things like this? Is it to lie upon in his winter den? One would almost think so. I only wish I could come upon that den, and find the thermometer again, and the ball of twine, and the harpoon line, and all the other precious things he has taken.

Thursday, December 5

It seems as if it would never end. But patience a little longer, and spring will come, the fairest spring that earth can give us. There is furious weather outside, and snow, and it is pleasant to lie here in our warm hut, eating steak, and listening to the wind raging over us.

Thursday, December 12

Lovely weather. But night and day are now equally dark. We walk up and down, up and down, on the level, in the darkness. Heaven only knows how many steps we shall take on that level before the winter ends. Through the gloom we can see faintly only the black cliffs, and the rocky ridges, and the great stones on the beach, which the wind always sweeps clean. Above us the sky, clear and brilliant with stars, sheds its peace over the earth.

Far in the west falls shower after shower of stars, some faint, scarcely visible, others bright like Roman candles, all with a message from distant worlds. Low in the south lies a bank of clouds, now and again outlined by the gleam of the northern lights; but out over the sea the sky is dark; there is open water there. It is quite pleasant to look at it. One does not feel so shut in. It is like a connecting link with life that dark sea, the mighty artery of the world, which carries tidings from land to land, from people to people, on which civilization is borne victorious through the earth. Next summer it will carry us home.

Tuesday, December 24

At 2 p.m. today 11.2 below zero F. And this is Christmas Eve, cold and windy out-of-doors, and cold and draughty indoors. How desolate it is! Never before have we had such a Christmas Eve.

At home the bells are now ringing Christmas in. I can hear their sound as it swings through the air from the church tower. How beautiful it is! Now the candles are being lighted on the Christmas trees; the children are let in and dance round in joyous delight. This is the time of rejoicing, and there is feasting in every cottage at home.

And we are keeping the festival in our little way. Johansen has turned his shirt, and put the outside shirt next to him; I have done the same, and then I have changed my drawers and put on the others that I had wrung out in warm water. And I have washed myself, too, in a quarter of a cup of warm water, with the discarded drawers as sponge and towel. Now I feel quite another being; my clothes do not stick to my body as much as they did. For supper we had fiskegratin made of powdered fish and maize-meal, with train oil to it instead of butter, both fried and boiled (one as dry as the other), and for dessert we had bread fried in train oil. Tomorrow morning we are going to have chocolate and bread.

Wednesday, December 25

We have got lovely Christmas weather, hardly any wind, and such bright, beautiful moonlight. It gives one quite a solemn feeling. It is the peace of thousands of years. In the afternoon the northern lights were exceptionally beautiful. When I came out at six o'clock there was a bright, pale yellow bow in the southern sky. It remained for a long time almost unchanged, and then began to grow much brighter at the upper margin of the bow behind the mountain crests in the east. It smoldered for some time, and then all at once light darted out westwards along the bow; streamers shot up all along it towards the zenith, and in an instant the whole of the southern sky from the arc to the zenith was aflame. It flickered and blazed, it whirled round like a whirlwind (moving with the sun), rays darted backwards and forwards, now red and reddish-violet, now yellow, green, and dazzling white; now the rays were red at the bottom and yellow and green farther up, and then again this order was inverted. Higher and higher it rose. Now it came on the north side of the zenith too; for a moment there was a splendid corona, and then it all became one whirling mass of fire up there. It was like a whirlpool of fire in red, yellow, and green and the eye was dazzled with looking at it. It then drew across to the northern sky, where it remained a long time, but not in such brilliancy. The arc from which it had sprung in the south was still visible, but soon disappeared. The movement of the rays was chiefly from west to east, but sometimes the reverse. It afterwards flared up brightly several times in the northern sky. I counted as many as six parallel bands at one time, but they did not attain to the brightness of the former ones.

And this is Christmas Day. There are family dinners going on at home. I can see the dignified old father standing smiling and happy in the doorway to welcome children and grandchildren. Out-of-doors the snow is falling softly and silently in big flakes. The young folk come rushing in fresh and rosy, stamp the snow off their feet in the passage, shake their things and hang them up, and then enter the drawing-room where the fire is crackling comfortably and cozily in the stove. How nice and comfortable everything is! One might fall ill with longing to be home.

Tuesday, December 31

And this year too is vanishing. It has been strange, but after all it has perhaps not been so bad. Far in up the fjord you can see the clouds of snow chasing one another over the ice in front of gusts of wind, and the snow-dust glittering in the moonlight. And the full moon sails silent and still out of one year into another. She shines alike upon the good and the evil, nor does she notice the wants and yearnings of the New Year. Once more a leaf is turned in the book of eternity, a new blank page is opened, and no one knows what will be written on it.

Wednesday, January 1

42.2 below zero F. So a new year has come, the year of joy and homecoming. In bright moonlight 1895 departed, and in bright moonlight 1896 begins. But it is bitterly cold, the coldest days we have yet known here. I felt it, too, yesterday, when all my finger-tips were frostbitten. I thought I had done with all that last spring.

Friday, January 3

Morning. It is still clear and cold out of doors. I can hear reports from the glacier. It lies up there on the crest of the mountain like a mighty ice-giant peering down at us through the clefts. It spreads its giant's body all over the land, and stretches out its limbs on all sides into the sea. But whenever it turns cold—colder than it has hitherto been—it writhes horribly, and crevice after crevice appears in the huge body. There is a noise like the discharge of guns, and the sky and the earth tremble so that I can feel the ground that I am lying on quake. I am almost afraid that it will someday come rolling over upon us.

Johansen is asleep, and making the hut resound. I am glad his mother cannot see him now. She would certainly pity her boy, so black and grimy and ragged as he is, with sooty streaks all over his face. But wait, only wait! She shall have him again, safe and sound.

Wednesday, January 8

Last night the wind blew the sledge to which our thermometer was hanging out over the slope. Stormy weather outside—furious weather, almost taking away your breath if you put your head out. We lie here trying to sleep—sleep the time away. But we cannot always do it. Oh, those long sleepless nights when you turn from side to side, kick your feet to put a little warmth into them, and wish for only one thing in the world—sleep! The thoughts are constantly busy with everything at home, but the long, heavy body lies here trying in vain to find an endurable position among the rough stones.

Tuesday, February 25

Lovely weather to be out in today. It is as though spring were beginning. We have seen the first birds, first a flock of six little auks (*Mergalus alle*), then a flock of four. They came from the south along the land, evidently through the sound in the southeast, and disappeared behind the mountain crest to the northwest of us. Once more we heard their cheerful twittering, and it roused a responsive echo in the soul. A little later we heard it again, and then it seemed as if they were perched on the mountain above us. It was the first greeting from life.

Friday, February 28

I have discovered that it is possible to get twelve threads out of a bit of twine, and am happy as a king. We have thread enough now, and our wind-clothes shall be whole once more. It is possible, too, to ravel out the canvas in the bags, and use it for thread.

Saturday, February 29

The sun high above the glacier today. We must begin to economize in train oil in earnest now if we are to get away from here, or there will be too little blubber for the journey.

Wednesday, March 4

When Johansen went out this morning the mountain above us was covered with little auks, which flew twittering from crest to crest, and sat all over the glacier. When we went out again later on, they were gone.

Friday, March 6

We are faring badly now. We have to sleep in the dark to save oil, and can only cook once a day.

Sunday, March 8

Shot a bear. Johansen saw ten flocks of little auks flying up the sound this morning.

Wednesday, March 25

There is the same dark water-sky behind the promontory in the southwest, stretching westwards almost to the extreme west. It has been there all through this mild weather with southwesterly wind, from the very beginning of the month. There seems to be always open water there, for no sooner is the sky overcast then the reflection of water appears in that quarter.

Tuesday, May 19

This earliest report of our journey was deposited in a brass tube that had formed the cylinder of the air pump of our Primus. The tube was closed with a plug of wood and hung by a wire to the rooftree of the hut.

"May 19, 1986. We were frozen in north of Kotelnoi at about 68°43′ north latitude on September 22, 1893. Drifted northwestward during the following year, as we had expected to do. Johansen and I left the *Fram* March 14, 1895, at about 84°4′ north latitude and 103° east longitude to push on northward. The command of the remainder of the expedition was transferred to Sverdrup. Found no land northwards. On April 6, 1895, we had to turn back at 86°14′ north latitude and about 95° East longitude, the ice having become impassable. Shaped our course for Cape Fligely; but our watches having stopped, we did not know our longitude with certainty, and arrived on August 6, 1895, at four glacier-covered islands to the north of this line of islands, at about 81°30′ north latitude and about 7° east of this place. Reached this place August 26, 1895, and thought it safest to winter here. Lived on bears' flesh. Are starting today southwestward along the land, intending to cross over to Spitsbergen at the nearest point. We conjecture that we are on Gillies Land."

Saturday, May 30

Lying weather-bound, stopping up the tent against the driving snow, while the wind flits round us, attacking first one side and then another.

Monday, June 1

Yesterday it at last grew a little calmer, and cleared up so that we had bright sunshine in the evening. We rejoiced in the thought of moving on.

Monday, June 15

We proceeded on our way in beautifully calm weather. As walruses swarmed on all sides, we did not much like paddling singly, and for some distance lashed the kayaks together. Towards morning we rowed for some time without seeing any walruses, and felt more secure. Then we saw a solitary rover pop up a little in front of us. Johansen, who was in front at the time, put in to a sunken ledge of ice, and although I really thought that this was caution carried to excess, I was on the point of following his example. I had not got so far, however, when suddenly the walrus shot up beside me, threw itself onto the edge of the kayak, took hold farther over the deck with one fore-flipper, and as it tried to upset me aimed a blow at the kayak with its tusks. I held on as tightly as possible, so as not to be upset into the water, and struck at the animal's head with the paddle as hard as I could. It took hold of the kayak once more and tilted me up, so that the deck was almost underwater, then let go, and raised itself right up. I seized my gun, but at the same moment it turned round and disappeared as quickly as it had come. The whole thing had happened in a moment, and I was just going to remark to Johansen that we were fortunate in escaping so easily from that adventure, when I noticed that my legs were wet. I listened, and now heard the water trickling into the kayak under me. To turn and run her in onto the sunken ledge of ice was the work of a moment, but I sank there. The thing was to get out and onto the ice, the kayak all the time getting fuller. The edge of the ice was high and loose, but I managed to get up, and Johansen, by tilting the sinking kayak over to starboard so that the leak came above the water, managed to bring her to a place where the ice was low enough to admit of our drawing her up. All I possessed was floating about inside, soaked through. What I most regret is that the water has got into the photographic apparatus, and perhaps my precious photographs are ruined.

So here we lie, with all our worldly goods spread out to dry and a kayak that must be mended before we can face the walrus again. It is a good big rent that he has made, at least six inches long. But it is fortunate that it was no worse. How easily he might have wounded me in the thigh with that tusk of his! And it would have fared ill with me if we had been farther out, and not at such a convenient place by the edge of the ice, where there was a sunken ledge. The sleeping bag was soaking wet. We wrung it out as well as we could, turned the hair outside, and have spent a capital night in it.

A Conversation with Ed Mathez and Gerry Elkan

This conversation, like the preceding one, took place in a staff conference room at the American Museum of Natural History. I arrived early, and spent some time in the museum's Hall of Planet Earth studying a sample of an undersea black smoker, a fairy-tale tower encrusted with shells. I watched a film shot from a submersible research vessel. Smokers dramatically belched black smoke as debris swirled around them. Sausagelike tubeworms covered them, along with mussels, spiky crabs, and clams that look like dinner plates. Occasionally a fish swam by. A scene like this, invisible to us, had been beneath the ice for a brief time as the Yamal *traveled from the North Pole to Franz Joseph Land.*

I was standing at the rail of the Yamal *when passenger Gerald (Gerry) Elkan remarked that we were, at that moment, passing over the midocean ridge, the spot where tectonic plates meet one another. "About a mile underneath us are heat vents sending out fluids that are about 700°F," he said. "And there are microorganisms called archaea that survive there and also in sea ice. They are sometimes called extremophiles." I was at first incredulous, then entranced, visualizing the boiling volcanoes and the frozen seawater, two extreme but inhabited environments layered over one another. Thinking about Nansen's survival at Cape Norway, I compared the survival of archaea in very hot or very cold environments to that of much more fragile humans.*

Gerry Elkan is a microbiologist whose research area is biological nitrogen fixation. He has taught since 1958 at North Carolina State University. When archaea were discovered in 1979, he began following the research about them and lecturing about them in his courses. In this conversation, he is joined by Edmund (Ed) Mathez, curator and geologist at the American Museum of Natural History. Ed Mathez was the principal scientist involved

Gerry Elkan

Ed Mathez

in developing the museum's Hall of Planet Earth, and was co-leader of the expedition that brought back the black smoker sample. The undersea black smokers were discovered in 1977. Our discussion ranged from the smokers and the archaea to a possible new ice age, and the new and pressing necessity for scientists to share information.

ED: An interesting question that arises from thinking about life in extreme environments is, does this shed light on where life began? I think one of the most profound ideas that has emerged over the last fifty years is the concept that life can originate as a consequence of normal chemical evolution. The implication is that life could have begun over and over again in many different places and many different times. All you need in this concept is the right set of physical and chemical conditions to produce the necessary precursors to life. And that leads to another interesting implication: that life may exist on many other planetary bodies.

GERRY: You could walk on both sides of that argument. There are a hundred billion stars, and if life arose in the chemical way that we now think it did (and it's pretty much accepted in principle now), you'd almost have to conclude that it really couldn't be unique to us. On the other hand, if there'd been a slight difference in the mineral content—suppose instead of carbon the base was silicon?

Would that have made life?

ED: There is a good, fundamental chemical reason that life is based on carbon and not on some other element such as silicon. It's simply that carbon engages in many different ways with other elements, and silicon does not.

So you think you'd need carbon.

ED: I think you'd need carbon. Regarding the existence of life beyond our solar system, I think most scientists accept the view that there are gazillions of potential environments and there is a high probability that in some of them life could have arisen. What you need is a fluid that has chemical properties like water. Water is a good solvent. It has a high heat capacity; it ameliorates changes in temperature.

Could the fluid be something else besides water?

ED: There aren't many fluids that have the properties of water.

As far as we know?

ED: I think we know.

Things are the same everywhere in the universe?

ED: I think it would be stretching things to say otherwise. We don't want to abuse science. There are vast realms of knowledge that are beyond our comprehension, but in science you're not free to think in dimensions that are forbidden by the fundamental laws of chemistry and physics.

You were co-leader of the expedition that brought back the black smokers on display downstairs, weren' t you?

ED: Yes. With John Delaney, a geologist at the University of Washington. It was a partnership between the museum and the university.

What, exactly, are black smokers?

ED: They're hot springs deposits. They were discovered only recently, in 1977, and they exist primarily along the fifty-two-thousand-mile-long volcano known as the midocean ridge. The midocean ridge is in the North and South Atlantic Ocean, the Indian Ocean, and the South Pacific. It passes through the Arctic. It's very deep in parts of the Arctic, actually. It is where the tectonic plates separate from each other. This is where about 80 percent of the earth's internal heat escapes to the surface.

It escapes out of the crack, because the plates don't align?

ED: In sort of an abstract sense, it's a crack. It's never just open. The upper sixty miles or so of the earth is broken up into plates that slip by each other, separate from each other, and converge. Where the plates separate, new plate is formed. The plates are relatively stiff because they are cold. They move around on a less stiff, hotter, deeper part of the earth. Heat rises to the surface primarily by circulating ocean water that convects through the system. Basically, the hot springs deposits exist along the midocean ridge because that's where the heat source is.

At the midocean ridge you have water that is as hot as 750°F being injected into the ocean that is 29 to 35°F. The hot water has a very high concentration of metals, hydrogen sulfide, and other nasty components, and it is acidic. Maybe it has a pH of 2. The cold water is alkaline, with a pH of about 8, and it has no metals—certainly not metals like iron or manganese that are coming out of the smokers. And all the stuff that is dissolved in the hot water starts precipitating.

So that's how you get the towers. How big are they?

ED: The first ones seen were about sixty-five feet tall, and the biggest ever seen was a hundred and fifty feet tall and forty feet across. It was named Godzilla, and later collapsed. In June 1998, we brought back one that is five feet tall and weighs five thousand pounds. It came from the Juan de Fuca undersea ridge, about two hundred miles west of Seattle. It was an expedition for both science and education—we would never run an expedition just to get a sample for an exhibit, especially one of this magnitude and this risk.

Why was it risky?

ED: No one had ever done anything like this before, or even close to this before. We're talking about working under seventy-two hundred feet of water! We did it because it is part and parcel of the tradition of the museum. Our exhibits capture people's imaginations because we go to frontiers and we do it for valid scientific reasons. The scientific reason here was to collect an organized sample of subsurface life in this extreme environment. The basic question was, how is the distribution of life related to the chemical and physical gradients that exist in the rocks?

GERRY: This niche of life has so many ramifications. We can learn so much about early life and unique ways of getting energy and nutrients.

Gerry, on our North Pole trip, you gave a short talk about the archaeabacteria that were on the ocean bottom under us, and yesterday you gave a talk on them here at the museum. What are archaea?

GERRY: They were discovered in 1979 by Carl Woese at the University of Illinois. Up until then we had two domains for classification of life: Prokaryota, or bacteria, and Eukaryota, which are plants, animals, fungi, and protozoa. Woese was studying relationships among Prokaryotes using DNA sequences, and in the hot springs at Yellowstone National Park he found organisms that seemed to be bacteria but genetically and biochemically were more closely related to Eukaryota.

We're part of the Eukaryota domain, aren't we?

GERRY: Yes. Archaea is a new domain, closer to humans than they are to bacteria, even though related to us only very distantly. Woese thought the organisms were very ancient life forms, and that is why he named them archaea. They live in boiling water and in ice, in undersea vents, salt lakes, sulfuric springs, and soda lakes. They live in the rumens of ruminant animals like cows. They don't need sunlight or oxygen.

It's very different from what I was taught in school. We learned you have to have sunlight and water to have life.

ED: Now we're saying you don't necessarily need sunlight. You have to have something to eat. You need a source of energy, but you don't necessarily have to have sunlight. I think that's a rather profound thought. The black smokers are a place where life can exist off the chemical energy of the planet itself.

GERRY: And a great deal of life. This was a big surprise, that it's so rich and diverse. Who would have thought that we would have this high population of life in the total absence of any photosynthesis or energy from the sun?

And the archaea are the beginning of that?

GERRY: They have a high population there, and other creatures live off them.

Were they really just formed from the chemicals? They don't eat something else?

ED: Formed is not the right word.

GERRY: No, no. They live by using the chemicals as a source of energy.

They eat the chemicals?

ED: They metabolize them. It's a process of creating the hydrocarbons that make them up. They are using hydrogen sulfide to reduce carbon dioxide to the organic parts of hydrocarbon. That becomes their bodies.

GERRY: They get a little energy from this. So they are living off what comes out of the smokers.

They're living off the things that are precipitated out of the seawater?

ED: Wait a minute. Minerals are being precipitated.

And that's not what they're eating?

ED: No, they're eating the chemical components. The hydrothermal fluid has compounds like hydrogen sulfide dissolved in it.

In the Hall of Planet Earth, near the smokers, there is a big caption that says, "Why is Earth Habitable?" Does this environment have something to do with the answer to that question?

ED: I have to tell you that we don't know that answer. We perhaps know parts of it, but to suggest that we know the answer to why the earth is habitable would be ridiculous. And even the partial answer is rather lengthy. The earth is habitable, for one thing, because there's water, and one reason we have water is that we have an atmosphere that contains a cold trap. The base of the stratosphere, about seven and a half miles above us—it varies in elevation depending on where you are in terms of latitude—is a cold trap. It traps water vapor, limiting the amount that rises into the higher portions of the atmosphere. That is really important because when water rises into the upper stratosphere, the ultraviolet radiation from the sun breaks those water molecules up into hydrogen and oxygen, and the hydrogen, because it's so light, escapes to space. So, if we didn't have that cold trap, we'd be letting our water into the stratosphere and the planet would dry out.

Is that what happened to Mars, do you think?

ED: Possibly. Early in its history.

Mars has tremendous carbon dioxide in its atmosphere, and there may have been water there once.

ED: Yes, absolutely. It's a possibility that Mars simply dried out when its hydrogen escaped. Earth is a planet of the right size, with the right composition, for the interior to remain hot. It has a certain concentration of radioactive elements that are the main source of heat. If this planet were much smaller, as Mars is, it would be cooling much more rapidly and it wouldn't have plate tectonics. That could be a reason that Mars doesn't have a surface supportive of life. It doesn't have a way to recycle carbon between the atmosphere and the solid part of the planet.

Could you explain the carbon cycle?

ED: Carbon dioxide is an essential greenhouse gas—without it the surface of this planet would be very cold. As CO_2 builds up, the surface heats up. CO_2 reacts in the weathering process with rocks and enters the oceans as carbonic acid. A higher CO_2 content in the atmosphere increases the weathering rate of rocks. The carbonic acid in the ocean is removed by the formation of shells, primarily. They die and settle to the ocean floor and form sediment. That sediment is buried and eventually emerges back into the atmosphere as carbon dioxide. The carbon cycle is a long-term thermostat. When CO_2 builds up in the atmosphere and the climate becomes warmer, the weathering rate increases. This causes CO_2 to be removed from the atmosphere more rapidly and, over the very long term, cools things down.

Does that mean we don't need to worry about putting extra CO_2 into the atmosphere?

ED: We definitely need to worry about it. The carbon cycle operates on a hundred-thousand- to a million-year time span. Rapidly dumping CO_2 into the atmosphere is, wihout question, causing warming, and our climate is characterized by a complex set of feedback systems. The build-up of CO_2 may be slow and steady for a while, and then one day it will reach a threshold, and climate will change dramatically. It is scary, actually.

Let's get back to the archaea now for a bit. Gerry, are they bacteria? I thought you said they weren't, but sometimes they are called archaebacteria.

GERRY: Sometimes they are called that, and sometimes the word *bacteria* is used in a general way that is meant to include them, because bacteria essentially are forms of microscopic life. But Archaea is a different domain. Apparently, the bacterial branch and the Archaeal branch arose separately. There has been an assumption about a common ancestor for all life. But I don't think there was a common ancestor, a cell that suddenly arose, as some books will tell you. The only thing we can say, I think, is that the archaea are probably not the precursors of bacteria.

They're separate, and that's what was identified by Woese?

GERRY: Woese's discovery was made using molecular biological techniques and computer programs. It's not about looking at cells or fossils or anything of that nature. When I was in graduate school, the fossil record of bacteria was zero because what you essentially have are tiny bubbles, since there are no bones or structures to fossilize. It was only when we got very precise analytical tools to be able to look at chemical reactions that people started saying, "This was once bacteria, not water or air bubbles."

ED: There are different kinds of information. The geological record is really quite mute about this issue of evolution—what evolved from what. But there is evidence of life 3.8 billion years ago. It's evidence that derives from the ratio of carbon 12 to carbon 13 in rocks. It's controversial because these rocks have been subjected to high temperatures and high pressures, and have been recrystallized not once, not twice, but three, possibly four times. We know for sure that life existed on the planet about 3.3 or 3.4 billion years ago. But the nature of that life, other than that it was microbial, is not clear. The evidence of Eukaryotic life goes back to about 2.7 billion years, but it doesn't tell us what evolved from what.

Gerry, in your talk yesterday at the AMNH, you said, "Back in Darwinian times we used to think such and such." Are we not in Darwinian times anymore?

GERRY: The theory of evolution as we have moved along was that the bacteria are primitive, and they gave rise to more complex organisms, and so on. We had a straight line of ascent. We thought modern human beings evolved from the earlier human beings whose fossils we found. Now, we know quite clearly that certain lines, like the Neanderthal line, died out. We didn't evolve from Neanderthals. The theory of evolution is fine. It's just that a single line of ascent isn't the way things occurred. Very recently, it's been discovered that humans and chimpanzees are totally unrelated to other forms of modern apes. Obviously they diverged some time farther back, but the chimps emerged together with humans and the others are another branch. In Darwinian days, up until about fifty years ago, we had little chemical or genetic information.

DNA was discovered.

GERRY: DNA was discovered about one hundred years ago, but the double helix was identified in 1953 and that opened the door to all this. Life has to have two components. One is a way of getting energy, which we've been talking about, and the other is to maintain itself by passing on genetic information. That genetic information is what we can now analyze. It's giving us a tool that Darwin didn't have. It turns out that elephants are very closely related to pigs. You would never have thought to put those two closely together. So it's a different dimension of analysis.

ED: Once life was established on earth, it had a great influence on how the earth itself evolved. This is something we've appreciated only in the last couple of decades, this interaction between the physical and biological parts of the planet.

At the beginning, archaea generated oxygen from the earth's chemicals and bacteria generated oxygen by photosynthesis.

Oxygen provided an environment where other organisms could live, and we've ended up with all these green trees and such. Is that too much of a jump?

ED: No, it's not too much of a jump, but the idea goes well beyond that. It's not just that we have produced oxygen. If life hadn't been able to modify the surface environment, that environment wouldn't have been able to support life and life would have died.

It would have started and then fizzled out?

ED: That's right. We touched on that when we talked about the need for an early greenhouse gas. In earth's early history, the sun was less luminous. The obvious question is, if the sun was less luminous, how come the planet didn't freeze? The first evidence of a major glaciation was 2.3 million years ago. So what happened the first few billion years?

GERRY: Methane. Bacteria and archaea produce methane. Thirty years ago we would have thought life was very sparse at that time. But now we think there was a humongous bloom of bacteria between two and four billion years ago.

You think that would have had to be the case, in order to build up to where we are now?

ED: No, that's not what we said. But it could have been.

GERRY: It's possible that fewer organisms over this great mess of time could have done it. During the first 80 percent of the life of the planet we had only bacteria.

If a glacial age came back, what would survive? If this were a doomsday scenario and humans couldn't survive, would the archaea and bacteria still be there and then they would start over?

GERRY: They've survived everything so far.

ED: It's only doomsday from our point of view. If you're a bacteria, you'd have a different point of view.

The bacteria would survive.

ED: Yes, I'm sure they would. And other organisms too. Because, don't forget, the planet is still warm. You're not going to stop plate tectonics with a measly little glacial age. What might do in humans might not do in many other forms of life.

Whatever did in the dinosaurs didn't do in mammals.

ED: And some dinosaur-like creatures survived.

We still have armadillos.

ED: And birds.

GERRY: Birds. And reptiles—gators and so on.

Armadillos and birds are warm-blooded.

GERRY: Some people think that dinosaurs were warm-blooded, too. I don't know.

ED: I would try to avoid that subject, myself! We've been talking around an issue that Gerry and I understand, but is a difficult concept for people outside the sciences. It is the scale of time. We talk easily about two billion years, but that's a fairly abstract concept. It's incomprehensible on the timescale of a human being's life.

That's true.

ED: A glacial age is just a moment—

GERRY: A blink—

People will orient to themselves. The way I see it, if a glacial age comes along, that's it for the human race. Will it ever come back?

ED: I would think so. Humans, or maybe I should say humanoids, have already lived through a glacial age.

GERRY: Some humans will adapt. It's not going to happen overnight.

No, not overnight. But from what I've read, it could be faster than most people think.

GERRY: There have been little glacial ages.

The Little Ice Age. We did adapt to that.

ED: But that's not what we're talking about. The best example is the Younger Dryas, which was a cold, near glacial time span of 1,300 years that began about 12,900 years ago. The planet had been emerging from the last glaciation and conditions had become quite temperate by about 13,000 years ago, although the ice caps were still quite extensive. Then within a span of a decade, maybe, temperatures plunged globally—significantly more than the Little Ice Age. I don't know the figures offhand, but the age is named for an Arctic flower, the Arctic dryad, that replaced a lot of Europe's vegetation during that period. Conditions remained cold for 1,300 years and then within the span of another decade, maybe less, the temperatures rose again.

Does anyone have any idea why that happened?

ED: It must involve the ocean, because the ocean carries enormous amounts of heat. The climate system is the consequence of interaction between the ocean and the atmosphere, and one of the important parts of that system is the North Atlantic, the Arctic area up near the North Pole. What happens in the North Atlantic is that warm surface water flows there from the tropics and keeps northern Europe warm. This includes the Gulf Stream, but it also includes the general surface flow northward. As that water liberates heat in the North Atlantic, it sinks because it becomes dense—the salinity increases. The current notion is that there is something called a Conveyor Belt that circulates the heavy, cold, salty water to the tropics where it is replaced by buoyant, warm, less salty water and the cycle continues. The balance of salt and fresh is critical in this theory. What many people think caused the Younger Dryas cooling is freshening of a large part of the Arctic. A huge freshwater lake was created by melt water from glaciers as the ice age gradually ended, but it was damned up by unmelted ice. When the dam melted and broke, a lot of freshwater poured into the ocean, causing the Conveyor Belt to shut down so that warm water no longer flowed past Europe. This brought back the cooling.

That's Wallace Broecker's theory, isn't it?

ED: Yes. Broecker and some others. We don't actually know if it happened that way. But it could have happened that way. And that could be a warning of what might happen if there are large-scale freshening events in the future.

And those could be caused by global warming—the burning of fossil fuels?

ED: Yes. As Broecker once said, what we're doing now is like taking a stick and poking a big, mean animal. We don't know what that animal will do. It's very important for our lives how the ocean and atmosphere interact to cause our climate. Also important is what Gerry and I have been talking about today, the interaction between the biological part of the planet and the physical part. Everything that exists around us on the planet is a consequence of complex interactions.

Scientists have their own specialties and each one goes deeply into a particular subject. But who puts it all together?

ED: I think we all try to put it together in our own context. But I don't think we understand very well the large-scale planetary systems from the point of view of geology. I don't want to speak for Gerry but I suspect not from the point of view of biology either. Although we're gaining new insight into understanding the natural world, that doesn't mean we're particularly knowledgeable.

GERRY: We're gaining insight more rapidly than we were in the past, and that is simplifying the picture and complicating it at the same time. The understanding that all of these systems have a profound influence on each other is a relatively new thing.

Really?

GERRY: In the past, biologists were biologists, engineers were engineers, and geologists were geologists. And we talked at each other, but we didn't talk to each other.

Now you are starting to talk to each other?

ED: Certainly, in the case of the undersea vents, we are talking to each other. No one knows anything. The biologist knows as much as the geologist. It's almost a new interdisciplinary science, if you will. It has to be seen in an interdisciplinary way. But my impression is that there aren't too many groups that are doing it to that extent yet.

GERRY: In effect, it's very difficult. I work with chemical engineers. We each do our own thing. We talk to each other, but I know the chemical engineer doesn't have a real notion of what I'm talking about biologically, and I have trouble understanding some of his concepts. We have different ways of looking at things, but we realize we have to work together. As the branches of science become more complex, there's a narrowing of information in a sense. I have to know less but in more depth. As my branch has become more and more complex, it's become necessary to work in teams. But I don't know that I always understand—although I try—what all these other team members are doing. In the past, you did your own stuff. And we realize we can't do that now.

CHAPTER SEVEN
CAPE FLORA

The Journal of Fritdjof Nansen
June 23, 1896

Tuesday, June 23

"Do I sleep? Do I dream?
Do I wonder and doubt?
Are things what they seem?
Or is visions about?"

What has happened? I can still scarcely grasp it. A few days ago I was swimming in the water for dear life, attacked by walrus, living the savage life which I have lived for more than a year now, and sure of a long journey before us, over ice and sea, through unknown regions, before we should meet with other human beings—a journey full of the same ups and downs, the same disappointments, that we have become so accustomed to.

Now I am living the life of a civilized European, surrounded by everything that civilization can afford of luxury and good living, with abundance of water, soap, towels, clean, soft woolen clothes, books, and everything that we have been sighing for all these weary months.

It was past midday on June 17 when I turned out to prepare breakfast. I had been down to the edge of the ice to fetch salt water, had made up the fire, cut up the meat and put it in the pot, and had already taken off one boot preparatory to creeping into the bag again, when I saw that the mist over the land had risen a little since the preceding day. I thought it would be as well to take the opportunity of having a look round, so I put on my boot again, and went up onto a hummock to look at the land beyond. A gentle breeze came from the land bearing with it a confused noise of thousands of bird voices from the mountain there. As I listened to these sounds of life and movement, I watched flocks of auks flying to and fro above my head. As my eye followed the line of coast, stopping at the dark, naked cliffs, glancing at the cold, icy plains and glaciers in a land which I believed to be unseen by any human eye and untrodden by any human foot, a sound suddenly reached my ear so like the barking of a dog that I started. It was only a couple of barks, but it could not be anything else. I strained my ears, but heard no more, only the same bubbling noise of thousands of birds. I must have been mistaken, after all; it was only the birds that I had heard. And again my eye passed to the island in the west.

Then the barking came again, first single barks, then full cry; there was one deep bark, and one sharper. There was no longer any room for doubt. At that moment I remembered having heard two reports the day before which I thought sounded like shots, but I had explained them away as noises in the ice. I now shouted to Johansen that I heard dogs farther inland. Johansen started up from the bag where he lay sleeping and tumbled out of the tent. "Dogs?"

He could not quite take it in, but had to get up and listen with his own ears, while I got breakfast ready. He very much doubted the possibility of such a thing, yet fancied once or twice that he heard something which might be taken for the barking of dogs. But then it was drowned again in the bird noises and, everything considered, he thought that what I had heard was nothing more than that. I said he might believe what he liked, but I meant to set off as quickly as possible, and was impatient to get breakfast swallowed. I had emptied the last of the Indian meal into the soup, feeling sure that we should have farinaceous food enough by the evening.

As we were eating, we discussed who it could be, whether our countrymen or Englishmen. If it was the English expedition to Franz Josef Land which had been in contemplation when we started, what should we do? "Oh, we'll just have to remain with them a day or two," said Johansen, "and then we'll have to go on to Spitsbergen, or else it will be too long before we get home." We were quite agreed on this point, but we would take care to get some good provisions for the voyage out of them.

While I went on, Johansen was to stay behind and mind the kayaks, so that we should run no risk of their drifting away with the ice. I got out my snowshoes, glass, and gun, and was ready. Before starting, I went up once more to listen, and look out across the uneven ice to the land. But there was not a sound like the barking of dogs, only noisy auks, harsh-toned little auks, and screaming kittiwakes. Was it these, after all, that I had heard?

I set off in doubt. Then in front of me I saw the fresh tracks of an animal. They could hardly have been made by a fox, for if they were, the foxes here must be bigger than any I had ever seen. But dogs? Could a dog have been no more than a few hundred paces from us in the night without barking or without our having heard it? It seemed scarcely probable. But whatever it was, it could never have been a fox. A wolf then? I went on, my mind full of strange thoughts, hovering between certainty and doubt. Was all our toil, were all our troubles, privations, and sufferings to end here? It seemed incredible, and yet—

Out of the shadowland of doubt, certainty was at last beginning to dawn. Again the sound of a dog yelping reached my ear, more distinctly than ever. I saw more and more tracks which could be nothing but those of a dog. Among them were foxes' tracks, and how small they looked!

It was with a strange mixture of feelings that I made my way in towards land among the numerous hummocks and inequalities. Suddenly I thought I heard a shout from a human voice, a strange voice. How my heart beat, and the blood rushed to my brain as I ran up onto a hummock and hallooed with all the strength of my lungs. Behind that human voice in the midst of the icy desert, this one message from life, stood home and she who was waiting there, and I saw nothing else as I made my way between bergs and ice ridges. Soon I heard another human shout, and saw, too, from an ice ridge a dark form moving among the hummocks farther in. It was a dog. But farther off came another figure, that of a man. Was it Jackson or one of his companions, or perhaps a fellow countryman? We approached one another quickly. I waved my hat; he did the same. I heard him speak to the dog, and I listened. It was English, and as I drew nearer I thought I recognized Mr. Jackson whom I remembered once to have seen.

I raised my hat. We extended a hand to one another with a hearty, "How do you do?" Above us was a roof of mist, shutting out the world around, beneath our feet the rugged, packed drift ice, and in the background a glimpse of the land, all ice, glacier and mist. On one side was the civilized European in an English check suit and high rubber water boots, well shaved, well groomed, bringing with him a perfume of scented soap perceptible to the wild man's sharpened senses. On the other side was the wild man, clad in dirty rags, black with oil and soot, with long uncombed hair and shaggy beard, black with smoke, with a face in which the natural fair complexion could not possibly be discerned through the thick layer of fat and soot which a winter's endeavors with warm water, moss, rags, and at last a knife had sought in vain to remove. No one suspected who he was or whence he came.

Jackson: "I'm immensely glad to see you."

"Thank you, I also."

"Have you a ship here."

"No. My ship is not here."

"How many are there of you?"

"I have one companion at the ice-edge." As we talked, we had begun to go in towards land. I took it for granted that he had recognized me, or at any rate understood who it was that was hidden behind this savage exterior, not thinking that a total stranger would be received so heartily. Suddenly he stopped, looked me in the face, and said quickly, "Aren't you Nansen?"

"Yes, I am."

"By Jove! I am glad to see you!" And he seized my hand and shook it again, while his whole face became one smile of welcome, and delight at the unexpected meeting beamed from his dark eyes. "Where have you come from now?" he asked.

"I left the *Fram* in 84° north latitude, after having drifted for two years, and I reached the 86°15′ parallel, where we had to turn and make for Franz Josef Land. We were, however, obliged to stop for the winter somewhere north of here. We are now on our route to Spitsbergen."

"I congratulate you most heartily. You have made a good trip of it, and I am awfully glad to be the first person to congratulate you on your return." Once more he seized my hand and shook it heartily. I could not have been welcomed more warmly; that handshake was more than a mere form. In his hospitable English manner, he said at once that he had "plenty of room" for us, and that he was expecting his ship every day. By "plenty of room" I discovered afterwards that he meant that there were still a few square feet on the floor of their hut that were not occupied at night by himself and his sleeping companions. But "heart-room makes house-room" and of the former there was no lack.

As soon as I could get a word in, I asked how things were getting on at home, and he was able to give me the welcome intelligence that my wife and child had both been in the best of health when he left two years ago. Then came Norway's turn, and Norwegian politics. But he knew nothing about that, and I took it as a sign that they must be all right too.

He now asked if we could not go out at once and fetch Johansen and our belongings, but I thought that our kayaks would be too heavy for us to drag over this packed-up ice alone, and that if he had men enough it would certainly be better to send them out. If we only gave Johansen notice by a salute from our guns, he would wait patiently, so we each fired two shots. We soon met several men: Mr. Armitage, the second in command, Mr. Child, the photographer, and the doctor, Mr. Koetlitz. As they approached, Jackson gave them a sign, and let them understand who I was, and I was again welcomed heartily.

We met yet others: the botanist, Mr. Fisher, Mr. Burgess, and the Finn Blomqvist (his real name was Melenius). Fisher has since told me that he at once thought it must be me when he saw a man out on the ice, but he quite gave up that idea when he met me for he had seen me described as a fair man, and here was a dark man, with black hair and beard. When they were all there, Jackson said that I had reached 86°15′ north latitude and from seven powerful lungs I was given a triple British cheer that echoed among the hummocks.

Jackson immediately sent his men off to fetch sledges and go out to Johansen, while we went on towards the house which I now thought I could see on the shore. Jackson now told me that he had letters for me from home, and that both last spring and this he had had them with him when he went north, on the chance of our meeting. We now found that in March he must have been at no great distance south of our winter hut, but had to turn there as he was stopped by open water, the same open water over which we had seen the dark atmosphere all winter.

Only when we came up nearly to the houses did he inquire more particularly about the *Fram* and our drifting, and I briefly told him our story. He told me afterwards that from the time we met he had believed that the ship had been destroyed and that we two were the only survivors of the expedition. He thought he had seen a sad expression in my face when he first asked about the ship, and was afraid of touching on the subject again. Indeed, he had even quietly warned his men not to ask. It was only through a chance remark of mine that he found out his mistake and began to inquire more particularly about the *Fram* and the others.

Then we arrived at the house, a low Russian timber hut, lying on a flat terrace, an old shoreline beneath the mountain, and fifty feet above the sea. It was surrounded by a stable and four circular tent-houses, in which stores were kept. We entered a comfortable warm nest in the midst of these desolate wintry surroundings, the ceiling and walls covered with green cloth. On the walls hung photographs, etchings, and photolithographs. Shelves were everywhere, containing books and instruments.

Under the roof, clothes and shoes hung drying, and from the little stove in the middle of the floor of this cozy room the warm coal fire shone out a hospitable welcome.

A strange feeling came over me as I seated myself in a comfortable chair in these surroundings. At one stroke of changing fate, all responsibility, all troubles, were swept away from a mind that had been oppressed by them during three long years. I was in a safe haven in the midst of the ice, and the longings of three years were lulled in the golden sunshine of the dawning day. My duty was done; my task was ended. Now I could rest, only rest and wait.

A carefully soldered tin packet was handed to me; it contained letters from Norway. It was with a trembling hand and a beating heart that I opened it, and there were tidings, only good tidings, from home. A delightful feeling of peace settled upon the soul.

Then dinner was served, and how nice it was to have bread, butter, milk, sugar, coffee, and everything that a year had taught us to do without and yet to long for. But the height of comfort was reached when I was able to throw off my dirty rags and have a warm bath. I got rid of as much dirt as was possible in one bout, but only succeeded in becoming anything like clean after several days and many attempts. Then clean, soft clothes from head to foot, hair cut, and the shaggy beard shaved off, and the transformation from savage to European was complete, more sudden than in the reverse direction. How delightfully comfortable it is to be able to put on one's clothes without being made greasy, but most of all to be able to move without feeling them stick to the body with every movement.

It was not very long before Johansen and the others followed, with the kayaks and our things. Johansen related how these warm-hearted Englishmen had given him and the Norwegian flag a hearty cheer when they came up and saw it waving on a bamboo rod which he had put up by my orders, so that I could find my way back to him. On the way here they had not allowed him to touch the sledges, and he had only to walk beside them like a passenger, and he said that of all the ways in which we had traveled over drift ice this, without comparison, was the most comfortable. His reception in the hut was scarcely less hospitable than mine, and he soon went through the same transformation that I had undergone. I no longer recognize my comrade of the long winter night, and search in vain for any trace of the tramp who wandered up and down that desolate shore, beneath the steep talus and the dark basalt cliff outside the low underground hut. The black, sooty troglodyte has vanished and in his place sits a well-favored, healthy looking European citizen in a comfortable chair, puffing away at a short pipe or a cigar, and with a book before him doing his best to learn English. It seems to me that he gets fatter and fatter every day, with an almost alarming rapidity.

It is indeed surprising that we have both gained considerably in weight since we left the *Fram*. When I came here I myself weighed about 205 pounds, nearly 22 pounds more than I did when I left the *Fram*. Johansen weighs over 167 pounds, having gained a little more than 13 pounds. This is the result of a winter's feeding on nothing but bear's meat and fat. It is not quite like the experiences of others in parallel circumstances; it must be our laziness that has done it.

So here we are, living in peace and quietness, waiting for the ship from home and for what the future will bring us, while everything is being done for us to make us forget a winter's privations. We could not have fallen into better hands, and it is impossible to describe the unequaled hospitality and kindness we meet with on all hands, and the comfort we feel. Is it the year's privations and want of human society, or is it common interests that so draw us to these men in this desolate region? I do not know, but we are never tired of talking, and it seems as if we had known one another for years instead of having met for the first time a few days ago.

Journey: Cape Flora

When Nansen and Johansen left the *Fram* on March 14, 1895, they took enough provisions to last them one hundred days. "In that time," Nansen wrote, "it seems to me that we should have arrived somewhere." By "somewhere" he meant somewhere civilized, a place where people lived, a place where food was available, a place where ships could be expected to call. Cape Flora, where he and Johansen arrived on June 23, 1896, was that place. The journey had taken 460 days.

Cape Flora is on a glacier-covered island in remote and uninhabited Franz Josef Land, and its civilization was entirely the creation of one man: Frederick Jackson. This spot at the tip of Northbrook Island, discovered and named by Benjamin Leigh Smith in 1880, had not been chosen by Leigh Smith as a place to stay. Instead, he had erected a hut (using material he had brought with him) on nearby Bell Island. After losing his ship, the *Eira,* off Cape Flora in 1881, Leigh Smith and his party overwintered there in a stone hut much like the one Nansen and Johansen built in 1895 at Cape Norway.

Jackson, on the other hand, had come prepared. He arrived at Cape Flora on September 10, 1894, in a steam yacht called the *Windward* with a house prefabricated in Russia of timber logs; he had erected it in advance to be sure he had all the numbered pieces, then broke it down again for transport. He named it Elmwood and described it in his journal as "the most suitable, best, and most comfortable house ever put up in this latitude." We know now that Inuit snow houses in Greenland provided competition as "most suitable," but this would have been beyond the understanding of Jackson and his countrymen at the time.

Jackson also brought with him a stable (there were four ponies), dog kennel (there were many dogs), three storehouses, and several tents (which he did not erect until the worst of the winter was past). Inside the main house was a communal space thirteen feet long by twelve feet wide, and seven feet in height. It was comfortably furnished. A corner was set aside for bathing, separated when in use from the main room by canvas screens. There were two private rooms, one for Jackson, the other shared by the doctor and the chief scientist. There was a kitchen, and a cook. The explorers, including the cook, the doctor, and Jackson, at first numbered eight, then nine—one man (a Finn) from the ship's crew joined the party before the ship departed.

The ship, with a crew of eighteen, overwintered in the harbor some distance from (and apparently quite independent of) Jackson's camp. It departed Cape Flora in early summer as soon as the ice was passable, and returned after the following winter had subsided. When Nansen and Johansen arrived, the *Windward* was expected "every day" and appeared almost six weeks later on July 26. "We heard of the wondrous X-Rays and color photography and a hundred and one other things which more than two years' total absence of news had accumulated," Jackson wrote. The ship had had a difficult trip back to England the year before, becoming locked in the ice. The captain had feared a second winter away from home and had stripped timber from her decks for extra fuel. He had managed to escape; this winter he would not remain at Cape Flora for long. He departed on August 8, 1896, with Nansen and Johansen aboard. The voyage was unusually ice free, and in only six days the *Windward* traveled the 750 miles to Vardo, Norway, where it left Nansen and Johansen.

Nansen's journal entries peter out after his arrival on Cape Flora, but in his book, *Farthest North,* he gives a recollected account of the trip home, his arrival, and his reunion with the *Fram.* Even before the *Windward* was securely anchored on August 14 in Vardo, Nansen wrote, he was in a small boat on the way to the telegraph station where he delivered a bundle of nearly a hundred telegrams ready to be sent. "The head of the telegraph office looked hard at me, and quietly took up the bundle. But as his eye fell upon the signature of the telegram that lay on the top, his face suddenly changed. He wheeled sharp round, and went over to the lady clerk who was sitting at the table. When he again turned and came towards me his face was radiant, and he bade me a hearty welcome." Nansen's joy at being back in Norway was tempered by worry about the fate of his ship, the *Fram,* which so far as anyone knew was still drifting in the Arctic ice. "She ought to be out of the ice by this time if nothing had gone amiss," Nansen fretted. He and Johansen went on to Hammerfest, about two hundred miles from Vardo, where Nansen was joined by his wife and his male secretary who had escorted her on her journey. In the harbor at Hammerfest was the yacht *Ontaria,* owned by English explorer Sir George Baden-Powell, who was just about to set out for Franz Josef Land to search for Nansen. Baden-Powell put his ship at Nansen's disposal, and Nansen, his wife, the secretary, and Johansen joined Baden-Powell and his wife on it.

On August 20, the head of the Hammerfest telegraph office made a trip out to the *Ontaria.* "With trembling hands I tore open the telegram: '*Fram* arrived in good condition. All well on board. Shall start at once for Tromso. Welcome home! Otto Sverdrup.' I felt as if I should have choked, and all I could say was, 'the *Fram* has arrived!'" Sverdrup was in Skjaervo, only a hundred miles down the coast, where he had heard the news of Nansen's whereabouts.

The next day at Tromso, farther down the coast, Nansen and Johansen met the *Fram*, "strong and broad and weather-beaten," with all her crew on board. A procession set out by sea to Nansen's home in Christiania, now the city of Oslo, about fourteen hundred miles away. First a tug, then the *Fram* "heavy and slow but so much the surer," and finally "the elegant *Ontaria* with my wife and me on board. We passed from town to town, from fête to fête, along the coast of Norway," Nansen wrote. "It was too beautiful to believe in. A feeling of dread came over me; but the silhouette of a woman's form, standing out against the glow of the evening sky, gave peace and security. "At a town near Nansen's home city, Nansen and his wife boarded the *Fram* for the homecoming. "It was on September 9th that the *Fram* steamed up Christiania Fjord and met with such a reception as a prince might have envied. The stout old men-of-war *Nordstjernen* and *Elida,* the new and elegant *Valkyrie*, and the nimble little torpedo boats led the way for us. Steamboats swarmed around, black with people. There were flags high and low, salutes, hurrahs, waving of handkerchiefs and hats, radiant faces everywhere, the whole fjord one multitudinous welcome. There lay home, and the well-known strand before it, glittering and smiling in the sunshine. The ice and the long moonlit polar nights, with all their yearning, seemed like a far-off dream from another world—a dream that had come and passed away. But what would life be worth without its dreams?"

Meanwhile, Jackson, far away in Franz Josef Land, continued his sledging and mapping, burying a Union Jack in a cairn at each island he discovered. His last pony died. His dogs were down to five. He was very well organized. Tinned food was inspected for spoilage before being eaten; water was boiled before drinking. When there was twenty-four-hour darkness, one train-oil lamp burned all night, and nine others were lighted when the clock said it was morning. Heat came from a stove that burned coal from Cape Flora's cliffs. Jackson arranged concerts and hunting contests to keep his men happy, and it seems that they were happy. In preparation for the *Windward*'s first return to Cape Flora, Jackson had asked every man to write a letter saying whether or not he wished to remain, and every one of them had wanted to stay. Three, nevertheless—for various reasons—had departed with Nansen and Johansen, leaving six in Jackson's party.

On July 22, 1897, when the *Windward* returned for a second time, it found Jackson and all his men alive and healthy after nearly three years on Cape Flora. Jackson had mapped to the southwestern extremity of Franz Josef Land, which he named

Cape Mary Harmsworth after the wife of his sponsor, Alfred Harmsworth, the founder of the *London Daily Mail.* In mapping to Cape Mary Harmsworth, Jackson had determined the nonexistence of a large stretch of land on the map drawn by Julius Payer, one of the discoverers of Franz Josef Land. This nonexistent land was called Gillies Land, the place Nansen had believed himself to be when he built his hut. Jackson also had serious doubts about the existence of Petermann Land and King Oscar Land, which Payer had mapped in the northern extremity of the archipelago. The nonexistence of those lands was discouraging for Jackson, who had planned to sledge to the pole by way of them. Jackson's patron, Alfred Harmsworth, did not yet have a report on this, but a North Pole attempt was what he wanted to finance, and he had become impatient with Jackson. The *Windward* brought notice that this would be its last trip to Cape Flora. Harmsworth did not, at the time, give Jackson his reason for withdrawing the *Windward*, but it turned out that he had decided to lend the ship to Robert E. Peary, the American who had plans to reach the pole by way of Greenland.

"I received among our correspondence certain communications which, together with the fact that no draught animals have arrived, leave us, I fear, no option but for the expedition to return to England," Jackson wrote in his journal on the day the *Windward* arrived. And on the next day: "I have been turning the situation over in my brain all day and night to endeavor to discover some method by which I can still carry on the expedition, but can think of none." Also delivered by the *Windward* were two fine Norwegian canvas kayaks, a gift from Nansen, sent with a copy of his book for each man. The book, *Farthest North*, had been published in Norway and (in translation) in England only a few months after Nansen's return. Jackson was so busy packing up his expedition, he did not have time to open it.

Nansen had been planning his book during the forty-two days he had spent on Cape Flora the year before. He had developed some of his negatives with the help of Jackson's photographer, and was relieved to see they had not been damaged by the walrus attack suffered at the end of his trip. He had had the presence of mind to ask Jackson to take his photograph, and that of Johansen, the first moment they had arrived, before bathing. And, at his request, other photographs were taken as well. Reenacted was the meeting of Nansen and Jackson, the meeting, as Nansen had put it, of a "wild man black with oil and soot" and a man in an English check suit smelling of scented soap. "Nansen re-dressed himself exactly as he was on that occasion, and in every way the scene was exactly reproduced, excepting that his hair and beard had been cut, and he was in a more cleanly condition," Jackson wrote in his journal. "I put on my brown leather coat, breeches, high leather boots, and round woolen cap, and carried my gun as upon that occasion. Misere, the dog that went out with me then, was also included in the group." Other photos were staged, too. Jackson wrote in his journal that he took three cameras down to a lake in a nearby floe and took about fifty photos of Nansen and Johansen dressed in their traveling clothes, "sailing, paddling, and dragging the kayaks, sledges, etc."

Nansen also had spent this time getting his maps together. "I showed Nansen my map, and he pointed out upon it to me where he had spent last winter," Jackson explains. "He afterwards copied from this map in making his own. He asked me what he should do about the country I had discovered to the north prior to his reaching here, and which he had since passed through. He would have to give a map showing his course; should he leave this blank and say that it will appear in my map?" Jackson delayed his reply, but considered it "very decent" of Nansen to ask. "Some would have published that portion of the map without consulting me—at all events, all that they knew of it."

Jackson knew every detail of it, and Nansen recognized this and was grateful for it. In return, Jackson was generous. On June 22 he wrote in his journal: "Yesterday I told Nansen that he might publish my map if he wishes to. I am also going to offer to allow him to name the land I discovered in 1895 north of Cape McClintock, which is in the neighborhood of his winter hut, as he has discovered very little to name, and I think it hard lines on the chap if he cannot name the capes and fjords in the neighborhood of his hut when he passed a winter under such hardships and privations, in lands which until he met me he had imagined to be his own discoveries. I shall have plenty to name without these. I suggested this to him, and he replied, 'This is not the right thing, I know.'

"I answered, 'I can't see that it matters, as it is a thing that only concerns you and me.' He thanked me for being so kind, and said he would consider whether he could accept my generous offer. I have offered him the naming of everything he could see from his winter quarters." Later Jackson added a footnote to that journal entry: "On reading Dr. Nansen's book, *Farthest North*, I find he has only availed himself of my offer so far as naming one of these spots—Frederick Jackson Island—after me, which I should never have consented to had I known of his intention." If Nansen had not named Frederick Jackson Island in the way that he did, there would be nothing in Franz Josef Land named after Jackson. Explorers, it seems, did not name the places they discovered after themselves.

It is interesting to think about the differences in temperament of Nansen and Jackson, both in their thirties, both achievers, both good, honorable people. Nansen was expansive, resourceful, making the best of whatever presented itself to him Jackson, more manipulative of his surroundings and less manipulative of how others might see him, was timid by comparison and (perhaps consequently) not so lucky. Jackson wrote in his journal, in fact, that he was struck by the "great luck" that attended Nansen. "I feel the greatest satisfaction at being the means of saving these brave fellows further perils and of sending them safely home," he continued. "I only trust that Dr.

Nansen's extraordinary immunity from penalty will not lead the inexperienced to suppose that they may go larking about within the polar circle with merely a dog and a gun, and that all things will be well with them. If they should fall into this error they will be sadly—I almost said fatally—deceived." In the Arctic, daring can easily be fatal if not accompanied by luck.

Nansen's daring, helped considerably by his writing skill and his sense of presentation, led to fame, which in turn led to a life in the public eye. He remained a celebrity all his life. Jackson, on the other hand, built a limited but controllable world in an uncontrollable environment, and in doing so he created accomplishment but not celebrity. Nansen's Arctic experience was to him "a dream that had come and passed away." Jackson left his settlement at Cape Flora with "not the smallest wish to go."

On Cape Flora today, one of Jackson's storehouses is still there: a shack, a weathered shelter used and modified by others after Jackson left and still standing despite one hundred years of storms. The structure is unmistakably Jackson's—in his book it is visible in nearly every photograph of his camp. The folded basalt cliff rising above the island's rocky, grassy plain is recognizable too. It is the background of the famous photograph of the Nansen-Jackson meeting. However, I knew nothing of Jackson and very little of Nansen when I arrived on Cape Flora and I did not recognize the shack or the cliff as connected to them.

Nevertheless, the island had an elegiac air. Cape Norway had been light in spirit, full of delicate beauty. Cape Flora, by contrast, was somber. Perhaps it was the rusted oil cans abandoned by generations of explorers. Perhaps it was the granite marker commemorating the three Italians who lost their lives when Umberto Cagni bettered Nansen's Farthest North record at the turn of the nineteenth century. The many bird feathers left after the meals of foxes surely played a part, as did the tomblike mound of ice inset with two ovals of older ice that pressed against a ridge of stones, the remains of Leigh Smith's hut. In the distance was an open ice-dotted sea. At our feet were fields of grass and moss, sprinkled with flowers and tiny mushrooms. In Jackson's book, there is a picture of these mushrooms. "New to Science, Discovered on Cape Flora" is the caption. Jackson, the careful cataloger, had also discovered fossilized tree trunks and ferns, evidence that Franz Josef Land, millions of years earlier, had had a much warmer climate.

Jackson was an expert hunter and killed polar bears and walruses routinely to stock his larder. But as he left Cape Flora he was saddened that a commercial walrus-hunting ship was already in the harbor. "It seems that someone from the *Windward* in 1896 had spoken of the large number of walruses to be seen here, and of the probability of its paying to take them," he laments. "I have a different opinion on that subject." Nevertheless, he supplied the captain a copy of the map that he had drawn. "He has only a small admiralty chart of these islands, which is useless to him," Jackson wrote. This was the beginning of a period during which polar bears and walruses were hunted almost to extinction in these lands.

The *Windward*, when it brought Jackson the news that he must leave Cape Flora, also brought a cache of supplies. But they were not intended for Jackson. The world's attention at the time was riveted on a Swede, Salomon Andrée who, with two companions, was setting out from Spitsbergen to attempt to reach the North Pole in a hydrogen balloon. In case something should go wrong, Andrée planned to make his way to Cape Flora, and supplies were delivered there for him. Jackson added his own stores to them and carefully sealed them inside Elmwood where they would be safe from bears. Andrée flew on July 11, 1897, and when Jackson left Cape Flora on August 6, his balloon had already crashed on the pack ice partway between Spitsbergen and Franz Josef Land. Of course, Jackson did not know this. No one knew what happened to Andrée and his companions until 1930 when their remains were discovered. They died unlucky deaths, possibly from carbon monoxide fumes from their Primus stove (Nansen's friend) burning in a tent in which they slept sealed up under drifts of snow.

As the *Windward* pulled away from Cape Flora, Jackson stood on deck under a clear sky. "The low midnight sun shone brilliantly," he wrote. "Our eyes could now follow with ease, as we luxuriously steamed along, the route Armitage and I, with our five surviving dogs, had so laboriously struggled along last spring. There to the northeast, at the head of Gray Bay, is the Peary Glacier (named by me after the Arctic explorer, Mr. Peary U.S.N.) up which we hauled our sledges foot by foot. And there to the northwest, at the base of the rocks of Cape Crowther, is the spot where bad weather kept us cooped up in our tent in wet clothes in the beginning of last May. It is difficult to believe now, with everything sunny and peaceful, that these are the same spots where all was drifting snow, bitter cold, and fiercely driving blizzard. And how we appreciate the comfort of the little cabin below, when we recall our camps upon that ice-bound land, when crouching over our smoky fat-lamp we swallowed our cocoa made with lukewarm water and devoured our lumps of frozen fat bacon. And yet I long for more sledging and more discovery. I leave my work with regret."

A Conversation with Olle Carlsson and Bob Headland

Robert (Bob) Headland is archivist and curator at the Scott Polar Research Institute at the University of Cambridge, Great Britain. In 1991, he was a lecturer on the first tourist trip by Russian icebreaker to the North Pole, and he has made the trip in the same capacity each summer (often more than once) since then. I met Bob Headland on his eighteenth trip to the North Pole. Olle Carlsson has been a guide on tourist ships in the polar regions, both north and south, for thirteen years. The summer following my North Pole trip, I went on an excursion along the coast of the island of Spitsbergen on the Polar Star, *a Norwegian icebreaker. On that trip, I met Olle Carlsson, who gave lectures on the history and wildlife of the area. When he is not traveling, he lives in Sweden.*

We began our conversation by talking about the presence in the Arctic of the Soviet Union before its breakup, and then shifted into talk about explorers of the polar regions. We discussed the arguments against Robert E. Peary's having reached the pole. We also talked about attempts on the North Pole by Salomon Andrée, who tried to reach it in a hydrogen balloon in 1897; Roald Amundsen, Lincoln Ellsworth, and Umberto Nobile, who passed over it in 1926 in a dirigible; Ralph Plaistead who traveled in 1968 by snowmobile; and Wally Herbert, who, in 1969, probably was the first to reach the North Pole by surface travel. We discussed Roald Amundsen at some length. Amundsen, the discoverer of the South Pole, had important experiences in the Arctic, including the one that possibly (but not certainly) ended his life.

OLLE: After I left the *Polar Star* last summer, I went to the *Molchanov,* a small converted Russian research ship, not an icebreaker.

Olle Carlsson

Bob Headland

On one day, we were in heavy ice for twelve hours on that little ship. It is a tough ship. Good Russian officers and crew. Russia had a fleet of about a dozen ships of that size that did many kinds of research, but they are all chartered now.

BOB: Charters are keeping the companies going. Those ships are well built. They are not icebreakers, but they aren't frightened of ice. They go into places other ships won't go near.

They're not doing research anymore?

BOB: Russian research has about 80 percent collapsed. No money. On one of the ships I was on recently I talked with a microbiologist who was still on board working as a stewardess. The ship was used for Russian government-sponsored research related to fisheries. Then it was chartered for a tourist trip, and some of the scientists stayed on to work for foreign currency.

OLLE: When I began working on the Russian ships, the small ones could take only thirty-five passengers because some of the space was given over to laboratories that we weren't allowed to touch. Today they can take fifty passengers because the laboratories have been made into cabins.

BOB: Even more important than the loss of the ships for research is the loss of the Russian polar stations. In 1991, there were 110, some on the islands, some drifting on the ice, some on the main land. Now there are only 4, all on the mainland.

Those stations were started under Stalin.

BOB: Yes, the first was Tichaya in 1929 on Franz Josef Land. Records were kept continuously. If you've got long continuous records of the polar regions, which are very vulnerable to climate change, you've got good data for your theories. It is a tragedy that the stations were disbanded so quickly. Almost any other country would have replaced at least the major ones with automated meteorological stations. But it's all gone.

We still need those stations.

BOB: We need science for an early warning. The best example of a success in this regard is the ozone hole, which is now repairing itself after CFCs [chlorofluorocarbons] were banned internationally in 1987.

That was accomplished by a global agreement, the Montreal Protocol, under the United Nations. CFCs were mainly used in refrigeration and in aerosol cans.

BOB: It's very good to have a success occasionally.

OLLE: Something similar was tried in 1997, with the Kyoto Protocol concerning global warming, but unfortunately the United States is not willing to cooperate in that. It was obvious that the depletion of the ozone layer was being caused by man. But in the case of global warming, scientists find it obvious that man is contributing heavily to it, but many other people do not.

BOB: I'm on the side of the scientists.

OLLE: I am too.

And I, also. But let's change the subject now. Bob, how many times have you been to the North Pole?

BOB: I think it's something like eighteen now. And quite a number of times through the Northeast Passage. I've just gone for the fourth time through the Northwest Passage. I strongly prefer the Northeast.

The Northeast Passage, like the Northwest, ends at the Bering Strait, but the Northwest Passage is through Canadian islands and the Northeast stays close to Russia.

BOB: Yes. I am rather keen on these trips. When Quark Expeditions ran the first Russian icebreaker trip to the North Pole on the *Sovetskiy Soyuz*, in theory I knew a lot about the area. But in practice it had been a closed area, Soviet territory. The papers and permissions we needed were daunting. I was on that trip in August 1991. The Soviet Union crashed at about that time, and Russia emerged. For me, it was the right time, right place. From then on I took a lot of interest in what was published about the area, and was asked to go on other Arctic trips as well. Once you go into the Russian Arctic you have a different sort of connection with the islands up there. And you realize very deeply the tragedy of the polar stations.

You said there are four left?

BOB: None are left on the remote islands. The last one closed in 2003. And it's more than that. In the last twelve years the Arctic has lost nearly half its population. In Siberia, the figure is probably three-quarters. Maybe the Scandinavian Arctic is stable, but in Canada and Alaska there has been withdrawal of personnel from the DEW [Distant Early Warning] Line stations. A sizable part of the military and scientific populations all over the Arctic is gone. Dikson, in Siberia, was a major port with at least ten thousand people living there just over a decade ago. Now the town has a population of less than two thousand. You can see the possessions of those who have gone packed in small containers sitting along the waterfront rusting away. All those Communist-built rectangular shoebox buildings are full of broken windows, and you can see makeshift chimneys pointing out of them. They were burning the doors and furniture before they left.

Olle, on our trip we passed an abandoned town on Spitsbergen. The Norwegian part of the island seems to be doing fine, but maybe the Russian part is not.

OLLE: The abandoned town we saw was Pyramiden, a Russian coal-mining town, a constructed community; it was state-owned, even down to the furniture. It closed in 1998.

They left everything there.

OLLE: Yes. Russia can get better quality coal from Siberia by rail. Pyramiden coal was high in sulfur. Barentsburg coal, from the main Russian town on Spitsbergen, is better, but still not very good. However, the Russians have asked for the right to reopen one of their oldest mines, close to Barentsburg. They think that with new technology they can develop another seam there.

You're an expert on the Spitsbergen area. How did you get into this?

OLLE: I have no scientific background at all. It was just a fascination that started with pictures of Antarctica taken by Stefan Lundgren, a commercial sailor who began going there in the early 1980s. When I saw his photos, I thought, "Is this place on earth? I have to see this place before I die." I was a schoolteacher then, at the high school level. I arranged slide shows for Stefan in the schools. I said, "These photos are amazing," and he said, "It's a pity they lie around collecting dust most of the time." I said, "You could make a book," and he said, "I can't write." "I can," I said. It was just taking a chance. I took leave from teaching for a year and we made quite a big book, an introduction to Antarctica. I wrote it, but it was based on his knowledge of being there, and on historical facts.

Did you go to Antarctica at that point?

OLLE: I wrote the book without having been there. I studied all the books I could find. I did all the background work I could, and then I looked at Stefan's pictures and wrote the book.

BOB: That was when I met you going up the stairs at the Scott Polar Research Institute.

OLLE: Yes, that's right. The book was published in 1990, and to have some kind of polar experience, I went to Spitsbergen before that. I was invited to give some lectures on a ship, and on that ship I became friends with the skipper—we almost immediately clicked. When the weeklong cruise was over, I looked at him and said, "I can't go home now." And he said, "No, you can't. Let's go to the office." I stayed on the ship the rest of the summer, doing odd jobs. That was thirteen years ago. I lecture, or lead trips, on ships going to Antarctica in the winter, and to Spitsbergen every summer, and also I have done the Northwest Passage, Greenland, and Iceland trips. Never Franz Josef Land.

Does anybody go to Franz Josef Land just for Franz Josef Land?

OLLE: Yes, but rarely. When Henry Kissinger was the U.S. secretary of state, someone said something about Svalbard to him and he said, "Where the hell is Svalbard?" Franz Josef

Land is even less known. It's hard to market it.

Another problem might be that Franz Josef Land is Russian. The Svalbard archipelago is technically international, but it is Norwegian so far as travel documents are concerned. I should point out that Svalbard is the name of the island group of which the island of Spitsbergen is a part. But the names Svalbard and Spitsbergen seem to be used interchangeably up there.

BOB: The regulars use Svalbard, but tourist promotions use Spitsbergen. Until Norway began administering the islands, Spitsbergen was the name of the largest island and also was used to describe the group of islands, so Spitsbergen is the name associated with the historic events that occurred there. Longyearbyen is the main town, the capital village. The first time I went there I was staying in the coalminers' dormitories. That was 1983.

The Spitsbergen Hotel was originally part of the coal miners' housing, wasn't it?

BOB: It was for the managers.

I stayed two nights there. Wood paneling and leather furniture. Everyone takes off their boots or shoes at the door.

OLLE: That's the tradition in Longyearbyen, to keep the coal dust and snow from coming inside.

Bob, I have a question for you. What happened to Jackson? I became involved with him by reading his book, A Thousand Days in the Arctic. *It's long out of print, but I found an old, falling-apart copy.*

BOB: Quite a good title, isn't it?

A good title, and quite a good book, but not as engaging as Nansen's. Jackson went back to England reluctantly. Did he ever return to the Arctic?

BOB: No. He advanced in the British army for many years, working as an engineer. He lived on a riverboat in the Thames and died there just before World War II. He became—what's the polite word for mildly eccentric?

He didn't seem the least bit eccentric in his book. In fact, the opposite.

BOB: His widow donated his diaries to Scott Polar, and we've also been given a portrait of him. It's very large, and I can't think of anywhere to put it up.

What happened to Elmwood? When we arrived on Cape Flora, there was only one small storehouse left of all the buildings Jackson took there.

BOB: Two of the octagonal observatory buildings ended up at Cape Tegetthoff, moved there by Walter Wellman in 1898 to use as a base for one of his many attempts on the pole. The storehouse remains because it was hauled up the hill by two explorers who stayed on Cape Flora over a winter. They moved the building so they could look out a great distance all around it. Georgiy Sedov's party took Elmwood, the main building, in 1914. They broke it up for fuel for their voyage back to Russia. They didn't bother with the storehouse because it had already been taken up the hill and it was small, but they did take the stable and the kennel as well as the main building.

A sad end for Elmwood. But it saved the lives of the Russians. I noticed Jackson's rather wistful comment that Nansen was lucky. I'm sure Jackson didn't think he, himself, was lucky. His sponsor expected him to go to the North Pole, but he didn't even try, did he?

BOB: I haven't put Jackson on my list of attempts. I've got seventeen attempts on the North Pole listed between 1894 and 1914, what I call the heroic period of exploration. Jackson determined the extent of Franz Josef Land. If King Oscar Land and Petermann Land had been there, he would have tried to go to the pole. But he wasn't prepared for lengthy travel on the drift ice. His primary interests were mapping and hunting. He had abundant food; he could have lasted another year if he'd had to. And he did have a bit of luck—he found his own coal mine to stoke the stove he brought with him.

His temperament was different from Nansen's.

BOB: Nansen certainly was lucky, especially in running into Jackson on his journey back from his Farthest North. There are indications from other diaries from the *Fram* that after two winters on the ship, Nansen was not displeased to leave it. Sverdrup was in command, and it might have been a mutual relief. There's an interesting thing in Johansen's diary. In February, after they had wintered in the hut, Nansen said to Johansen, "We've known each other long enough. We should speak to each other using our first names." They'd been sleeping in the same bag for almost a year as Dr. Nansen and Lieutenant Johansen!

OLLE: That also occurs in the Swedish Antarctic Expedition of 1901-03. It was the etiquette of the times. But from reports I've read, Nansen was often melancholy and not so easy to get along with.

He doesn't seem to have been an arrogant person though.

BOB: In Norway, he was a kingmaker.

OLLE: Very much a driving force. Norway was still subject to Sweden when he came back from his expedition, and he used his fame to work for its independence. He was interested in politics as well as science.

Didn't Nansen originally suggest the idea of polar drift stations?

BOB: Nansen suggested it, and Otto Yulyevich Shmidt took up the suggestion and produced one for the Soviet Union. That was the first Arctic Ocean drift station, in 1937. It was commanded by Ivan Papanin.

Wasn't Shmidt the one who claimed Franz Josef Land for Russia?

BOB: Yes. He was called the "Commissar of Ice" in the Soviet press. Shmidt later narrowly missed being purged. He survived only because he was stuck in the ice at the time of the purges in his department, and he came back a hero. In 1991, on my first trip on a Russian icebreaker, there were still commissars. In the sauna, where everyone wears the same uniform, there was often talk about the crew's country, what was wrong, what was right, and questions about my country. Then suddenly someone would come in and everyone began talking about ice conditions. You knew who that fellow was.

Did the commissar on the ship hold meetings extolling the virtues of Communism? That was normally part of a commissar's job.

BOB: Yes, he did, for the crew. There were warnings about the terrible capitalist tourists on the ship.

OLLE: The commissars held the rank of first officer, and after the collapse of the Soviet Union, the first officers disappeared. There are no first officers on Russian ships now, only second and third officers, and first mates.

Do either of you know if the Soviet Union seriously considered sending missiles to the United States over the pole?

BOB: The Soviets had capacity for war across the Arctic. I saw great fuel storage tanks on Graham Bell Island in Franz Josef Land, for example. If aircraft were to land there, they could get out quickly. There were submarine bases. The West's response, in 1955-57, was the Distant Early Warning Line, a great military radar network of fifty-eight sites across the top of Canada and Alaska. Some of them are now closed down, and some have been incorporated into a new network called the North Warning System.

OLLE: Also, the U.S. Air Force built the Thule Airbase in Greenland in the mid-1950s under an agreement with Denmark, which controls Greenland. Building it was a monumental project. The Thule base is located near Cape York, not far from where the Polar Eskimos live, and it is still very active. Five thousand American service people are stationed there. The Polar Eskimo population is about three hundred.

BOB: In the Cold War, air bases were also built in Alaska to face-off the Soviet Wrangel airbase.

I hadn't realized that Russia owns Wrangel Island. It is right off Alaska.

BOB: I think the Soviets kept their part of the Arctic closed because they wanted to give the impression to their own people that they were protected. In truth, there was very little there. Much of the work of the Soviet stations was scientific. But no one knew how much or how little military there was because no one was allowed in.

What was going on in Spitsbergen at that time?

BOB: The 1920 international treaty that gave Norway jurisdiction over Spitsbergen very largely held during the cold war. All countries had equal access, as they do now. Spitsbergen was not militarized. In Barentsburg, the Russian mining town, there was always a suspicion of Soviet activity. One fellow wrote about a Soviet military installation there, but what he had done was find an extremely well guarded blockhouse surrounded by barbed wire and he put one and one together and came up with twenty-three. It was in fact the explosives storage for the mines.

OLLE: The international treaty has held surprisingly well. During World War II there was a hefty debate about Spitsbergen in Moscow. Molotov, the cocktail guy, was arguing that they should attack the Germans there and occupy it. And then of course after the war they wouldn't have left. But there weren't many Germans there, and nothing happened. The Germans did destroy Longyearbyen and Barentsburg, but both towns had been evacuated soon after the Germans occupied Norway. Germany set up a few weather stations on Spitsbergen, and there was some resistance activity by Norwegians.

BOB: Russia and Norway have a history of fighting over the Arctic islands. Before the war, there was a race between them for possession of Franz Josef Land. The Russians won that because they had the better icebreakers, and were able to establish a permanent station, Tichaya. That was in 1929.

OLLE: There are still a couple of islands of uncertain ownership, Victoria Island, and White Island, where Salomon Andrée's remains were found. They are geographically part of Svalbard, but were not mentioned in the Spitsbergen Treaty of 1920, and Russia assumes them to be part of Franz Josef Land. In 1930, the Norwegian ship that found Andrée's remains possibly was on a secret mission to claim White Island and Victoria Island, but the find overshadowed that idea and nothing came of it.

Andrée crashed his balloon in 1897, thirty-three years before his remains were discovered. He was supposed to trek to Cape Flora if something bad happened, which it almost certainly was going to do.

BOB: There was a food depot on Cape Flora, and also Andrée was carrying silver dollars, gold rubles, and sovereigns, in case he landed in Alaska, Russia, or Canada. He had a tuxedo with him too.

OLLE: He had to be dressed for the welcoming party.

BOB: There was a possibility that he would meet the czar.

OLLE: He had planned that part thoroughly, but he didn't test his ballast ropes. He made some last-minute changes in how their segments were connected, and didn't test them.

BOB: One and a half turns of the balloon after takeoff, and he lost the bottom portion of his ropes. But he had the most modern communications possible—

Pigeons! And the poor pigeon that managed to fly off with a message was shot by a sailor on a whaleboat.

OLLE: At least someone on board realized this was an odd bird for the Arctic and the ship turned around and got the bird out of the sea. The message at that point was that all was well.

BOB: Andrée's flight is just beyond living memory. The change from using pigeons for communication to bouncing something off a satellite occurred within a lifetime.

Do you think Andrée died from fumes from his Primus stove? That was a new invention at the time. When their remains were found, it looked as if the men had had everything they needed for survival. One of the three had died and been buried, but the others weren't starving or injured.

BOB: Carbon monoxide, hypervitaminosis, and trichinosis are the three theories. It was probably a combination.

OLLE: I think the trichinosis idea is strong. They recovered a camera in 1930 and developed the film. Andrée was posing with a bear they had killed.

But Nansen ate bear meat all the time.

BOB: One badly infected bear could do it. Also hypervitaminosis, too much vitamin A from eating bear liver, is possible. Considering Andrée's naiveté, he probably thought the liver was delicious.

OLLE: Andrée had enthusiasm but not experience. Above all, I think he and his companion gave up. Cape Flora was about two hundred miles away, and apparently they were on the way there. But it was the end of August, and they saw no way out, facing the winter. Andrée was not an explorer. He was fired by nationalistic feelings at the turn of the century.

He wanted to be the first at the pole.

BOB: He was a balloon fanatic, and he was starting on the right track. The first people indubitably to see the pole did it from an airship, a dirigible.

That was the Norge *in 1926. Amundsen, Ellsworth, and Nobile.*

BOB: Roald Amundsen initiated the project, Lincoln Ellsworth basically financed it, and Umberto Nobile designed the airship and piloted it. When they got to the pole they threw down first the Norwegian flag, then the American flag, and then an enormous Italian flag. Weight was an issue. Amundsen and Ellsworth brought only the necessary clothes, but Nobile was resplendent in a uniform with gold braid when they took off their flying suits, exited the airship in Alaska, and were greeted by the press. Amundsen never forgave Nobile for that.

I can see how Amundsen would be upset. He and Ellsworth looked like passengers, not explorers.

BOB: The conceived plan of using a dirigible was Amundsen's, though. He and Ellsworth had tried the year before, in 1925, with heavier-than-air aircraft and crashed.

So they were the first ones to know what the pole looked like. There was no Open Polar Sea.

OLLE: That's right. And they didn't see land anywhere nearby.

BOB: The *Norge* passed over the pole and landed in Alaska. The Eskimos told of seeing a flying whale.

Didn't Nobile try to go back a second time?

BOB: Two years later Nobile went back in the *Italia.*

He wanted to do it again for Italy.

OLLE: Yes, and Mussolini was very keen on it.

BOB: The *Italia* reached the pole, and on the way back everything went wrong. It was too heavy and it iced up, various problems. It broke into two pieces when it crashed. One section with about a third of the crew in it vanished and was never seen again. The other section landed and the radio operator was eventually able to make contact. There were a variety of rescue attempts, ships setting out for the spot, small planes flying in, one of which crashed. There is an excellent picture of this small aircraft upside down at a 45-degree angle the wrong way and the airship survivors in the background.

OLLE: It was a Swedish pilot. He was rescued later with the crew of the *Italia*.

BOB: The first person rescued was flown out. It was Nobile with his lap dog. Mussolini didn't think he should have left his crew, and this is one thing that I agree with Mussolini about.

The others got out by ship, didn't they?

BOB: The Soviet Union had a powerful coal-fired icebreaker, the *Krassin*, and it rescued them. That convinced Stalin that Russia should build icebreakers that could go anywhere in the Arctic.

Wasn't the Krassin *built in Russia?*

BOB: No, it was built in Newcastle, Britain. Stalin started the building program for icebreakers after that.

Didn't Amundsen join the rescue effort? That was how he died, wasn't it?

BOB: It's not certain that he died, although that is what the record says. On the 18th of June, 1928, Amundsen took off in a seaplane, the *Latham*, with a crew of four, ostensibly to try to rescue Nobile. A close friend of his who had been with him at the South Pole described later how Amundsen went through his pockets and gave the friend a number of peculiar things: buttons, string, bits and pieces, and said, "Goodbye. I might not see you again." The *Latham* took off with a lot of supplies, collapsible kayaks, food, rifles, that sort of thing. She was in radio contact with the station on Bear Island, which is between Spitsbergen and Norway, and then she went off the air. A year previously a *Latham*-type aircraft, with an extra fuel tank in the nose, had broken a pontoon on landing and the crew had taken out the forward fuel tank and successfully put it on the strut to use as a pontoon. A fuel tank with the same sort of cuts was found later on the beach at Bear Island. So the *Latham* must have been damaged near Bear Island and remained in the sea there for the hours needed to do this work. I'm prepared to think that Amundsen might have abandoned the *Latham* at that time, taking a kayak, with the ostensible idea that he could continue the search and rescue that way. Subsequently, on Spitsbergen, a trapper's cabin was found to have panels in its construction that were identified as being parts of the *Latham*.

Oh!

BOB: So she crashed, probably on takeoff after the modification.

The great question is whether Amundsen was aboard. There's a theory that suggests he was on a beach on Bear Island. One of the search parties heading for the Nobile situation was a Newfoundland sealer chartered by Lincoln Ellsworth.

That's a coincidence!

BOB: Maybe not. It might have arrived by arrangement on a beach on Bear Island.

Why would Amundsen want to fake his own death?

BOB: He considered, not without reason, that he should be a national hero, and he'd run up debts all over the place. He was being hounded and dragged through the courts for debt collection. He regarded himself as underappreciated and persecuted. There are all sorts of theories about what happened to him in later life.

He might have started a new life in Newfoundland. Maybe people wouldn't have recognized him there.

BOB: It's a speculation.

OLLE: Or he might have died with the airplane crew, as the papers reported.

BOB: The plane crash wouldn't have been part of the plan. I suspect he had a cover story ready, and at some point he would have left in a kayak to proceed with the search. The aircraft crew would have flown back and reported where they left him. Money might have changed hands for this. He had food and a rifle and could have waited on the beach on Bear Island until the sealer arrived. It's a little like a World War II espionage novel, isn't it?

This speaks to Amundsen's character. From what I know, it doesn't seem to be in character that he would have gone to rescue Nobile.

BOB: Very much not in character. There was a big hate there, and Amundsen was good at hating.

OLLE: If the rescue couldn't benefit him, he probably wouldn't have attempted it. It's an interesting theory. I hadn't heard it before.

Amundsen was a genuine polar hero. He was the first to go through the Northwest Passage, and the first to get to the South Pole.

BOB: The Northwest Passage was very well done. The *Fram* expedition to the South Pole was something else. In 1909, when news was all over the place of first Cook and then Peary claiming to have reached the North Pole, Amundsen probably believed those claims. If he didn't believe one, he believed the other. He had arranged to borrow Nansen's ship to do essentially the same expedition that Nansen did, but to start considerably farther east so he would drift considerably closer to the pole. With that plan, he might have been able to make it to the pole. He sold the expedition to backers on his plan for scientific research, continuing the bathymetry that Nansen did very well, proving the depth of the ocean up there. Amundsen told Nansen that was what he was going to do. He told the new king of Norway and got his support. There were public notices, press reports, articles in scientific journals. The crew believed they were going north. But Amundsen was deceiving everyone. He was intending to go to the South Pole.

OLLE: Maybe it is too strong to use the word *deceiving*? In the beginning he was planning to do exactly what he said with the *Fram*.

Did he tell Nansen that he changed his mind or ask permission?

OLLE: No, he didn't.

BOB: He changed his plan about a year before he left. Preparations were being made for him in the south, but he didn't tell anybody. He was deceiving, or at least misleading, everybody involved.

The reason for the secrecy and deception was Robert F. Scott?

BOB: Scott had announced his expedition to the South Pole in 1908 and was getting prepared. Amundsen made his decision to go there a year later and he left Christiania [Oslo] on August 9, 1910, eight weeks after Scott's ship had left England. Amundsen's first stop was the island of Madeira, between Portugal and Africa, on September 6. That was when he announced to the crew what was happening.

He did warn Scott, didn't he, by sending him a telegram?

BOB: "Beg inform you proceeding Antarctica. Amundsen." That was actually sent by his brother, dispatched from Oslo in October, when Amundsen knew he would be beyond recall.

Where was Scott when he received it?

BOB: In Melbourne, Australia. Amundsen was well under way, and Scott had no idea where he was and neither did anyone else. Scott's backers weren't worried; they thought it would take Amundsen months to get there. "The *Fram* has no more sailing qualities than a haystack," one of them said. But Amundsen arrived at the Ross Ice Shelf in Antarctica on January 14, only ten days after Scott. Scott's expedition had many objectives, including geophysical observation and mapping, although the South Pole was the objective of greatest public interest. There is a version of this story that shows Amundsen as being very efficient and getting to the South Pole with no trouble at all and back in ninety-nine days, and Scott as the bumbling idiot who killed everyone. That version is biased, I believe. I think it is right to say it was a race only insofar as Amundsen was racing. Scott's expedition was doing side-valley mapping, scientific data gathering—

So you don't think Scott was racing?

BOB: He certainly wanted to get there first, no doubt about that, but it was a slow, careful, scientific expedition. Amundsen was racing; Scott was exploring. They both wanted to get there first.

But Amundsen clearly was more efficient.

BOB: He didn't get off to an efficient start. The first attempt was a false one. The weather was abominable. They were in trouble, and retreated in disorder. Among the last men to make it back to camp was Hjalmar Johansen.

Nansen's Johansen? Was he on Amundsen's expedition?

BOB: Yes. He was the most experienced polar explorer in the group, even more experienced than Amundsen. He rescued the stragglers in that false start, and when they returned he found Amundsen had had a bath and was eating a meal comfortably in the base hut, having abandoned several of his men in the blizzard. Johansen expressed an opinion that was quite critical. Amundsen never spoke to him subsequently.

OLLE: Amundsen excluded him after that. He sent Johansen on a side exploration. He didn't take him to the pole.

BOB: Amundsen's hate was so strong and Johansen's character so different that Johansen committed suicide shortly after that expedition. He shot himself in a cheap hotel behind the railroad station in Oslo.

Oh, poor Johansen! He was such a resourceful person when he was with Nansen.

BOB: Amundsen's idea of commanding men was less than ideal. Scott's expedition went on in an organized fashion. You know the story. They arrived at the South Pole to find the Norwegian flag and a note from Amundsen. There are many reasons why they died on the return. The extremely severe weather was one.

I've heard that Scott was ill, and the two of his men who were still alive at that point could possibly have made it back if they had been willing to leave him. But they were honorable and died together.

BOB: With those temperatures, they might not have made it back in any case. There are so many might-have-beens. Sometimes you're lucky, sometimes not.

It is probably because of Amundsen's deception that the permanent station at the South Pole carries Scott's name as well as his. The Amundsen-Scott station. History makes judgments about behavior as well as about accomplishment. Speaking of that, could we talk a little bit about Peary?

BOB: I'm not at all happy about Peary and the North Pole.

He had in previous instances falsified data. One of his maps resulted in the death of an explorer who followed the map a few years later.

Lots of people made poor maps, saw mirages, whatever.

BOB: Yes, but when you haven't got definite information, you use little things like "existence dubious" or "position doubtful."

Peary was never doubtful about anything. That's a failing, but it doesn't mean he didn't get to the North Pole.

BOB: No. But his previous Farthest North can't be sustained. The records are just confabulated. On the claimed North Pole circumstance, his diary was usually fairly well kept, but in this case it had blank pages and paper inserted. It should be continuous, especially since this is the only evidence there is. He sent back the only fellow who could competently back up his navigation, and at that moment his distances started doubling.

That's suspicious. But Henson was there. He was a witness, and perhaps Peary was out of it by that time because of his difficulty walking without toes. Henson said he and the Eskimos knew they were at the pole because of the position of the sun and their experiences of distances in the Arctic. That's the argument I read.

OLLE: It's pretty weak.

BOB: Henson was a practical and knowledgeable fellow, but accuracy of navigation in the situation would require use of instruments. And although Peary took latitude readings, he didn't calculate longitude. There was a case made that longitude calculation is unnecessary, saying Amundsen didn't do it at the South Pole, but that has a particular problem. The person who claimed that had merely read Amundsen's published account in English. If you read the Norwegian version you will see that he did the longitudes. He didn't consider it of enough importance to the general reader to put in the English version.

So you really need to do longitudes?

BOB: Yes—the Navigation Foundation's interpretation aside.

That foundation analyzed Peary's photos and said they could tell from the angles of the sun that they were made within five miles of the pole.

BOB: The criticism of the Navigation Foundation's findings came from the U.S. Naval Institute of Annapolis. The institute held a symposium—I believe in 1994—dealing with the North Pole question. Various persons addressed it and the consensus reported in the institute's journal was unfavorable to Peary. Unfortunately, for reasons I don't know, the results of that symposium were only published in summary. But they came out against Peary for many reasons: inadequate documentation, the distances doubling—

The distance-time relationship is damaging, except that in April 2000 two men, Paul Landry and Paul Crowly, made the trip in close to Peary's time.

BOB: With modern equipment. The type of equipment Peary used at the beginning of the century can't be compared with the modern, light, low-friction sledges of our time.

But no one was breaking the trail for them.

BOB: Peary didn't have a trailbreaker at the time that his distances doubled. And he couldn't have used the same trail on the way back because the ice drifts. He wouldn't have ended up at his ship if he did that.

The incendiary thing about this is that Henson was black, and it seems to be racially biased to maintain that he could not be a witness.

BOB: He was a witness to what was done, and I should think he believed Peary so he thought they were at the pole.

OLLE: He wanted to be at the pole. He and the Eskimos thought they were there. And Peary set up his instruments and told them they were. Of course, Henson believed Peary. He respected Peary. He never doubted that they had been at the pole. But Peary still might have lied about it.

BOB: I don't believe Peary. The kindest thing you can say is "not proven." But consider this: Amundsen probably believed Peary, and possibly believed Cook, and that affected his decision to go to the South Pole.

If he had kept to his original plan, Amundsen might now be celebrated as the discoverer of the North Pole. In the route that he had planned, he would have been taking advantage of information about the drift of the sea ice discovered by the Fram. *I was interested to read that Cook used that information. Sverdrup, the* Fram's *captain, helped design his route to the pole. Do you think there was any possibility that Cook was successful?*

BOB: Peary's documentation is inconsistent, but Cook's is nonexistent. He stored his papers on the way back, and they were lost—some say by foul play on the part of Peary henchmen. Cook had falsified other claims in the past. Cook and Peary probably both lied—I think that word is reasonable. If they had not done so,

Amundsen would have continued with his North Pole plan and, considering his determination and the course he had planned, he'd very likely have made it. Scott's expedition going to the South Pole would have continued—it was planned before any of this happened—and they would have made it, as they did. And the morale factor might have kicked in, the excitement of having been first versus the disappointment of making it there to find Amundsen's note. Morale plays a large part. It could perhaps have brought Scott back. It's a terrible armchair speculation, isn't it?

Was Peary even close to the pole? When he took the readings and realized they weren't there, although Henson and the Eskimos thought they were, why didn't he just tell them to push on?

BOB: I suspect they were a degree away. Seventy to eighty miles. Too far.

OLLE: Back and forth doubles it. By the way, the book Peary wrote about the pole was ghostwritten, and the ghostwriter took some of it from journals of other people on other trips because Peary didn't cooperate well with her. If you were absolutely sure that you did it, you would reach out for that fame in good conscience, wouldn't you, and be open about it?

Yes, that makes sense.

BOB: There's nothing wrong with using a ghostwriter. Very few explorers were gifted writers like Nansen. But Peary's relationship with the ghostwriter wasn't forthcoming, and that is odd. A somewhat parallel situation happened more recently. Ralph Plaistead's trip by snowmobile in 1968 is listed in some of the literature as the first surface trip to the North Pole. He was at the North Pole, no doubt about it, but there's a bit in the middle where the snowmobile couldn't get over a lead and his Twin

Otter picked him up and dropped him on the other side. How far on the other side is the question. Plaistead has declined to write anything about this expedition. He went twice. His first trip is described in a detailed book that tells how he abandoned the effort. The book came out first in the United States, then in Britain. At the end of the British edition there is a paragraph that says he repeated the trip the next year and successfully reached the pole. Plaistead has never published any details. The problem is that his aircraft dropped him much farther along than the end of the lead, possibly almost a degree farther. As a result of the Cold War ending, information from the DEW Line stations is becoming available, and we now have reliable reports of everything flying in the Arctic. There are even reports of geese that someone thought might be a Russian presence. Plaistead's aircraft operated in radio silence, but we now have credible information where the aircraft landed and took off and landed again. And consequently we conjecture why Plaistead has never published an account.

Wally Herbert was the first to reach the North Pole by surface, wasn't he? He walked completely across to the other side.

BOB: Yes. That was in 1968-69. He's still alive, living in Scotland. Wally Herbert started his career working in Antarctica in the British Antarctic survey. Sir Vivian Fuchs had done a trans-Antarctic expedition, and Wally wanted to do the same in the Arctic. They knew each other. Fuchs had revived the idea behind Ernest Shackleton's failed trans-Antarctic expedition of 1914-16 and, in cooperation with Sir Edmund Hillary, he successfully crossed the continent of Antarctica in 1958 using tracked vehicles. Wally was a dog man. He went by dog sledge from Barrow, Alaska, to Svalbard with three companions and was supported by airdrops, parachute only, no landings. They left Barrow late in the year when the ice was solid, went as far north as they could and wintered on the ice, drifting quite a long way. When the light returned they began sledging again, reached the pole in April, and continued on to Svalbard. They had trouble reaching Svalbard because the ice was breaking up, but they did reach the exposed rocks at the tip of it. And then they had done it—Alaska to Svalbard, over the top on foot. They were in radio contact all the way and the navigation was correct and checked. It is very strongly probable that they were the first persons to go by surface to the North Pole.

That was sixty years after Peary's trip, and twenty-one years after the twenty-four Russians—the ones who most likely were the first to set foot on the pole—had arrived by plane. Perhaps it was actually impossible to reach the North Pole the way Peary and Nansen tried to do it, with dogs, without communication, carrying everything, no drops, no air support. Maybe if Amundsen had tried, he wouldn't have been able to do it either. Do you think it was possible to get to the North Pole in Peary's time?

BOB: If everything had worked extremely well, it is not inconceivable. But no one was able to do it.

The drift makes the situation very different from the South Pole.

BOB: The beauty of the South Pole is that thirty-three days after Amundsen left, Scott arrived and they backed each other up. Scott's calculations were confirmed by Amundsen, and Amundsen's by Scott. Nothing drifted. There's no fuss about the South Pole but the question of who was first at the North Pole is still an issue.

And there's a permanent station at the South Pole. That would be impossible at the North Pole.

BOB: Here's a hobby horse of mine: I'm very keen to distinguish between explorers and adventurers. Exploration is geographical research—finding new things. Adventurers use a map and go into places that someone else has explored. Lots of adventurers call themselves explorers. I don't like this. With modern communications, if something happens you can get a helicopter in to get you out. But some modern adventurers get themselves into dangerous situations and they risk not only their own necks but other people's. There's nothing wrong with adventuring so long as you don't go beyond the limits of safety or at least the limits of sanity.

Are there any explorer things left to do up there?

BOB: The new areas are the ones newly open, the Russian Arctic. Many of those areas are not mapped in detail, and good maps are needed, especially for the study of climate change.

Scientists are using everything they can get.

BOB: Mapping is valid and useful exploration, with adventure thrown in.

OLLE: Adventuring is valid too. I have a friend who has adventured out there—Liv Arnesen, who was the first woman to ski solo and unsupported to the South Pole. She skied across the Greenland ice cap too.

Does she think of herself as an adventurer?

OLLE: Oh, she does. This is a highly personal thing, and she just has to do it.

BOB: In the summer of 2003, the *Yamal* wasn't able to reach the North Pole in the time allowed.

I heard that!

BOB: She made it three times subsequently in 2003, but the first trip couldn't be completed.

Were the passengers upset about it?

BOB: Many of them were not. Apart from reaching the pole, there is significance in the journey: bashing through the ice, the atomic power, unlimited electricity, heat, how the whole thing works by steam. Great amounts of ice being pushed out. When you're sitting in your window, craning your neck out—

I remember. It's mesmerizing. It is really about unremitting power. Bob, I noticed you went swimming at the pole, jumping in through the ice. Did you do that on all of your eighteen trips?

BOB: The one time I didn't there was a nasty cough running around the ship. The Russians like to do it. Throw down some vodka, jump in, and then go to the sauna. It is one of the things you do. You've got this tremendous depth of water, almost three miles, below you. The last time I jumped in, I dove and I was able to see beneath the ice for a fraction of a second, very dark with blue streaks coming through. I turned around and there was the other view, the rather shiny propellers, the dark rudder, and the bottom of the ship. A quick look as I was coming to the surface. The propellers move very slowly even when the ship is stopped, and they keep the swimming hole clear. One time I was amazed to see a ringed seal poke its head out, more or less after people had stopped jumping in. There's always a question as to whether seals follow the ship. Did you notice those little black fish in our wake, sometimes jumping up on the ice?

Yes. I saw one on the ice. That would encourage a seal to follow. Animals normally aren't ever at the pole, are they?

BOB: We've seen bear and fox prints there, but it is likely they were made far away in that piece of ice before it drifted to the pole.

Do you think the polar bears are doomed? Will they become extinct?

OLLE: There is a significant effect on them from global warming, since the ice builds up later and later each year.

BOB: They are very strong and intelligent animals.

OLLE: But very vulnerable because they are so adapted to this environment that there is only a small niche for them. It's true that there is a lot of strength and intelligence in these animals, but once you take the ice out from under their feet—

So you think they're in trouble.

OLLE: For the hunt, they are dependent on the sea ice.

BOB: We don't need to think of them becoming extinct, but they might become zoo specimens only. They do breed in zoos. It is a refuge, but a sad way to save them for the children.

OLLE: If it gets cold again, the people can release them. Provided people are still around.

BOB: With everything freezing in a new ice age, people will not be very well adapted. They might not want to let *them* out!

CHAPTER EIGHT

SPITSBERGEN

Journey: Spitsbergen

In a remote harbor called Signehamna on the island of Spitsbergen, about seven hundred miles from the North Pole, passengers from a Norwegian icebreaker surrounded a few pieces of rusted metal. Some of us stood; some sat on the ground. It was the summer following my trip to the North Pole, and I had returned to focus for seven days on Spitsbergen, an island in the Svalbard archipelago. Our young Norwegian leader leaned back on his hands, a rifle across his knees in case a polar bear should appear. "In this place on June 23, 1943, exactly sixty years ago today," he began—and we settled down for a story. Midway through World War II, a German weather station had been established here, manned by four men who lived undetected in this spot for eighteen months, frozen in for the winter and resupplied in June by submarine. About a hundred miles away, the island's two main towns, Russian Barentsburg and Norwegian Longyearbyen, had been evacuated of their populations, leaving only a 152-man Norwegian garrison in Longyearbyen. With the ice breaking up in early summer, a small party from there set off in search of the German station, discovered it, and found it unoccupied but full of supplies.

Four Norwegians stayed hidden near the station while one man took the small boat to get reinforcements. Soon a lone German appeared carrying a camera and carefully holding some plants. The Norwegians confronted him; he fled. They heard a shot from behind a large piece of ice; he had killed himself. In the weather station, the Norwegians found his botanical notes and preserved plant specimens. The film in his camera, developed later, yielded pictures of plants and birds.

The dead man's three German companions had been in the station when the Norwegian boat had approached and had radioed for help before hiding themselves outside. A German submarine responded, arriving at about the same time as the returning Norwegian boat with its driver and two reinforcements. There was a gun battle, and one of the Norwegians was killed. The other two hid behind an ice floe in the freezing water while the three remaining Germans from the weather station raced to the submarine, jumping from floe to floe. The submarine took them on board and quickly dived. One German and one Norwegian were dead. The incident is known as the Battle of Signehamna.

On September 8, 1943, just before the ice isolated Spitsbergen for the winter, the German high command sent a battleship and nine destroyers there in retaliation for the Battle of Signehamna. Barentsburg and Longyearbyen were demolished. Six of the 151 Norwegians there were killed, 41 were taken prisoner, and the rest withdrew to the mountains. The next day, September 9, the German fleet returned to its base in occupied Norway, without encountering the British fleet sent to intercept it. Three other German weather stations in the Svalbard archipelago continued to operate. Two of them were evacuated in September 1945, months after the war was over.

As we crossed the ice-scarred land between the former weather station and the harbor where our rubber dinghy was pulled up on a beach of gravel and ice, I wondered where the Germans had found places to hide themselves. My mind struggled to understand why this immense treeless landscape seemed familiar. Never before have I been in a place like this, I thought, and then realized I had seen something like it in dreams. The space was so large in relation to myself that I found an exhilaration in it. The only visible objects were the people in our small group, our rubber boat pulled up on shore, and—in the sea—our ship, the *Polar Star,* diminutive in the distance.

Compared with the Russian *Yamal*, a great Cossack of a ship, the Norwegian *Polar Star* is a ballerina. She is strong. She can break ice, but only to a point. She is a tourist ship that divides her time between the Arctic and the Antarctic. Her territory as she makes her way up the coast of Spitsbergen is very different from the *Yamal*'s—despite her name, she has no ambition to reach the pole. On the *Yamal*'s route, people are never encountered, but the *Polar Star* finds them here and there. She occasionally shares a fjord with another ship, and she visits two towns. In addition, we saw the homes of three isolated souls.

One of those homes was a sailboat, frozen into the still-solid ice of a sheltered cove. A well-known craftswoman lives there, our leader told us, with her boyfriend. At the end of each summer, she sails her boat here and parks it in a spot she likes. Then the couple waits for the ice to form around the boat; once that happens, they can walk across the ice to land, where they can ski and snowshoe. The ship has no visitors except polar bears, foxes, and reindeer. The woman spends the winter making intricate silver jewelry, and when summer comes and the ice thaws, she sails back into Longyearbyen where she sells some of her winter's work to the shops there and sends the remainder out to galleries and shops in cities farther afield.

The second home that we saw was clearly a home, a comfortable-looking wood cabin with a chimney puffing smoke. It was surrounded by a small outbuilding, a pile of wood as tall as the outbuilding, and a towerlike scaffolding with seal meat drying out of reach of bears. As we passed by it in our dinghies (we did not plan to land), I was surprised to hear a crackle in the walkie-talkie carried by our guide. "Little rubber boats," said a disembodied voice.

"Yes," our guide answered. "I am receiving you."

"Come a little closer," said the voice, "and I will bring my toilet bucket out to empty over you."

"Well, I guess he wouldn't be living out here if he liked company," our guide said to us, and then had a short conciliatory conversation in which he learned that another group of rubber boats had been there the day before and scared the nesting ducks off their eggs. All around his cabin the man has built boxes where eider ducks nest. He protects the ducks from foxes, and they cooperate with him: when he approaches, the female moves over in her nest so he can collect down from it. He makes a living selling the highest quality eider down for jackets and pillows.

On our week-long trip, there was beauty everywhere, but perhaps the most beautiful moment was in Magdelenefjord when unusual steady sunshine illuminated the glaciers slung between mountains that illustrate the island's name—Spitsbergen means "pointed mountains." For most of the trip, the sun was intermittent. It came in and out of clouds when we docked at the town of Ny-Ålesund on June 21. Norway, Germany, Japan, Italy, France, and the United Kingdom have permanent research stations here—we were told to stay on the main road and be careful not to disturb instrument markers. Ny-Ålesund looks like a newly minted New England village. The only hint of its history as a coal mining town is the presence of an abandoned locomotive with open boxcars. Science has replaced mining as the primary activity here; nearly every house has near it a scientific instrument of some kind—an insulated box, an antenna, a weather ball, a reflective panel. As our group crowded into the store to buy souvenirs and mail postcards from the northernmost post office in the world, a young woman in blue jeans waited in line at the cash register with a tube of toothpaste in her hand.

June 21 was Midsummer Day, the summer solstice, the day on which the sun is at its highest point in the sky, and the scientists of Ny-Ålesund were celebrating the holiday. I thought of Nansen and Johansen marking Midsummer Day on June 24, 1895, "with great festivities." We heard rock music and saw young people below the road near the shore, holding drinks, standing in groups. When the recorded music stopped, there was singing, at first just a few voices carrying a folk tune in the cold air. The tune grew stronger and people raised their glasses to the sun. For a moment, it came out from behind the clouds.

As we straggled down the road on our way back to the *Polar Star*, I paused to look at a barnlike house with a small antique-looking tower behind it. The tower was not inconsistent with other pieces of scientific equipment nearby, but it did not really fit. Olle Carlsson, the lecturer on the *Polar Star,* caught up with me. "It's from 1926," he said. "The *Norge* was tethered there before it flew over the pole. And, later, the *Italia*, when it tried to do the same and crashed."

"Did Salomon Andrée bring his hydrogen balloon here?" I asked.

"No, he started out at the northern tip of Spitsbergen, closer to the pole. That was in July 1897. There were a lot of tourists in Spitsbergen in 1897. They came up here by ship for Andrée's launch. Even the King and Queen of Sweden came," he replied. "And did you know that Andrée had been up here the previous summer, and he boarded the *Fram*? It stopped at Spitsbergen after it had freed itself from the ice and was on the way home."

Andrée was in the inner circle of explorers (scientists of a hundred years ago). I tried to imagine how he must have felt as he went aboard the *Fram* and talked with Sverdrup and the other men who were returning in 1896 from three years drifting near the North Pole locked in ice. A year later, Andrée crashed his balloon in the ice and he and his two companions lost their lives. "Shall we be thought mad or will our example be followed?" he wrote in his diary. "I cannot deny that all three of us are dominated by a feeling of pride. We think we can well face death, having done what we have done. Isn't it all, perhaps, the expression of an extremely strong sense of individuality which cannot bear the thought of living and dying like a man in the ranks, forgotten by coming generations? Is this ambition?"

As the *Polar Star* continued on her way through fjords lined with the compressed snow that is glacial ice, Andrée remained in my mind. This is where he died, I thought, not exactly in this spot, but in a spot like this—the archipelago of Svalbard is 60 percent covered by glaciers. Unlike sea ice, glacial ice does not support life; as I searched it with my binoculars, nothing moved but an occasional bird that flew past the lenses in a blur.

Only one species of bird, the Svalbard ptarmigan, remains in these islands year-round, but there are birds in abundance in summer. They come here to have their young, and the steep cliffs where they nest to be safe from foxes are layered with green under bare ledges above. With our binoculars we picked out glaucous gulls, dovekies, little auks, and thick-billed murres (Brünnich's guillemots). The elegant, large murres against gray cliffs streaked with red and yellow minerals like rays of light and scumbled with whiteness like clouds reminded me of angels painted on a Renaissance ceiling. "Why do the birds only sit on the white rocks?" a passenger asked. The white rocks, lower down, have turned green with vegetation that spreads to more accessible places and is the birds' gift to this harsh place.

The largest beneficiary of vegetation fertilized by the birds is the Svalbard reindeer, which has come back from near extinction since Norwegian law protected it in 1925. If Santa Claus lives at the North Pole, this must be his reindeer, but it is hard to imagine such a sturdy, short-legged animal flying through the sky. "It looks like a '49 Buick," a passenger remarked.

We saw two groups of walruses, one on sea ice, the other on the shore. We got close enough to the ones onshore to experience their powerful smell, but stayed well back, knowing of their unpredictability and also that they will abandon traditional haul-out spots after interference by tourists. A large male gloriously stretched out on the beach, but most of the animals lay touching one another. They are thigmotactic, Olle explained—liking body contact. He pointed out one with a tag, visible through binoculars, on one of its flippers. Walruses were hunted for their ivory here until 1952 when Norway enacted a law to protect them; by that time they had become difficult to find. Now scientists estimate that there are about two thousand individuals in the Svalbard area, and tagging has shown that some have moved here from Franz Josef Land and east Greenland.

Our most exciting wildlife sighting was a pod of beluga whales, right underneath us at the moment the ship passed from clear water into loose floes of ice. *Beluga* is Russian for "white" and that is the color of these whales, which look like long pieces of ice moving fast, barely under the water. Even to those of us standing on the deck, carefully observant, they were invisible until the word spread among us where they were and what to look for. We strained to hear their clicking, squealing sounds. Beluga whales are small, about fifteen feet long, and weigh about a ton each. They travel in groups and talk to one another with a large vocabulary, swimming often under thin ice and using their flat heads to lift or break the floes so they can breathe. Because they swim so near the surface, their sounds can be heard above the water—"sea canaries" was what the whalers called them. Their almost transparent blubber was in demand two centuries ago to make especially clean-burning oil for lamps and is still occasionally used for that purpose by the Polar Eskimos.

The word *train* in the train oil that darkened Nansen's skin and clothing comes from a mid-sixteenth-century Dutch word for "tear," and in the seventeenth and eighteenth centuries train oil, the oil rendered from marine animals, was considered the best oil for lubrication and lighting in Europe and America (other oils used for those purposes were from vegetable products like olives and rapeseed). Performances of Shakespeare's plays in the 1570s were lighted by candles, with wick trimmers constantly running back and forth across the stage, but a hundred years later, footlights and sidelights of train oil were common in the theater, and train oil lamps were in the homes and on the streets of the great cities of the Western world. Much of that oil came from Spitsbergen.

William Barents, who discovered Spitsbergen in 1596, saw whales there, and Henry Hudson, in the summer of 1607, reported that hundreds of enormous bowheads crowded the relatively warm fjords, a calving spot for females. Bowhead whales weigh between fifty and one hundred tons, and an individual can live two hundred years. They feed on surface plankton and have baleen—or what was called whalebone—a network of fringed plates of flexible material, hanging from their upper jaws. Whalebone was in demand for women's corsets, and this was a secondary market to the huge one for oil.

Approximately twenty-four thousand bowhead whales were killed in Svalbard between 1611 and 1670. On Amsterdam Island, northwest of the large island of Spitsbergen, there was a Dutch whaling town called Smeerenburg (Blubbertown) where fifteen whale ships would anchor each summer. Two hundred men slept ashore and worked the cauldrons where blubber was rendered into oil. By 1670, Spitsbergen had no whales and Smeerenburg was a ghost town. Friedrich Martins, a surgeon on a whaler, described visiting it in 1671. He saw a thousand human corpses, evidence of the difficult life there, on nearby Deadman's Island, "frost knawing forever on [the] bleaching relics, yet eternally preserving them." In 2002, Olle told us, there was excitement in Longyearbyen because a bowhead whale had been sighted off Spitsbergen, the first anyone could remember. The entire world population of bowhead whales today is around eight thousand five hundred. Bowheads, with other endangered whales, have been protected since 1946 by the International Whaling Commission, but commercial whaling had largely stopped almost a hundred years earlier because whales had become scarce and another product had risen to take their place. It can be argued that the whales were saved by petroleum.

The petroleum age, which may now be close to its end, had its beginning in 1858 when the first oil well in the United States was drilled in Titusville, Pennsylvania. This was not the first production of oil for fuel, but it started the rapid commercialization of it. In the United States, until then, oil had been seen mostly as an undesirable by-product of drilling salt wells, but oil wells had been drilled in China as early as AD 347, and there had been an oil industry in medieval Persia. A Canadian geologist, Dr. Abraham Gesner, distilled kerosene from oil in 1849, and in 1857 a kerosene lamp, the forerunner of the Primus stove, began to force whale oil lamps from the market. A modern-style oil well drilled by a Russian in Baku, Azerbaijan, the area of the earlier Persian wells, preceded the Pennsylvania well by eleven years. Nevertheless, it was after oil was exploited in the United States that automobiles were developed to use it, electricity was generated by it, and many of our other necessities of life became dependent on it.

Now, oil is becoming scarce and two-thirds of its proven reserves are in Saudi Arabia and four other Middle Eastern countries. Perhaps the United States (or some other country) will find another product to develop, one that does not require the burning of fossil fuels. A product like that could save many more species than whales—perhaps it would save even ourselves. Is it too much to ask that our resources be directed to that end rather than to extracting whatever oil might be available in the Arctic?

In the late 1970s, a group of scientists studying polar bears became concerned about the possible effects on them of an oil spill and deliberately enticed three bears to enter a pool onto which they had poured oil. The bears had no experience with oil and were not suspicious of the pool. When they came out, they began to shiver; the oil had reduced their natural insulation. They licked themselves just as they would have licked seal oil from their fur. Two of them died. The third was quickly cleaned and now lives in a zoo. The press, when it discovered the experiment, was outraged, and the scientists were surprised to find the outrage directed at them, with no mention of what they had learned.

The relationship I had developed with the polar bear that visited the *Yamal* was so clear and strong that all through my trip on the *Polar Star* I searched eagerly for a bear. It was late June, the right time of year for mothers to be leaving their dens with their cubs. When the ship moved into the pack ice, there were tracks. The bears were there, if only we could see them. Finally, someone saw one, a yellow spot he said, pointing to the shore.

My binoculars helped me pick it out. The bear was alone, and moving slowly, arthritically, its fur strongly yellow, often a sign of age. I watched it for a long time. The next day there was a mother with a cub, also far away, picking their way along the shore, up and down hillocks, the mother waiting, looking back, if the cub fell behind. And later another mother, this time with two cubs playing like puppies. They all stayed on shore, too far away to photograph, but the ice in front of us was so solid that the *Polar Star* could not proceed. For sure, this year, the bears would walk out on the ice and find the seals they need.

My son and his wife and daughter accompanied me on this trip, and, before catching the plane for the first leg of our journey home, we stayed for a day in Longyearbyen. I photographed the university, a single long building that crouches animal-like on the tundra. The one hundred students there are all studying Arctic subjects. The town, entirely rebuilt since World War II, is workaday, with many same-size houses looking like pieces in a Monopoly game. After a time, the town's austerity—a consequence of the lack of trees—began to seem like spaciousness to me. Snowmobiles were parked everywhere, some with covers that made them look like clogs. On Spitsbergen, roads do not link one town to another. Svalbard, overall, has an area of about twenty-four thousand square miles (about the size of West Virginia), and there are only four inhabited towns. All four towns have air strips, but the population does not use air travel extensively. People travel the twenty-five miles from Longyearbyen to Barentsburg by foot or by ship in summer or snowmobile in winter. Sveagruva, a hundred miles by sea from Longyearbyen, is a small mining town that ships coal and minerals to Europe. Ny-Ålesund, seventy-five miles up the coast, is reached by ship. In Longyearbyen, the network of gravel streets within the town converges into one road as houses thin out. We took a taxi as far as we could go. The road ends in two radio telescopes and a dog kennel, the new Arctic and the old, side by side.

POLAR STAR

A Conversation with Camille Seaman and Lisa Ström

On my trip on the Polar Star *and second visit to Spitsbergen, the summer after my North Pole trip, I was accompanied by my son, Kevin Parker, his wife, Camille Seaman, and their daughter, Tala Powis Parker, three years old at the time. The family lives in Berkeley, California, where Kevin owns a business. Camille Seaman, thirty-three years old in 2003, is a graduate of the State University of New York at Purchase, where she majored in photography. In Berkeley, she is a website designer. Lisa Ström, at the time of this conversation, had been living year-round in Longyearbyen, Svalbard, for two years, and was twenty-five years old and a student in* UNIS *(the University Courses on Svalbard). In addition to her studies, she is a tourist guide, working at the dog kennel at the end of the road in Longyearbyen. Her permanent home is in Sweden.*

CAMILLE: I bet we listen to the same music. What's your favorite group?

LISA: Smashing Pumpkins.

CAMILLE: Out of Seattle. My favorite right now is Radiohead. It's the same genre. Smashing Pumpkins and Radiohead are both bands that sort of address the anxiety of the modern world, as we know it. An anxiety about what to do with your life in this world. You've chosen to be here, in this community, which seems to be very young.

LISA: Yes.

CAMILLE: Just looking around downtown, a lot of people seem

Lisa Ström

Camille Seaman

to be young and quite hip. They obviously feel strongly about their own identity. That's what the music is about: making your own definition of what your life should be and not having to apply some social thing to it. I was pretty blown away by this community and the other one we were in, Ny-Ålesund.

LISA: They're very different. Here the community is like the mainland but smaller scale. At Ny-Ålesund there are only researchers. There are no schools, no children, just research people staying there. There are more people there in summer, about one hundred people. In winter maybe only twenty.

How many people live here in Longyearbyen year-round? A lot of them are researchers, too, aren't they?

LISA: About nineteen hundred. There are many researchers but also miners and other workers. There is still one functioning coal mine. The university has about one hundred students. You have here all the things you find in other communities: children's schools, hospital, movie house, swimming pool, stores, cafés, Internet.

Would you stay here if you didn't have the Internet?

LISA: If everything were the same as now but just without the Internet, I would stay. We have telephones. But the Internet is more immediate.

CAMILLE: How did you find out about Svalbard, to decide to go to the university here?

LISA: It was the Internet. When I finished gymnasium, high

school, in Sweden at the age of eighteen, I wanted to continue studying, and I was interested in whales. I had never heard anything about Svalbard. It was by chance that I printed a page while searching on the Internet, the last page of something about whales. It was a discussion on ice. I thought, what is this? There was mention of a university on Svalbard. It had four courses of study: Arctic biology, Arctic technology, Arctic geophysics, and Arctic geology.

Which one did you take?

LISA: Technology. I took engineering in Sweden so I could come into the technology course here. I studied in Sweden for three years, took one year off, and then came here.

CAMILLE: And what is the coursework like here?

LISA: It includes a lot about pollution. A lot of pollution comes up here in the atmosphere. And also it includes studying ice and permafrost, their interaction with buildings and platforms. Quite a bit of that has to do with exploring for oil in the Arctic. There's a lot of interest in the possibility of finding oil up here, and we studied how ice will affect construction and how oil accidents will affect the Arctic. It is not known very well how oil will degrade or spread here, or how effective oil cleanup can be made in ice.

A friend of mine who works at the American Museum of Natural History told me that oil companies often pay for Arctic science. He says it's good science. The oil companies want to find out all they can about the Arctic because this is the next oil frontier.

LISA: I know one PhD student whose work is paid for by an oil company. She's actually working with plankton, looking at the lowest form of life in the food web, to see how it will be affected.

CAMILLE: That's good. At least they're concerned.

Camille, you had an interest in the Arctic even before this trip, didn't you?

CAMILLE: I have to be honest. I didn't know Svalbard existed until you told me about it. I never even thought to look that far. I thought Greenland and part of Canada were the Arctic, and maybe some parts of Russia. And Alaska, of course. In the United States, we have Alaska. I was booked on an Alaska Airlines flight from San Francisco to Los Angeles and the airline had oversold the flight. They said, "If anyone will give up their seat on this flight we will give you a roundtrip ticket anywhere we fly." I said, "I'll do it." I had always wanted to see Alaska.

LISA: A free ticket to Alaska!

CAMILLE: I arranged to go as far north as I could to a place called Kotzebue. It's just inside the Arctic Circle, below the Bering Strait—not as far north as Svalbard, but pretty far north. I thought about going to Nome, which was part of the gold rush, but I wanted to see an Eskimo town. Also, there was a strange movie partly set in Kotzebue called *Eye of the Beholder*. KD Laing was in it, and a lot of Eskimos. It was weird—artsy. The town seemed very strange.

Was it very strange?

CAMILLE: Oh, yes. Even the plane ride was strange. I changed planes in Anchorage and there was this huge stuffed polar bear standing in the airport. I thought, "Whoa, where am I going?" The plane from Anchorage to Kotzebue was a small jet, a 737, but inside it was divided in half. The forward part was all for cargo, and the back part had seats for about twelve people. All these Eskimos were getting on in their parkas with huge ice chests to stow in the cargo part. I went in April, and it was still very cold. The sun only set for about two hours; it would go down around 1:30 a.m. and come up around four. We landed on a frozen runway, and I thought, "Now you're somewhere." I was on the plane dressed just like I am now, with a fleece sweater and light shoes, almost slippers. All my warm clothes were in my suitcase, which unfortunately never showed up.

LISA: Oops. Oh, dear!

CAMILLE: It was minus 30°F.

LISA: That's cold, especially if dressed like that.

CAMILLE: The Eskimo women who worked in the airport loaned me clothes. I had a parka, a fur hat, gloves, pants, even boots. One of them put me in a cab with her sister, who is the town taxi driver, and we drove from one end of the town to the other, picking up people and letting them off. The town is one mile long. But the most amazing part of my journey was the day I decided to go out walking on the frozen sea ice. I don't know what I was thinking—I think I wanted to see where the ice ended and the ocean became visible. I was walking and walking, and every once in a while someone would come up on a snowmobile and say, "Are you okay?" And I'd say, "Yes, I'm just going for a walk."

There were twigs marking the way, stuck in the ice. It was like being on the moon because you have to be completely covered, even your face; it's so cold. The ice is very dry. It doesn't feel like the snow I know from my childhood growing up in New York.

LISA: It's like that here too. It is a nice sound the snow makes when you walk on it.

CAMILLE: I felt very alone and in touch with being in such a foreign place, so much so that I was made to deal with my own planet. It was the first time I said hello to the earth as this really big thing. I walked and walked, and then a Russian woman and an Eskimo man came by and said, "We'll give you a ride." They each had a snowmobile, and I got on the back of the woman's. After we had been going about five minutes, very fast, I tapped her and said, "How far is the ocean? "She said, "About twenty-two miles." I said, "Stop, stop!" I knew I was going to have to walk back. Even in those few minutes we had gone far enough that I couldn't see the town anymore.

LISA: Snowmobiles go so fast, and that means you will travel great distances in a short time.

CAMILLE: When they were totally out of sight and I was alone again on the ice, I panicked. I thought, What if there is a white-out and I can't find my way? What if there is a polar bear? Actually, there was snowmobile traffic on the ice. But I walked back for three hours before the next snowmobile came by and said, "Are you okay?" Everyone I saw stopped. They must have thought I was crazy.

Three hours in that cold!

CAMILLE: The walking was fine. I was dressed for it.

LISA: It's the same here. But you must not panic. You have to be prepared for surprises, and bring extra clothes, food, windbag, shovel, rifle, signal pistol, and so on. Whiteouts come so fast. The weather changes quickly. The wind can be totally still, and in minutes suddenly it's a blowing storm and if you don't have the equipment with you to dig down into the snow, things can move very fast until you're not alive anymore. And the same with the polar bears. Here you shouldn't go out of town without a rifle. I don't know anyone personally who has been attacked by a polar bear—it very seldom happens. But in 1996, I think, there were two girls walking on the mountain that you can see right there, out the window. They went for a walk without a rifle and met a polar bear that was very hungry. This was in summertime and the bear had probably been without any food for a long time since it was not able to get out on the ice. One of the girls died, and one was able to save herself. After that, no more incidents with bears have happened.

CAMILLE: I've never even held a gun.

Even if you had a rifle and a bear came after you, do you think you could kill it? It would be hard to kill.

LISA: If a bear comes and you see it hunting you, I think you will shoot it.

CAMILLE: To be a guide, did you have to take classes in shooting?

LISA: Yes. Anyone planning to go out of town should take a rifle course. The university requires a one-week survival course: how to behave in the Arctic when you go outdoors. It's about snowmobiles, and rifles, and how to make tent camps. They teach it from scratch, how you should dress, what you should take. It's dangerous. You might be planning to go for just half a day, but if something breaks down or something happens, you would be far from civilization.

CAMILLE: One of the Eskimo women who loaned me clothes took me on her snowmobile late in the night—the sun was close to the horizon. And the snowmobile just died. And we were nowhere. But, again, there was traffic. Within ten minutes a man came by and he couldn't fix it but he had a sled attached to his snowmobile and was able to give us a ride back.

LISA: Here, in the high season, if you go on snowmobile treks you'll probably meet someone. But if you choose to go someplace where many people don't go, you have to plan very carefully. You must have the ability to dig in or walk back. You should always bring extra equipment such as a tent, an emergency beacon and maybe a satellite phone, and the things that I talked about before. Even though you are just out for a day trip, a tent and extra food and clothes should be with you. And polar bear protection is needed.

You don't go by yourself.

LISA: Some people do, but mostly on routes where there is a lot of traffic.

CAMILLE: It's not like getting in a car and putting on your seatbelt. It's beyond that. This could easily be the end of your life if you don't pay attention to the rules. When you were growing up in Sweden, did it snow very much where you were living?

LISA: Yes, in the wintertime. But I live near the ocean, and the Gulf Stream is coming along there. It's a small place about seventy-five miles from Göteborg. In the wintertime we had a lot of snow but, actually, there's not so much anymore. You can really see the change. We used to build big ice castles when I was a child, and you could go downhill on sleds, but now the children can't play that way. There's not enough snow.

CAMILLE: We used to build igloos where I grew up on Long Island, but they don't have that much snow anymore either.

It's not a very long time ago. Fifteen to twenty years.

CAMILLE: I really thought I was finished with the Arctic after my Alaska trip. Then Kathan went to the North Pole, and I thought, how adventurous!

It was not as adventurous as it appeared.

CAMILLE: Nine out of ten friends of ours that we told we were coming up here this summer said, "Why? Why are you doing that?"

LISA: I recognize that. Many of my friends said, "So what are you going to do up there? It's just cold." But you can never understand what's up here if you don't come here. It's the atmosphere, the energy of the place. You need to be here to understand.

CAMILLE: The stillness. It's beautiful.

But it's not beautiful in the conventional sense. Not picture-post-

card beautiful, like the Alps for example, with big peaks and sunsets, and trees. For another example, the tourist trips to Antarctica are much more popular than those to the Arctic because the scenery there is so much more dramatic.

CAMILLE: What's the definition of *dramatic*? It's something we've been fed for hundreds of years in paintings and photographs and movies. And sometimes when you get to the picture-perfect place, it's disappointing. Svalbard is beautiful in the way Baja California is. It's a coastal desert, rugged and beautiful because it is what it is. It's not dressed up. You have to be there. It's the whole experience. It's not just a picture.

Here, in Spitsbergen, it's dark for months.

LISA: Yes. The polar night starts at the end of October when the sun goes below the horizon, and there is twilight until mid-November. Then it is totally dark, except for the moon and the Northern Lights, for three months, until mid-February.

Do you like that?

LISA: Yes, I do like it. It's our quiet time. But this year I will go home in September and be away until January. That will be a change. I've been here year-round for two years in a row now so I need some traveling, and for me it's best to do it in the dark time because the tourist season is when it is light. I will take this time to travel to Mongolia. I will go by horseback and travel in the northwest part of the country. Then I will come back to Svalbard.

What do you actually do with the tourists here in Svalbard?

LISA: I work for a small company, one owner with approximately three employees. We do long trips with dogs. If the snow is good, we start to train the dogs in January, and then the first guests come in February or March.

There's not much snow right now in town, but we can see plenty up higher. Do you do anything up there in summer?

LISA: In Longyearbyen now the winter is over, but in other places in Svalbard it is still winter. But our company doesn't do dog trips in summer because it's a lot of work to bring the dogs, sleds, and all the equipment to where there is enough snow.

So your season is only from March to when? May?

LISA: Yes, late May. We train the dogs a bit in summer as well. We have them pull a wheeled cart on land. It keeps the dogs in shape and they like to do it.

Everything I've read about sled dogs says that they're independent and difficult to control.

LISA: That's true. It's important to have a really good leader dog to control the others. They're lovely animals. When you go with them and you have a nice relationship with them, it's wonderful. We go out in places where snowmobiles are not allowed, and we have only our dogs to rely on.

Are you planning to make a career out of this, or are you going to go back to Sweden and do something else?

LISA: I don't know. I really like the dog sledging. But I've been studying now for five years, and maybe it's time to try to use what I've learned. But to sit inside too much, like I'm doing now with my thesis, is quite hard. To be out with the dogs is much better. I don't think I can leave the cold and the snow. Maybe the northern part of Sweden would be the place to live, in a small town. I don't think I can live in a bigger town than Longyearbyen. I even moved out from Longyearbyen six miles down the road, closer to the dog kennel.

What do you do for fun?

LISA: Up here? I'm too busy with my thesis. It should be finished right now but the dogs take all the time. In the summer you work all the time, and when you're not working you sleep. But in the dark season there's a lot of relaxing.

CAMILLE: You have good friends here?

LISA: Yes, but as soon as you get to know most of the people from the university, they go home. The courses are one year, or half a year. Two friends of mine stay here for the winter. When I began working as a guide I got to know other guides, and most of them stay here or come back for the next season.

CAMILLE: I felt an affinity for the guides on our ship. There were eight all together, most of them young. Some of them seem to have boyfriends or girlfriends who are also guides. They make a life that way. It's a sought-after position. I was told that every summer, there are about a hundred applicants from all over the world.

What is your thesis subject, Lisa?

LISA: It's about pollution in the Arctic, especially PCBs, to analyze and quantify these. I have the Arctic char as my source.

The fish?

LISA: Yes.

CAMILLE: Is it frightening?

LISA: It depends on where the fish come from. The fish I am using from Spitsbergen are not so contaminated, but in fish from Bear Island, which is not far away, PCBs have been measured in very high amounts.

There is a lot of concern about PCBs in farmed salmon in the United States. I think that is because they are fed fish meal traded on the world market and often made from contaminated fish.

LISA: Up here, it is the effects of PCBs in the polar bears that are frightening.

I read that they have found some female polar bears with male organs because of PCBs.

LISA: That's true. PCBs have harmful effects on the reproductive system, nervous system, endocrine system, and immune system. Children in some areas were exposed to high levels through their mothers' breast milk, and some researchers correlate this with poor performance on learning and memory tests. PCBs were also found to cause cancer in test animals. PCB production was banned in the United States in 1976 by the Toxic Substances Control Act, and in Canada and most other developed countries they were banned in 1977. In 2000 a worldwide treaty was adopted in Johannesburg requiring disposal of old appliances containing PCBs to be completed by 2028. But PCBs are still in soil and in the atmosphere. They do not break down readily. They can travel long distances in the atmosphere.

What are PCBs? What were they used for?

LISA: They are synthetic organic chemicals developed in the 1930s. There are no known natural sources. PCBs were used in lubrication oil, and as plasticizers in paints, caulking for sealing windows, rubber products, and some plastics. They were used in fluorescent lights. The strongest use was in electronic components, for insulation, and in circuit boards for computers. Most people have low levels of PCBs in their blood because nearly everyone has been environmentally exposed. All the dump fields continue to release PCBs, and if there is combustion it is much worse. They still come out into the atmosphere, even though they're not being produced anymore.

Getting rid of something like that takes a long time, but at least we are seriously working on it. It shows that correcting large-scale environmental problems is not a hopeless cause.

LISA: In 1968 a lot of people in Japan became sick, mainly with liver damage, because rice oil became polluted with PCBs. That was the beginning of action.

CAMILLE: I would think birds would be affected.

LISA: Some birds. The glaucous gulls have the highest PCBs, even higher than polar bears, because they eat everything. They are scavengers.

Do you think there's hope for laws against other pollutants?

LISA: Yes, I think so. I hope so. The PCBs have been replaced by other chemical compounds, and some of those have gone wrong as well.

A lot of people are studying the environment. All the people in your university, for example.

CAMILLE: I went to art school, and about twenty people I knew there gave up on art and switched to environmental studies. Hopefully we can learn fast enough to keep from seriously poisoning ourselves.

Do you feel optimistic?

LISA: Yes. I think you need to feel optimistic.

CAMILLE: I agree. Otherwise, what's the point? I think the planet, no matter what we do to ourselves, will go on without us. But if we're going to survive, I can see that places like Svalbard are very important. As more people become aware of what's happening to the planet, there will be change. I was really glad to see so many birds up here.

LISA: There is a lot of activity now. In winter it's totally quiet, but now it is exploding. It's nice to hear the bird noises on the road. I think that PCB production was stopped soon enough that it will not be permanently harmful. You see these effects in the polar bear, but the damage will decline in time.

Another problem for the polar bear is getting enough seals as the ice declines.

CAMILLE: I saw a television program about a place called Churchill in northern Canada. The bears can't get out on the ice soon enough so they wait there, and tourists come to see them. The bears are thin. They can't get the proper nourishment, so they come into the town to try to find food. Does that sort of thing happen here?

LISA: It's not common here for bears to come into Longyearbyen. This is not a regular route for them. The bear population is denser on the east coast of the island than on the west coast where Longyearbyen is located. The bears move onto the drift ice in the east, and the ice drifts from east to west. They follow the ice and usually go on land farther south than Longyearbyen. Then they trek back over the land and the glaciers to the east coast again. That's their normal trek.

CAMILLE: This is off the road for them.

LISA: But this year has been extraordinary because four or five bears have come into town, and one was shot. A lot of people in the town didn't like it that this bear was killed. It was a young male. He was on the ice on the fjord, eating a seal. And then he was full and satisfied, but he wouldn't leave. The Sysselmannen, the governor of Svalbard, sent people to try to chase him away, but he kept coming back. Finally the governor sent a helicopter to shoot him. The bear didn't come into the village. He stayed on the fjord and everyone went down to look at him.

CAMILLE: Why did they shoot him?

LISA: The governor thought he was a threat to the people. Maybe it was right to shoot him. You never know with bears. He kept coming back. Of course, they don't want polar bears to get in the habit of coming here. But there are different opinions in town about how they behaved with this specific bear. He was right down there at the shore. It was only about two weeks ago. There were other bears earlier in the season, mothers with cubs, but they just passed by and went away.

They don't go for the garbage here?

LISA: No, generally they do not. They go into cabins on the outskirts of town, looking for food, and they are curious. Researchers put instruments into the ice, something sticking up from the ice, and the polar bears come and investigate the instruments.

A friend I met on the North Pole trip e-mailed me a satellite photo from a navy site of a polar bear batting at a submarine tail fin that was sticking up out of the ice.

CAMILLE: The crew must have thought, "What is going on up there?"

LISA: Bears investigate everything.

What about global warming?

LISA: The predicted effects on the Arctic are terrifying.

You were both optimistic.

CAMILLE: I am hoping that soon we will start putting more money into alternative energy sources. I know it's possible to develop them, but right now we're stuck on petroleum.

LISA: There's so much money involved in petroleum. But I am

still optimistic because petroleum won't last forever. I think alternate sources will be developed.

If it's going to be done in time, it will take some laws.

CAMILLE: I am going to vote for people who want to do something about global warming, and there are a lot of people in the United States like me.

LISA: I think a change in thinking is beginning. It used to be the opinion all over the world that if a community bought and sold more goods and used more natural resources, it would become richer.

That's still the mentality of the U.S. government.

LISA: In Europe, I believe people are beginning to think that we need to find another way to proceed.

CAMILLE: This fleece sweater I'm wearing used to be empty plastic soda bottles. That's what the fabric is made from. It is happening. There is slow change.

What happens to the garbage here?

LISA: Some of it is transported to the mainland for recycling: glass, plastic, batteries. All other things go in the garbage dump. They dig it down. Some of it blows away or turns into liquid and goes into the ocean, but most of it comes up again. Everything comes up again in permafrost. It doesn't break down. Maybe in a thousand years—

Whatever we throw away here stays a thousand years. It's a shocking thought.

CAMILLE: Yesterday we were on a beach where miners abandoned tools a hundred years ago and they are still lying there intact.

Maybe it's not good that tourism is increasing. Tourists will make more waste.

LISA: It is important to think in ecotourism terms. Tourists are important for this community. I do not know how long coal mining will be efficient here, and then all that is left will be the researchers and the tourists.

What about Russia? Might the Russians drill for oil, perhaps in Barentsburg? If they do, maybe they won't be ecological about it?

LISA: Maybe the Russians think about the environment, but they don't have money. Every human being thinks about his own livelihood before he thinks about nature, especially if he's just living to stay alive. Thinking about the environment is a luxury. Here we have Norwegian law, but Norway doesn't own Svalbard. It manages it under a treaty, and Russia has rights here. Barentsburg is an entirely Russian town.

The Russians still do coal mining there, don't they?

LISA: Yes. And there is also some coal mining here in Longyearbyen. Our power plant runs entirely on local coal. It is not so clean, not up to the standards of the mainland. If that plant were on the mainland of Norway, it would have to put in a cleaning system for the pollutants.

I'm surprised that they don't have to do it here.

LISA: I think they believe that if they put such restrictions on the power plant in Longyearbyen, they would have to do it in Barentsburg, and they know Barentsburg can't afford it. If cleaning systems were required of the Russians, the town might die. But Norway can afford it, and it is not the fault of the people in Barentsburg that they are poor. Sometimes the poor get blamed for what the rich are doing.

CAMILLE: That's what happens globally. At the Kyoto conference on global warming [in 1997] the U.S. should have been the leader. We have been the leader in this sort of thing in the past, and we are the biggest polluters. But now we are saying we won't agree to lower our emissions unless the third world is held to the same standards. Europe is going ahead and cutting emissions, with the idea that others will come on board later. In the past, we've done that sort of thing—you were just telling us about the PCBs, for instance, where the U.S. took the lead. And it worked.

It also worked with the protocol on protecting the ozone layer by banning CFCs, chloroflourocarbons, the chemical that used to be in aerosol cans and in refrigerators. That protocol was adopted in Montreal in 1987 in the same sort of conference that was held in Kyoto. It's now beginning to be successful. You have to do something to start.

CAMILLE: Lisa is doing something.

She's studying the problems. But what happens after that?

CAMILLE: Research is what fuels the possibility of laws. What am I doing?

What are you doing?

CAMILLE: I felt very alive walking on the beaches here or on the squishy permafrost. It feels like something living. You begin to acknowledge the environment in a way that will have to be reciprocal.

LISA: People come back here year after year because they get so much from Svalbard.

CAMILLE: It's such an extreme place. You guys live extreme: dogs, and ice, and polar bears, that's your daily life. I had no idea. My expectation was that we would see mostly forty- to sixty-year-olds here, very weathered looking.

LISA: The average age here is thirty-five.

CAMILLE: And I heard that there's a large population of children under five.

LISA: Yes.

CAMILLE: This is where people want to bring up kids.

Is there a feeling of escape? Do you want to escape the rest of the world?

LISA: It's not an escape. I don't think so. I can read the newspaper and listen to the news, and I do that when there are big news events. But there are other things that maybe you don't want to affect you, and they do affect you because you hear them over and over. It's like being brainwashed. Maybe Svalbard is an escape from that.

CAMILLE: Here you're bombarded by basic elemental concerns, and where we live there's a constant commercial bombardment. I can see why you want to move that aside and say, "Show me what's real." This place is real.

Conclusion

Now that this book has reached its conclusion, it remains for me to try to describe how my trip to the North Pole has affected my way of being in the world. I must attempt this, since earlier I asked others to do it. Camille Seaman walked out on the sea ice in Alaska, wanting to see where the ocean became visible, and "said hello to the earth as this really big thing." John Elton, fifty-five years older than Camille, had a feeling of being "one with immensity" as he stood at the rail of the *Yamal* on the way to the North Pole. A year later he said that he hadn't shaken that feeling, and doesn't want to shake it. Ed Staak jumped into below-freezing water at the North Pole and discovered that his body temperature became warm again very quickly—nature heals itself in many ways. And Fred Sandback, on a trip by small plane to the pole, found that being in a place "a little bit beyond nomenclature" was "indeed, very moving." Naming things gives us control over them. What does it mean to be in a place where there is nothing to name? My experience contained elements of the experiences of all these people.

For days, the *Yamal* had been moving through the ice, cutting a jagged blue swath that mended almost immediately behind her. Day and night for the better part of a week, I had looked out in every direction to the horizon and seen only ice. Then the polar bear appeared: large, alone, confident, moving unhurriedly toward our ship. When the *Yamal* left him, we went forward noisily, cracking the ice before us. The bear stood still and watched. I kept my eyes on him until he was a speck, unrecognizable in the expanse of ice but nevertheless a living presence there. Since then I have had a sense of equilibrium available to me that had not been there before. It is not always with me, but whenever I notice that it is missing, I can usually find it again by taking a moment to—in Nansen's words—"possess my soul with patience." I think that the immensity of the view, the continuous sunlight, and the many days that had passed without seeing trees, plants, birds, or life of any kind had set up my consciousness to grasp, through seeing the bear, the graceful interconnection of living things.

What happened to Nansen in later life? When Norway became independent, he was offered the job of prime minister, but turned it down, saying that he was a "scientist and an explorer." He did accept the post of ambassador to London, where he served from 1906 to 1908. He went to London with plans to mount an expedition to the South Pole at the end of his time there, but at some point was approached by Englishman Robert F. Scott, seeking advice—which Nansen freely gave—for his own planned South Pole expedition. Nansen later began an affair with Scott's wife, Kathleen, and when Norwegian Roald Amundsen asked for the loan of the *Fram* for an expedition to the North Pole, Nansen agreed, knowing that giving up the *Fram* meant giving up his plans for a future expedition in the south. After Amundsen secretly switched his course and beat Scott to the South Pole, Nansen wrote Amundsen a letter of reproach, although he supported him publicly, writing that he admired "a deed that lifts us above the grey monotony of daily life."

Nansen and Amundsen were very different men, not to mention Johansen who touchingly pulled off Nansen's boots in the Arctic when he could not do so himself, and committed suicide after having confronted Amundsen in Antarctica. Two very different men claimed to have discovered the North Pole. Frederick Cook seems not to have cared what people thought of him, and in the years after he announced his conquest of the pole he slipped from being a hero to being reviled, perhaps unfairly. Robert E. Peary, after his North Pole announcement, became a famous hero as he had wished, but he seemed to take no pleasure in his fame. Matthew Henson, Peary's African-American associate, was eventually inducted into the Explorers Club in New York, but could not afford to go to its meetings because they included meals paid for by individual members.

Many of the early explorers had the nature of scientists, doggedly accumulating information and returning to the ice one summer after another. Benjamin Leigh Smith and Frederick Jackson, between them, determined the extent of most of Franz Josef Land after its discovery by Julius Payer and Karl Weyprecht. Weyprecht later laid the foundation for the first International Polar Year, which initiated a pattern of international scientific cooperation in the Arctic and the Antarctic. Otto Sverdrup not only commanded Nansen's *Fram* in its polar drift, but also discovered and mapped a large part of Arctic Canada. Georgiy Sedov, a romantic, mapped a good deal of the Russian coast but lost his life pursuing the North Pole. Salomon Andrée, also a romantic, pioneered travel by balloon and died "dominated by a feeling of pride" after crashing in the ice. The romanticism of Sedov and Andrée contrasts with the prudence of George Nares who set off for the pole in a government-sponsored expedition and returned early after sending home a telegram: "North Pole impracticable." These men, different as they were, created groundwork for understanding the Arctic.

Wally Herbert, the first person indisputably to reach the North Pole by surface travel, did so in 1969, the year that Neil Armstrong became the first person to set foot on the moon. From that year forward, reaching a great symbolic place where no one has been before is beyond the resources and idiosyncrasies of individuals and their patrons. As I write this in 2004, there is talk in the United States of trying to send people to Mars, and public desire for a lift above "grey monotony" may sanction spending a great deal of public money on the project.

At the end of World War I, Fridtjof Nansen was appalled to learn that half-a-million prisoners of war who had fought for

Germany and its allies were languishing in prison camps, mainly in Siberia, with no interest by any country in their plight. As Norway's delegate to the League of Nations, and later as the league's high commissioner for refugees, he worked to repatriate them. Because of his heroism in the Arctic, known throughout the world through his popular book, no diplomatic door was closed to him. He was successful in repatriating the POWs, even though, as one of his biographers said, "his appeals to the magnanimity and charity of politicians were met with pettiness and intrigue, callousness and apathy, and sheer human inertia." He also aided resettlement of two million refugees, mainly from the Russian Revolution, and took on the problems of Greek and Turkish refugees from a war between their two countries. When he received the Nobel Peace Prize in 1922, he wrote to a friend that he "was forced by chance into this work which was not mine at all." When he died at the age of sixty-nine in 1930 he was working to bring about a disarmament conference. "My scientific work has convinced me that everything goes in cycles, in waves," he wrote. "It is my consolation, even if the periods of decay can be long, and the wave troughs deep, that a crest comes again, if only one can wait."

A sense of enormous time is quickly gained in the Arctic, a place of enormous space where one day is much like another but things can change rapidly. If the United States undertakes to send people to Mars, many scientists believe the project will drain money from more urgent scientific research. "If the only goal is glory, and to plant a flag somewhere, then you send people to Mars," said a planetary scientist and geophysicist who advocates unmanned, robotic space exploration. "If you have some serious purpose other than planting a flag, then people are basically in the way."

People, individual idiosyncratic people, are very much needed, however, to create groundwork for understanding human-caused alterations in earth's natural mechanisms. Needed individuals include scientists who accumulate information and make informed judgments about what that information means, and—equally important—ordinary people who are willing to press for laws to bring damage to our environment under control. With rollbacks in 2003 of some provisions in the Clean Air Act, and continued refusal since 2001 by the U.S. government to consider any form of cooperation with the Kyoto Protocol on climate change, we are in a trough, to use Nansen's metaphor. Nevertheless, work is being done. A crest will come again. If only we can wait.

Dedication

This book is for Tala,
with fingers crossed for the future.

Time Line

1300 Approximate beginning of the Little Ice Age.

1596 William Barents discovered Spitsbergen.

1607-10 Henry Hudson explored the Arctic, seeking a route to China. He noted whales in Spitsbergen and discovered Hudson Bay in Canada.

1611-70 Twenty-four thousand bowhead whales were slaughtered in Spitsbergen.

1616 William Baffin sailed from England to Canada, where he met the Polar Eskimos, who thought they were the only people on earth.

1831 Captain James Ross discovered the Magnetic North Pole.

1845 Sir John Franklin led an expedition to the Northwest Passage. His entire group of 129 men perished.

1849 Dr. Abraham Gesner distilled kerosene from oil. Kerosene eventually replaced whale oil as the preferred fuel for lamps.

1850 Approximate beginning of the global warming phenomenon.

1852 Elisha Kent Kane, ship's doctor on an expedition searching for Franklin, said he had seen the Open Polar Sea. In the following year Kane commanded an expedition attempting to reach the North Pole by the (nonexistent) Open Polar Sea.

1858 The first commercial oil well was drilled in the United States.

1860-61 Isaac Hayes, in a ship called the *United States* attempted to reach the North Pole by way of the Open Polar Sea.

1869-71 A German expedition, in ships called the *Germania* and the *Hansa,* tried to reach the pole via the Open Polar Sea.

1871-73 Charles Francis Hall, in the *Polaris,* searched for the North Pole and the Open Polar Sea for the glory of the United States.

1872-74 Karl Weyprecht and Julius Payer, for the Austro-Hungarian Empire, attempted to reach the pole and the Open Polar Sea in the *Admiral Tegetthoff*. Instead they discovered Franz Josef Land. Walking home on drifting ice, they spent two months traveling nine miles.

1875-76 George Nares led a British attempt on the North Pole and sent back a telegram: "North Pole impracticable." He said the Open Polar Sea did not exist.

1879-82 An American ship, *Jeannette,* captained by George Washington De Long, tried to reach the pole and the Open Polar Sea and sank near the Bering Strait. A pair of oilskin trousers and other relics from the wreck were recovered on the other side of the pole.

1880-82 Benjamin Leigh Smith made two trips from England to Franz Josef Land and lost his ship, the *Eira*, on the second one.

1882-83 The first International Polar Year.

1882 The Primus stove was invented by Frans Lindqvist in Sweden.

1893 Fridtjof Nansen deliberately trapped his ship, the *Fram*, in an Arctic ice floe, hoping it would drift to the North Pole. His drift theory was inspired by the oilskin trousers that had drifted past the pole from De Long's ship, the *Jeannette.*

1894 Englishman Frederick Jackson set up a semi-permanent camp on Cape Flora in Franz Josef Land.

1895 Nansen and Hjalmar Johansen left the *Fram* in command of Otto Sverdrup and set out to walk to the pole. They set a new Farthest North record and turned back.

1896 Nansen and Johansen happened upon Cape Flora after a year and three months on the ice. They were rescued by Jackson and returned to Norway on his ship, the *Windward.*

1897 Salomon Andrée, a Swede, tried to go to the pole by hydrogen balloon. Frederick Jackson returned to England from Cape Flora on the *Windward.* Nansen's book, *Farthest North,* was published in Norway and England.

1898-99 Walter Wellman, an American newspaperman, made his second of five unsuccessful attempts on the pole, this time from Franz Josef Land.

1898-1902 Otto Sverdrup, commander of Nansen's ship the *Fram*, used it to discover and map the Sverdrup Islands in Canada. Robert E. Peary took the *Windward*, formerly Jackson's ship, on his first of three attempts on the North Pole and lost eight toes.

1899-1900 The Duke of Abruzzi (Italy) attempted to reach the pole from Franz Josef Land, celebrating the turn of the century with fireworks there. His associate, Umberto Cagni, bettered Nansen's Farthest North.

1909 Robert E. Peary claimed to have discovered the North Pole on his third attempt to do so. Frederick Cook claimed to have discovered the North Pole in the previous year, 1908.

1905 Roald Amundsen was the first to go through the Northwest Passage.

1911 Roald Amundsen, beginning his journey in Nansen's ship, the *Fram*, beat Robert F. Scott to the South Pole.

1912 Milutin Milankovitch discovered cycles of climate based on variations in the earth's orbit and axial tilt.

1913-1914 Georgiy Sedov attempted to go to the North Pole in the

Sveta Foka through Franz Josef Land. He died but his crew returned.

1914 Otto Sverdrup searched unsuccessfully in Franz Josef Land for Sedov's lost expedition.

1926 Roald Amundsen, Lincoln Ellsworth, and Umberto Nobile flew over the North Pole in a dirigible called the *Norge*, taking off from Spitsbergen. They were probably the first people to see it.

1928 Umberto Nobile piloted a dirigible, the *Italia*, to the North Pole, then crashed. Eight crew members died. Roald Amundsen joined the rescue operation and then vanished.

1929 Otto Yulyevich Shmidt claimed Franz Josef Land for the U.S.S.R., which established the Tichaya Station there.

1930 The remains of Salomon Andrée and two companions who tried for the pole in a balloon in 1897 were discovered on White Island between Spitsbergen and Franz Josef Land.

1932-33 The Second International Polar Year.

1941 Ivan Cherevichny reached the Northern Pole of Inaccessibility by air.

1946 The International Whaling Commission was established by the world's fourteen main whaling countries to manage the conservation of whale stocks. It banned the hunting of bowhead and other endangered species of whales.

1948 Twenty-four Russians led by Alexander Kuznetsov landed at the North Pole by aircraft. They were probably the first people to stand there.

1952 Norwegian law protected walruses on Spitsbergen. The Soviet Ministry of fisheries put restrictions on hunting walruses in Franz Josef Land.

1956 The Geomagnetic North Pole was proven to exist.

1957-58 The International Geophysical Year.

1958 The Soviet Union and France began drilling ice cores at the Vostok station in Antarctica. The first submarine, the nuclear-powered USS *Nautilus*, reached the pole but did not surface.

1959 The first submarine surfaced at the North Pole. It was the nuclear powered USS *Skate*.

1968 Ralph Plaistead traveled to the North Pole by snowmobile, assisted by airplane.

1969 Wally Herbert, the first person indisputably to reach the North Pole by surface travel, arrived there by dogsled on a journey from Alaska to Spitsbergen over the ice. Neil Armstrong was the first person to walk on the moon.

1972 The U.S. Congress enacted the Marine Mammal Protection Act.

1973 The International Agreement on Conservation of Polar Bears and their Habitat was signed by all the countries where polar bears live.

1974 The U.S. Congress enacted the Clean Air Act.

1975 The Convention on International Trade in Endangered Species (CITES) came into force. As of 2003 it has been adopted by 164 countries, each of which has enacted domestic legislation to prohibit trade in products derived from wild animals and plants whose survival is threatened.

1976 The U.S. Toxic Substances Control Act banned production of PCBs. Canada and other countries banned their production in the following year, 1977.

1977 The Russian nuclear-powered icebreaker *Arktika* reached the North Pole, the first surface vessel to do so. Undersea hot springs called black smokers were discovered.

1979 Archaeabacteria, life forms that arise from chemicals and live in extreme environments like sea ice and the heat of black smokers were discovered.

1985 Wallace Broecker put forward the theory of the Great Ocean Conveyer Belt. It raises the possibility of a new ice age as a consequence of the warming and freshening of salty ocean waters in the Arctic.

1987 The United Nations Montreal Protocol on Substances that Deplete the Ozone Layer was adopted.

1989-93 Ice cores that show climate changes over 110,000 years were drilled in Greenland by the United States and a consortium of European countries. Clear evidence of rapid climate change events was found.

1991 Russian nuclear-powered icebreakers began taking tourists to the North Pole.

1995 An ice core was drilled at Vostok in Antarctica that is yielding evidence of climate shifts over the past 400,000 years.

1997 The Kyoto Protocol to the United Nations Framework Convention on Climate Change was drafted in Kyoto, Japan by 160 nations, including the United States. In the terms of the Protocol, the industrialized nations agreed to cut emissions of greenhouse gases to a level 5.2 percent below their 1990 levels in the period 2008-2012. The Protocol will go into effect when it is ratified by fifty-five nations that together account for 55 percent of the industrial world's greenhouse gas emissions. As of November 2003, 120 countries have ratified the Protocol. They include Canada, Denmark, Norway, Sweden, Switzerland, Great Britain, the European Union, and Japan. Together they account for 44.2 percent of emissions. Russia is considering ratification. The United States announced in 2001 that it would not consider ratifying the Protocol.

Notes

The Journal of Fridtjof Nansen

The excerpts in this book from the journal of Fridtjof Nansen were taken from the first edition in English of Nansen's *Farthest North*, published by Archibald Constable and Company, London, in 1897. I could not find a translator credit in the volume. Nansen's book intersperses his journal entries with explanatory and recollected text, and I have used only material from the journal except for an occasional cluster of words inserted from the explanatory text as needed for clarity. As much as possible, I have used whole sections of the journal. Throughout I changed Nansen's word *lane* to *lead* to bring the terminology in line with modern usage, and in a few places have modernized other words (substituting *where* for *whither*, for example). Occasionally I have modernized punctuation. *Farthest North* is readily available in an abbreviated version published by Modern Library, New York, with an introduction by Roland Huntford. Some of the material I chose from the 1897 edition is not included in the Modern Library edition.

Introduction

The explorer I mention in the first paragraph who walked for two months to travel nine miles was Karl Weyprecht, who—with Julius Payer—discovered Franz Josef Land. I talk more about their journey in Chapter Five. I found the information mentioned here, and the quote, in Fergus Fleming's book *Ninety Degrees North: Quest for the North Pole* (p. 126).

Chapter One: The Polar Bear

My understanding of sea ice and melt water pools comes mainly from E. C. Pielou's *A Naturalist's Guide to the Arctic* (pp. 65-69). Throughout my book I have used E. C. Pielou as the authority for the spelling of wildlife names. The rudimentary information on polar bears in this chapter is mostly from *The Arctic: A Guide to Coastal Wildlife* by Tony Soper (pp. 100-104).

Nansen, in his journal, says that the bear that visited the *Fram* was "a thin little one-year-old." It is worth noting that the bear must have been nearly three years old, since we now know that cubs stay with their mothers until the age of two and a half in the area where Nansen traveled.

In the conversation, Sonja Gustafson got her information about Nansen's affair with the wife of South Pole explorer Robert F. Scott from Roland Huntford's biography, called *Nansen* (pp. 558-569). On page 35, in the conversation, I quote from an early book of Scott's. I found the quotation in Jeannette Mirsky's *To the Arctic! The Story of Northern Exploration from Earliest Times* (p. 10). Mirsky cites Scott's 1905 book, *The Voyage of Discovery,* as its source. Nansen's ship, the *Fram,* is on display at the Fram Museum in Oslo, reached by boat from the downtown docks.

Chapter Two: The Ship

My information about the *Yamal* comes mainly from an information sheet given to the passengers by Robert Headland, courtesy of the Scott Polar Research Institute, Cambridge, England.

In the conversation, Larry Braden's quote from Lewis Carroll comes from *The Hunting of the Snark,* 1876. The Borneo base on the drift ice near the North Pole began operation in 1994. A description of life there can be found in Christopher Pala's book, *The Oddest Place on Earth: Rediscovering the North Pole* (p. 154 and throughout). The material that Janet Landfried read that argued for Robert Peary and Matthew Henson having discovered the North Pole was a photocopied chapter I sent her from S. Allen Counter's book, *North Pole Legacy: Black, White, and Eskimo.* The chapter is titled "The Controversy: Did Peary and Henson Reach the North Pole First?" (pp. 189-209). The quotation about Peary and Cook that I mention on page 83 is from the Danish explorer Peter Freuchen. I found it in Counter's book (p. 203).

In the conversation, the newspaper article claiming that the threat of global warming is exaggerated that Larry Braden mentions is from *The Gazette,* Montreal, April 22, 2003. It concerns the Montreal Economic Institute, which can be found on the Internet at www.iedm.org. The information that Janet Landfried mentions about the preservation of the boreal forest is from the *New York Times,* "Canadians, in Rare Alliance, Agree to Conserve Woodlands," December 1, 2003. My information about the Global Climate Coalition came from Spencer R. Weart's book, *The Discovery of Global Warming* (p. 168). I did not read the book Larry Braden mentions, *The Skeptical Environmentalist* by Bjorn Lomberg, and it is not in the bibliography.

Chapter Three: The Weather

On page 89, I mention an observation Matthew Henson made about Arctic snow. I found it in *A Negro Explorer at the North Pole: The Autobiography of Matthew Henson* (p. 86). The general information about ice in this chapter comes mostly from two books by E. C. Pielou: *A Naturalist's Guide to the Arctic* and *After the Ice Age: The Return of Life to Glaciated North America.* The article in the *New York Times* about open water at the pole appeared on August 19, 2000. The two scientists who made the trip on the *Yamal* that year and were interviewed by the newspaper were Dr. James J. McCarthy, director of the Harvard Museum of Comparative Zoology, and Dr. Malcolm C. McKenna, a paleontologist at the American Museum of Natural History. A discussion on the website of the *New York Times* (www.nytimes.com) on August 29, 2000, suggested that the reports were not as surprising as they might seem. "What was really unusual was that over a period of two weeks we never had a day of what would be considered normal ice," Dr. McCarthy said. "When we reached the pole and found open water, that simply punctuated what we were seeing everywhere."

I obtained the measurements of decline in ice thickness and ice area as reported by submarines and weather satellites over a long period of time from an unpublished paper by Gunter Weller titled "The Weather and Climate of the Arctic." This paper, available through the Geophysical Institute, University of Alaska, Fairbanks, was helpful to me in trying to develop an understanding of the subject. Consequences of diminishing ice thickness as measured by U.S. Navy submarines are discussed in an article on the website of the *Christian Science Monitor* (csmweb2.emcweb.com), "Arctic Ice Cap: It's Thinner Than We Thought," November 17, 1999. More information on Radarsat-2, the Canadian radar satellite, can be found at www.space.gc.ca. NASA also has a satellite, IceSat, studying changes in the earth's climate using lasers (www.icesat.nasa.gov).

On page 93 I quoted Paul Mayewski about the problem of holding together specialized teams of people for scientific work. This is from Mayewski's book about drilling ice cores in Greenland, *The Ice Chronicles: The Quest to Understand Global Climate Change* (pp. 38-39). The information I reported on page 93 about the Greenland Ice Sheet Project Two also came from Mayewski's book, as did the information about Rapid Climate Change Events (p. 85). The information on the Vostok, Antarctica, ice cores comes from Spencer Weart's *The Discovery of Global Warming* (pp. 130-131).

My information about the Younger Dryas period came mainly from *Principles in Paleoclimatology and Earth History* by Thomas M. Cronin (p. 205). Trying to read this book led me to the observation I made in the text that students of climate change must learn a language nearly unintelligible to others. Cronin cites sources rigorously, however. If you doubt that global warming exists or that human activities are a major factor in it, I recommend this book, and that of the more readable Spencer Weart, as sources of abundant specific evidence that probably will change your mind. I also encourage you to look at the website of the Fridtjof Nansen Institute (www.fni.no) in this regard.

Wallace Broecker's theory of the Great Ocean Conveyor Belt is discussed in many of the books I read (listed in the bibliography), but the interpretation I found easiest to grasp is in Myron Arms's science-based travel book *Riddle of the Ice: A Scientific Adventure into the Arctic* (pp. 120-131). Some of my information on the Little Ice Age came from E. C. Pielou's *After the Ice Age* (pp. 308-310). Most of it came from *The Little Ice Age: How Climate Made History 1300-1850* by Brian Fagan. The stories about the French cavalry, the rural beggars, and the "Great Dying of the Beasts" are there, as is the quote I used on page 98 from a writer in fourteenth century Flanders (p. 41). The gift of the polar bear to the king of Denmark, the story of the ship captain who sighted the floating head of a mammoth, and the information about fourteenth-century real estate records are from this source. Fagan also presents an excellent explanation of Wallace Broecker's theories (Fagan, pp. 55-58). Paul Mayewski, in *The Ice Chronicles,* discusses whether or not the Little Ice Age is over (Mayewski, pp. 133-143). My direct quote from Wallace Broecker on page 101 is from Myron Arm's *Riddle of the Ice* (p. 134). The direct quote from Robert E. Peary is from his book, *The North Pole* (p. 257).

In the conversation, the website I mention on page 129 from the Greening Earth Society can be found at www.greeningearthsociety.org. The quote from Senator James M. Inhofe is from the *New York Times,* "Politics Reasserts Itself in the Debate Over Climate Change and Its Hazards," July 5, 2003. The strategist for the Bush administration who recommended use of the term "climate change" in preference to "global warming" was Frank Luntz. "Over the last several months, the Republicans have subtly altered their language," the *New York Times* reported ("Democratic Field Tries to Add Punch to the Environment Issue," July 2, 2003). The article in the *Economist* that I mention on page 138 regarding the McCain-Lieberman Climate Stewardship Act is on page 35 of the issue published on January 18, 2003 issue. When first introduced, as covered by this article, the bill was called the American Investments for Reduction of Emissions Act.

Chapter Four: The North Pole

A photocopied article regarding the twenty-four Russians who were probably the first to stand at the North Pole was sent out to participants in advance of the North Pole trip. It was written by Christopher Pala in April 1999, but appears to be unpublished in the version sent to us. Pala relates the information in a different form in his book, *The Oddest Place on Earth* (pp. 228-235). I obtained my understanding of latitude and longitude mainly from NASA's website: www-istp.gsfc.nasa.gov/stargaze/Snavigat. Information on the various North Poles was provided in fact sheets given out on the North Pole trip by Robert Headland, courtesy of the Scott Polar Research Institute.

Chapter Five: Franz Josef Land

Much of my information on Franz Josef Land came from the Bradt *Guide to Spitsbergen, Svalbard, Franz Josef Land, Jan Mayen* by Andreas Umbreit. Umbreit gives the ocean and air temperatures, the number of abandoned buildings on the Tichaya base, the number of babies born there, and other informative material (pp. 179-190). The story of Georgiy Sedov is in many books on the Arctic, with his first name spelled in several ways. I have used the spelling given by Richard Vaughan in *The Arctic, A History.* Sedov's ship is often called the *Foka,* but I have used its full name, *Sveta Foka,* as directed by Robert Headland. Headland also encouraged my use of *Admiral Tegetthoff*, Weyprecht's ship, rather than the abbreviated *Tegetthoff* used by most writers. My retelling of the stories of explorers in this chapter is based on many sources (listed in the bibliography), but Richard Vaughan's book has been a major one, as has Jeannette Mirsky's book *To the Arctic!* Because both these authors are careful in citing sources, they seem reliable to me. Lectures given aboard the *Yamal* by Robert Headland, and discussions with him, were an important source for my understanding of the subject.

The information that American Matthew Maurey originated the idea of the Open Polar Sea, an idea expanded later by the German geographer August Petermann, is in *The Ice Finders: How a Poet, a Professor, and a Politician Discovered the Ice Age* by Edmund Blair Bolles (p. 5) as is the quotation on page 212 from the orders given by the U.S. Navy to an 1852 expedition that they should contact U.S. officers in China after traversing the pole (p. 6). I found the quotations from the journal of Julius Payer that I used on pages 214 and 215 in Jeannette Mirsky's *To the Arctic!* (pp. 177-178).

My information on Barbara Bodichon came from two websites: spartacus.schoolnet.co.uk and lycos.co.uk/HastingsHistory. Searching the web and thinking about Benjamin Leigh Smith and his sister led to my observation about connections between exploration and the suffragette movement in Victorian England. The quote I used on page 220 from Frederick Jackson about the nonexistence of a land route to the pole is from his journal, *A Thousand Days in the Arctic,* published in 1899. The quote I used from the Duke of Abruzzi on page 220 also came from Mirsky (p. 184), who lists Abruzzi's *On the Polar Star in the Arctic Sea,* 1903, as its source. The information about the annexation of Franz Josef Land by the Soviet Union is from Vaughan (p. 206). Mirsky, in various places, gives the numbers of bears and walruses killed by the various explorers.

My estimate of the number of polar bears alive today comes from *Polar Bears* by Ian Stirling (p. 77). The walrus figure comes from the website of the U.S. Fish and Wildlife Service (www.e7.fws.gov). Information about the thick-billed murre comes from E. C. Pielou, *A Naturalist's Guide to the Arctic* (p. 235) and from Soper (p. 78).

In the conversation, the book Al Duba mentions that gives a story of the origin of the name Ahnighito for the large meteorite now on display at the AMNH is *Dinosaurs in the Attic: An Excursion into the American Museum of Natural History* by Douglas J. Preston (p. 40). It provides other information on the meteorite, including the letter from Mrs. Peary to the museum asking for payment for it. My information about the Eskimo sons of Peary and Henson is from Counter's *North Pole Legacy.* The quote from Donald MacMillan that I relate on page 298 is from the same source (p. 202). The two men I mention who made it to the pole in 2000 using Peary's route and taking four days longer than he did are Paul Crowley and Paul Landry. Their trip is described on the website www.northpole1909.com/landrycrowley.

Chapter Six: Cape Norway

The material in the early part of this chapter is from the recollected portions of Nansen's *Farthest North.* The information about plants in the Arctic is mostly from E. C. Pielou's *A Naturalist's Guide to the Arctic* (pp. 85-91). Additional information about the AMNH expedition to bring back a black smoker can be found on the website of PBS (www.pbs.org/wgbh/nova/abyss/mission/birth), which produced an episode of its NOVA television series on the expedition. Additional information on the black smokers is available on the website of the

American Museum of Natural History (www.amnh.org). Information on archaeabacteria can be found at www.ucmp.berkeley.edu/archaea.

Chapter Seven: Cape Flora

The quotation Nansen uses to begin his diary entry on Tuesday, June 23 is from a poem titled "Further Language from Truthful James" by Bret Harte, the American writer of the far west. It was published in 1870 and is written partially in dialect. The information about Frederick Jackson's situation at Cape Flora and all the direct quotations from him are from his book, *A Thousand Days in the Arctic.* I have taken the material from the first edition, published in New York and London by Harper and Brothers in 1899. The information about Nansen's trip home is from *Farthest North.*

Chapter Eight: Spitsbergen

The story of the Battle of Signehamna is told here as I remember it related by Bjorn Hendriksen, our trip leader on the *Polar Star.* I found it in a slightly different form in Vaughan (p. 234). The quote from Salomon Andrée that appears on page 417 is from Mirsky (p. 307). She cites *Andrée's Story, the Complete Record 1897-1930*, published by Viking Press in 1930, as its source. The quote is from Andrée's diary, written in 1897 and recovered from the ice in 1930.

The figure of twenty-four thousand bowhead whales slaughtered in Spitsbergen when the town of Smeerenburg was active between 1611 and 1670 is probably conservative. Kieren Mulvaney in *At the Ends of the Earth: A History of the Polar Regions* (p. 57) gives that figure as the number estimated to be there in 1611 when the Muscovy Company began systematic slaughter, and he has found records showing that between 1660 and 1912 ninety thousand bowheads were killed over a total of twenty-three thousand voyages to Spitsbergen. However, Smeerenburg itself was out of business by 1670. Mirsky devotes a chapter to Smeerenburg, and the quote I used from Friedrich Martins is from that chapter (p. 57). She got it from a book by Lord Dufferin, *Letters from High Latitudes* (undated).

I got the figure that two-thirds of the world's proven oil resources are in Saudi Arabia and four other Middle Eastern countries from the *Economist,* October 25-31, 2003, "The End of the Oil Age." This was the *Economist*'s cover story on that date. The header to the lead article is "Ways to break the tyranny of oil are coming into view. Governments need to promote them." The experiment I relate concerning the exposure of polar bears to oil spills comes from *Polar Bears* by Ian Stirling (p. 148). You can find further geographic and historic information about Spitsbergen on a map titled "Spitsbergen Explorer," Ocean Explorer Publications (e-mail: info@oceanexplorer.net). My statement that the Montreal Protocol on the Protection of the Ozone Layer is beginning to be successful is based on an article in the *New York Times*, July 30, 2003 "Ozone Layer Is Improving, According to Monitors."

Conclusion

The quote from Nansen on page 472 regarding Amundsen's South Pole discovery is from his introduction to Amundsen's book, *The South Pole.* The Nansen biographer whom I quoted on page 474 is A. R. Christophersen, from an address given in 1961 on the occasion of the centenary of Nansen's birth. I found it on the website of the Fritdjof Nansen Institute (www.fni.no). I found the quote from Nansen on page 474 in Roland Huntford's biography, *Nansen* (p. 650). Huntford found it in a letter of Nansen's replying to the congratulations of a friend. Scientist Norman Sleep, whom I quote on page 474 about possible travel to Mars, is quoted in the *San Francisco Chronicle,* January 10, 2004, "Plan for Men on Mars has its Boosters, Detractors."

Bibliography

American Museum of Natural History 2001. *The Official Guide*. London: Scala Publishers.

Arms, M. 1998. *Riddle of the Ice: A Scientific Adventure into the Arctic*. New York: Doubleday.

Berton, P. 2000. *The Arctic Grail: The Quest for the Northwest Passage and the North Pole, 1818-1909*. New York: Lyons Press.

Bolles, E. B. 1999. *The Ice Finders: How a Poet, a Professor, and a Politician Discovered the Ice Age*. Washington, DC: Counterpoint.

Bryant, J. H. 2000. *Dangerous Crossings: The First Modern Polar Expedition 1925*. Annapolis, MD: Naval Institute Press.

Conefrey, M. 1998. *Icemen: A History of the Arctic and Its Explorers*. New York: MacMillan.

Cookman, S. 2000. *Ice Blink: The Tragic Fate of Sir John Franklin's Lost Polar Expedition*. New York: John Wiley.

Counter, S. A. 2001. *North Pole Legacy: Black, White, and Eskimo*. Montpelier, VT: Invisible Cities Press.

Cronin, T. M. 1999. *Principle of Paleoclimatology: Perspectives in Paleobiology and Earth History*. New York: Columbia University Press.

Dowdeswell, J., and M. Hambrey 2002. *Islands of the Arctic*. Cambridge: Cambridge University Press.

Fagan, B. 2000. *The Little Ice Age: How Climate Made History 1300-1850*. New York: Basic Books.

Fleming, F. 2001. *Ninety Degrees North: The Quest for the North Pole*. London: Granta Books.

Henson, M. 2001. *A Negro Explorer at the North Pole: The Autobiography of Mathew Henson*. Montpelier, VT: Invisible Cities Press. (orig. pub. 1912.)

Hisdal, V. 1998. *Svalbard: Nature and History*. Olso: Norsk Polarinstituit.

Hjelle, A. 1993. *Geology of Svalbard*. Oslo, Norway, Norsk Polarinstituit.

Huntford, R. 2001. *Nansen*. London: Abacus.

Imbert, B. 1992. *North Pole, South Pole: Journeys to the Ends of the Earth*. New York: Harry N. Abrams

Jackson, F. 1899. *A Thousand Days in the Arctic*. New York and London: Harper.

Kjaernet, T., and I. Gjertz 2001. *Svalbard*. Norway: Aune Forlag As.

Lopez, B. 1986. *Arctic Dreams*. New York: Vintage Books.

Lundgren, S., and O. Carlsson 1999. *Svalbard: The Land Beyond the Northcape*. Stockholm: Ice Is Nice.

Malaurie, J. 2003. *Ultima Thule: Explorers and Natives in the Polar North*. New York: W.W. Norton.

Mathez, E. A. 2001. *Earth: Inside and Out*. New York: New Press.

Mayewski, P. A. 2002. *The Ice Chronicles: The Quest to Understand Global Climate Change*. Hanover, NH: University Press of New England.

McCannon, J. 1998. *Red Arctic: Polar Exploration and the Myth of the North in the Soviet Union 1932-1939*. New York: Oxford University Press.

Mirsky, J. 1970. *To the Arctic! The Story of Northen Exploration from Earliest Times*. Chicago: University of Chicago.

Mulvaney, K. 2001. *At the Ends of the Earth: A History of the Polar Regions*. Washington, DC: Island Press.

Nansen, F. 1999. *Farthest North: The Incredible Three-Year Voyage to the Frozen Latitudes of the North*. New York: Random House. (orig. pub. 1897.)

Nansen, F. 1897. *Farthest North: Volume I*. London: Archibald Constable.

Nansen, F. 1897. *Farthest North: Volume II*. London: Archibald Constable.

Niven, J. 2000. *The Ice Master: The Doomed 1913 Voyage of the Karluk*. New York: Hyperion.

Pala, C. 2002. *The Oddest Place on Earth: Rediscovering the North*

Pole. Lincoln, NB: Writers Showcase.

Peary, R. E. 2001. *The North Pole*. New York: Cooper Square Press. (orig. pub. 1910.)

Pielou, E. C. 1991. *After the Ice Age: The Return of Life to Glaciated North America*. Chicago: University of Chicago Press.

Pielou, E. C. 1994. *A Naturalist's Guide to the Arctic*. Chicago: University of Chicago Press.

Preston, D. J. 1986. *Dinosaurs in the Attic: An Excursion into the American Museum of Natural History*. New York: St. Martin's Press.

Soper, T. 2001. *The Arctic: A Guide to Coastal Wildlife*. Guilford, CT: Globe Pequot Press.

Stark, P. 2000. *Ring of Ice: True Tales of Adventure, Exploration, and Arctic Life*. New York: Lyons Press.

Stirling, I. 1998. *Polar Bears*. Ann Arbor: University of Michigan Press.

Swaney, D. 1999. *The Arctic*. Victoria, Australia: Lonely Planet.

Umbreit, A. 1997. *Guide to Spitsbergen, Svalbard, Franz Josef Land, Jan Mayen*. London: Globe Pequot Press.

Vaughan, R. 1994. *The Arctic: A History*. London: Sutton.

Weart, S. R. 2003. *The Discovery of Global Warming*. Cambridge, MA: Harvard University Press.

Wilson, R. C. L. et al. 2000. *The Great Ice Age: Climate Change and Life*. New York: Routledge.

Index

Page references to the Nansen journal sections are in italics.